DANCING *with the* ENEMY

Rosie at the harbor of Scheveningen

DANCING *with the* ENEMY

My Family's Holocaust Secret

Paul Glaser

ONEWORLD

A Oneworld Book

First published in Great Britain and Australia by
Oneworld Publications 2015

Originally published in the Netherlands as *Tante Roosje* by
Uitgeverij Verbum, Laren, in 2010.

A CIP record for this title is available from the British Library

ISBN 978-1-78074-753-8
ISBN 978-1-78074-754-5 (eBook)

Book design by Michael Collica
Printed and bound in Denmark by Nørhaven

Oneworld Publications
10 Bloomsbury Street
London WC1B 3SR
England

Rosa Regina Glaser
at age seventeen, 1931

Once his name is revealed, the calamity begins.

—LOHENGRIN SAGA

Based on an ancient myth, Wolfram von Eschenbach's thirteenth-century poem *Parzival* lauds the heroic deeds of the swan knight Lohengrin, who followed the Rhine River to Kleef, a small city on the German–Dutch border near Nijmegen, where he defended the honor of a noblewoman named Elsa. They married and were happy together, but Lohengrin forbade Elsa to ask about his origins and real name. Years later, unable to contain her curiosity, Elsa asked the forbidden question and thereby mired herself in misfortune.

CONTENTS

FOREWORD

This is the true story of my aunt Rosie.

I have narrated her experience based on her diary, photographs, wartime letters and notes, personal interviews, and archival research.

Immediately after the war Rosie reported those who had betrayed her to the police. Their reports and numerous witness statements also found their way into her archive.

As the oldest of my family's postwar generation, I have cast my aunt's story in book form. It shows what strength of character and optimism can mean when it comes down to the crunch. Pass it on.

DANCING *with the* ENEMY

PAUL

The Suitcase

In 2002 I attended a conference in Krakow for hospital directors. For once the event was scheduled while my wife Ria's students were on holiday, and she had been able to join me for the trip. We had never been to Krakow before, so we had arranged to stay on after the conference for three extra days with a few other directors. I'd been looking forward to it. Our first day would be spent sightseeing, enjoying the city's ancient streets. The following day was reserved for exploring the neighboring salt mines. On the third and final day we planned to visit Auschwitz, World War II's largest concentration camp, and the adjoining camp in Birkenau.

As the final day approached, I grew increasingly uneasy about visiting the camp. The evening before the planned trip I told my wife I was in no mood for the excursion. I had never been to a concentration camp. The documentaries I had seen during my school days had been enough. Was I trying to rationalize a deeper impulse? I told the group they could count me out.

At breakfast the following morning, a few colleagues tried to persuade me to make the trip after all. How could I not be interested, they argued. And it's only a stone's throw away. Out of solidarity I let them convince me. That morning I boarded the bus with mixed emotions.

After an hour's drive we arrived at a vast flat terrain. The place seemed immense. Wooden barracks extended as far as the eye could see. Our guide was a young man with short blond hair who welcomed us with a broad smile. After introducing himself, he led us through the camp gate with the words *Arbeit Macht Frei* suspended above our heads. Countless people were murdered here, our guide informed us, most of them Jews. Men, women, children, even babies. I felt like a disaster tourist. What was I doing there? Why hadn't I stood my ground that morning and stayed behind in the city?

With undiminished enthusiasm, the guide steered us past a number of stone buildings, stopping at a wall where people were executed on a daily basis. We then entered an adjoining building where Dr. Carl Clauberg conducted his medical experiments. The building had also been used to accommodate prisoners, and our guide led us to their dimly lit quarters, where confiscated property was piled behind glass.

One display contained an enormous quantity of spectacles; another contained piles of human hair, some of it still braided. While my colleagues lingered, my wife and I proceeded to the next room, which was filled with suitcases. Prisoners were obliged to mark their baggage to make sure it didn't get lost, at least that's what they were told, so each piece of luggage bore its owner's name and country of origin.

My attention was quickly drawn to a large brown suitcase situated at the front. Astonishment glued me to the spot. The suitcase was from the Netherlands and was inscribed with the name "Glaser" in large letters, a relatively unusual name in my country. My wife read it as well and took my hand. In the display window

I saw our reflection superimposed over the tableau, a suitcase going nowhere with my name on it. Silence engulfed us.

A moment later the voices got louder, signaling the group's approach. "I'm not in the mood for this, let's get out of here," I told my wife, and we hurried out of the room toward the exit. The fresh air did me good. After a while, everyone joined us outside. "Did you see it? The brown suitcase with your name on it?" someone asked. I had been dreading that question, secretly hoping that no one would have noticed the suitcase or read the name. I felt awkward and confused, and just before I attempted an answer someone else chimed in, "Did you have family here during the war?" I responded reluctantly: "My name? Yes, I saw it too. I have no idea who the suitcase might have belonged to," I lied. More questions followed, but I managed to brush them off. To my relief the guide cut in and we continued the tour. But my thoughts were with the suitcase.

At dinner that evening the group chattered spiritedly. Under normal circumstances I would have joined them without a second thought, but that night I was quieter than usual and went up to my room early.

As I lay in bed, I couldn't erase the image of the suitcase from my mind. Why had I been so evasive with my friends? Why did I beat about the bush when I knew precisely what to answer? I finally made a decision. The following morning I was still convinced: it was time to go public with the family secret.

ROSIE

Love's Broken Wings

Rosie and Boy in the countryside

IT WAS EARLY September of 1933, and Boy and I were enjoying a fine Sunday afternoon ambling through the center of Nijmegen. Every now and then I peered out of the corner of my eye at our reflections in the shop windows. People might have mistaken us for a couple. No big surprise. Boy was twenty-one and I would be nineteen the following week. A longing for love briefly bubbled to the surface. Boy was my chum. We danced together, played tennis, went swimming. But apart from an occasional amorous dally in the countryside, we were just good friends.

The honk of a passing car nudged me back to reality.

"Rosie, that car's honking at you," Boy said, stopping for a moment.

"Oh is it? Lovestruck drivers don't interest me one bit."

"The driver looked as if he knew you. Who was it?"

"No idea," I said indifferently. "Let's go."

We were passing time before we went to the Vereeniging later that night, where we had arranged to meet friends to go dancing. I went to the Vereeniging at least twice a week. It was a famous spot in Nijmegen—a magnificent building full of chambers, corridors, and bars. The great hall could accommodate 1,600 people, and in the winter it was used for concerts, operas, operettas, revues, and theatrical performances. The foyer was simply splendid: a mahogany dance floor, snug burgundy furniture, and a rotating mirrored ceiling. There was a winter café with light music and an excellent dance band in the summer. International cabaret acts performed every other week.

As a child I had often heard my parents talk about the Vereeniging and gazed at the building longingly as I crossed Keizer Karelplein. It seemed so magnificent, a place for grown-ups. You had to be at least sixteen to enter, and a member to boot.

I acquired my father's membership card by a quirk of fate. After his mother died he went into mourning for a year and my mother, the product of a narrow-minded upbringing, found it unthinkable to go out alone. I didn't want to hurt my father's feelings so I tried not to show my delight, but this was a real gift.

Every Thursday I would join my mother for a wonderful concert in the Vereeniging's grand hall. I enjoyed them immensely, especially the piano soloists. They gave me the chance to familiarize myself with all sorts of classical compositions, as well as the kinds of people in attendance. For a young girl like myself, this was a thrilling taste of adult life, and I wanted more.

There was always plenty to observe: Ladies who would spend the entire concert consuming sweets, driving everyone else mad with the constant rustling of paper. Elderly gentlemen armed with opera glasses, unashamedly scouring the audience instead of the podium. People in handsome evening wear with little interest in classical music, who would fall into a peaceful sleep minutes after the concert had started. There were also fanatical music lovers who followed the score note by note, eager to spot a conductor's mistake.

And then there were the intermissions, when people walked up and down the long mirror-lined corridors, assessing their reflections as they headed to the foyer where coffee was served.

I enjoyed every moment, so much so that my mother would often ask: "Rosie, are you looking for someone?"

"No, Mother," I'd reply. "I'm just enjoying the audience. It's like being at the zoo. Look around: I see monkeys, donkeys, foxes, owls, pigs, elephants, parrots, and hawks."

Getting my first taste of adult life wasn't the only thing that made the Vereeniging special. It also brought me back to my first love, dancing, which I had come to love as a girl when my family lived in Germany.

Shortly after World War I, my father joined Margarine A.G. in Kleef, Germany, the first foreign subsidiary of the Van de Bergh family. Three thousand people were employed making Blue Band margarine. My father quickly made a career for himself and was promoted to manager.

When life in Kleef started to stabilize once again—after a war that had ended in such disaster for Germany—we lived for quite some time in a fancy hotel by the name of Bollinger, which also housed a number of Belgian officers who kept the town under occupation.

As a five-year-old girl I was free to roam the hotel and everyone was nice to me. One evening I heard music and voices coming from the grand hall: "And one, and two, and three, and four, feet together—and three and four . . ." Behind the glass doors,

Kleef, 1930

shuffling feet glided past in the half light. Wearing patent-leather shoes and white kid gloves, youthful students with blushing faces surrounded Liselotte Benfer, a ginger-haired woman, small and fragile, swathed in a black tulle evening dress. She gave dance lessons to the young people of Kleef. After the war, after so many years of deprivation, they were eager to learn. "The gentlemen will now bring the ladies to their place," she instructed, and a long procession of couples, arm in arm, made its way to the ladies' side, where each gentleman performed a shallow bow, met with a curtsy. "Five-minute break," she decreed.

With my mouth half open I gazed longingly through the glass. That's it, I thought. I want to learn to dance.

One morning I was sitting with my mother in the hotel breakfast room when the same pretty young woman sat opposite our sumptuously arrayed table with a cup of black coffee and a slice of rye bread. It wasn't jealousy that repeatedly drove her gaze in our direction, it was hunger. My mother understood. She had seen the German dance teacher around the hotel and had overheard some suggestive remarks about her. But that was none of her business. She put together an extra breakfast plate—crispy Dutch rusk with cream cheese, fresh fish—and moments later I offered it to Liselotte Benfer with a German curtsy.

"Is that for me?" she asked. "How sweet. But first let me thank your mummy."

An animated conversation followed, giving me the chance to study my idol more closely: her pretty little feet, her fine silk stockings, her well-tailored linen dress, her delicate, slender fingers and cameo ring, her ginger hair held together by a single clip. She didn't need fancy clothes. She was incredibly beautiful.

The best part of this encounter was that I was invited to join the next dance class. When Fräulein Benfer appeared in the grand hall that night with me at her side, her students stared in surprise. "This is Rosie, and she is our new dancer," she explained. Despite my age, I quickly learned the first steps and danced as if my life depended on it. It absorbed me completely. After a while, when the officers in the hotel would ask what I wanted to be when I grew up, I answered, "Fräulein Benfer."

As Boy and I continued our stroll, a young man sitting on the ledge of a tall sash window waved and motioned us to come inside.

"Shall we?" Boy asked. "He's a friend of mine. A decent guy, you'll see."

Inside the large furnished apartment, Boy introduced me to Wim Vermeulen. "What would you like to drink?" Wim asked. Minutes later we raised our glasses to new friends and good health.

Wim was charming, an entertaining raconteur and an attentive listener all in one. On his desk I spotted several photos of the same girl, who I assumed to be his girlfriend. As I stared at the pictures I sensed my cheeks getting warm, not at the sight of the photos, but because I was certain Wim was staring at me.

Caught red-handed. The conversation continued. "What are you doing tonight?" he asked.

"Off to the Vereeniging," Boy replied.

"Come with us," I blurted out.

"May I?" Wim asked with a smile. "I don't want to be a bother."

"You're no bother at all," I said. "We'd really like you to join us."

There was something attractive about Wim, not only his handsomeness but also his manners, his attitude, and his slicked-back hair. He was taller than me and a little older, thin and agile. I was curious.

That evening Boy and I were sitting at a table in the Vereeniging waiting for Wim when I spotted him at the door with a girl, probably the one from the photos on his desk at home. But when they came closer I recognized her.

"I saw her by the cloakroom," Wim said as he arrived at our table, "and because she was alone I asked if she cared to join us."

"No need for introductions," I announced, relieved. "We've

Rosie, far right, at the tennis club

known each other for ages." I gave my tennis partner Lydia a wink. Boy knew Lydia too and we burst out laughing. They grabbed a chair.

Over drinks, Wim told us about his work as a civil aviation pilot. I was struck by his enthusiasm. "I come from a family of four," he explained. "My father died a long time ago and now I'm living here in Nijmegen in a couple of rooms. That's where we met this afternoon. I like it here, especially the good company, just like now," he said with a smile. "I have to make regular trips to the airport in Eindhoven for my work. It's a bit far, but I have a car. It takes about two hours door to door. I don't have to drive there every day. Sometimes I have a week off and stay here in Nijmegen. Other times I'm away from home, traveling all over. I've even flown as copilot to the Dutch East Indies a few times. The return trip takes a couple of weeks, with lots of stopovers in between for fuel and maintenance, and rest of course. It's exciting work." He looked at me with another smile.

Rosie and Wim, 1935

Wim and I spent a lot of time on the dance floor that evening. We didn't say much, just gazed into each other's eyes. It felt instantly good. At the end of the night we made a date to go cycling.

It wasn't long before we were seeking out each other's company at every possible moment. With Wim I felt calm and safe. I didn't need to go out of my way around him, and he was always himself, with no pretension. After a while I began to realize he was crazy about me. And I felt something deeper than the infatuation I'd experienced with previous boyfriends.

Since the time I was young I had always been very anxious

around boys. My parents never told me much about the opposite sex or about love, and I didn't have an older sister or brother I could ask for advice or confide in. I had to discover it all for myself. Most of my knowledge came from books, but my curiosity went hand in hand with an enormous amount of fear. If only I had someone I could talk to about it.

I met Lydia at the tennis club when I was fourteen. She was a sturdy girl in those days, always expensively dressed, nails varnished and polished, a touch of powder, rouge, lipstick. She was six years older than me and infinitely more experienced.

"It's bliss, a real man," she told me one day. "It was a bit scary at first, but now and then I do it with our waiter, at home behind the bowling alley. If my mother ever got wind of it I'd get a thrashing and he would be sacked. But we're always careful. We always get off at Fratton. Otherwise babies, you know?"

"Yes, of course," I said, blushing. "But you really love him, don't you? Surely you're planning to get married?"

"Get married?" Lydia screeched. "Not at all. He's already married, but his wife is sick. Anyway, I don't love him. He's only a waiter. I'm worth more than that, don't you think?"

"But . . . but . . ." I stammered, "why do such a thing?"

Lydia shrugged. "No idea, to be honest. He's just such a wonderful kisser, it makes me forget about everything else."

While my mother was still convinced that I didn't know the anatomical difference between boys and girls, this was the company I kept. But at age fourteen I didn't have a boyfriend to kiss me or whisper tenderly in my ear. Finally, with Wim, I did.

Distracted by my feelings, I stopped paying attention to my parents. We were headed for a major rift anyway. Their endless criticism of my friends was awful to endure: some were below my station or too free with boys, others had the wrong father, you name it. I was also beginning to lose interest in the work I did for my father's business. When we had moved back from Germany I had taken the entrance exam for the secondary school but failed abysmally. My Dutch wasn't up to it. So I concentrated on the language and then my father sent me to a commercial school to train for the business. I'd been doing the same work for years, but I'd been careless lately and my father had every reason to be angry.

Rosie's parents, Falk and Josephine Glaser, 1909

Rosie and her brother John, 1931

And then there were my aunts, who drove me up the wall. My family wasn't all that interested in its Jewish heritage. My parents were assimilated into Dutch society and didn't practice their faith. I certainly didn't. But my aunts kept telling me that I should try to date Jewish boys, and when I paid no attention they nagged even more.

A particularly heated row with my father was the final straw. Afterward, I raced to my room, tossed some clothes into a suitcase, and screamed, "I quit, and I'm leaving this house right now." I slammed the front door and walked away. The farther I got from home, the calmer I became. My father was right. I had found it difficult to concentrate on the invoicing and it had been a mess for quite a while. As I made my way to the city center, it began to dawn on me that I had another reason to leave home, and perhaps it was the real reason. Wim. That night, I stayed at his place.

The following day I left Nijmegen for Eindhoven, rented a room, and started looking for a job. Within a week I landed a position with a clothing manufacturer, handling correspondence and dealing with the representatives.

Eventually Wim and I decided to move in together in Eindhoven, since it was closer to his work. We found a place on Stratum Street in the town center, close to the main square. Neither of our families approved of the arrangement because we weren't married, and they made sure we were aware of it, but we paid no attention. We simply saw them less often. It was our life, after all, not theirs.

Rosie, Wim, and their friend Franz, 1934

Time passed and every now and then I heard a report from the home front. The biggest news was that my father's business had gone bankrupt because of the economic crisis, forcing my parents to move from Nijmegen to Den Bosch, where my father found work as an agent/broker for the textile manufacturer Venmans. As a home, Nijmegen was gone forever.

But life was good for Wim and me. We couldn't get enough of it. Our apartment was comfortably furnished, and on summer evenings we enjoyed sitting on our huge balcony, which overlooked a pretty park on the Dommel stream. I'd started playing piano again, much to Wim's delight, and my love for dancing also blossomed. We registered at the dance school and attended every ball in the city. Modern dances, often from America, added an extra accent to the rhythm of our lives. We made new friends and regularly traveled to Germany, although there was nothing very foreign about the country for either of us. Some of his family came from Germany and I had spent part of my childhood there.

Rosie and Wim at home on a Sunday morning, 1936

What struck me when we visited Germany was that the atmosphere had changed. When my family lived in Kleef, unemployment was rampant and the country was depressed. But now that

Wim and Franz in Düsseldorf, 1934

the National Socialists had been in power for two years, with Hitler at the helm, people seemed enthusiastic. Unemployment was receding, prosperity was on the rise, and Germans felt a new sense of pride. All the government buildings were decorated with Nazi flags and banners bearing swastikas and photos of Hitler.

German Jews were less enthusiastic. The new rulers had reduced them to second-class citizens. But it didn't affect me, so I didn't give it much thought.

In addition to our trips to Germany, we visited the World's Fair in Brussels, spent weekends in elegant Paris, and strolled Belgium's fashionable beaches in Knokke and Blankenberg. We gambled at the casino in Scheveningen on the Dutch coast. We enjoyed the pubs and musicals of London.

Rosie and Wim in Blankenberg, Belgium, 1936

As a copilot Wim was sometimes gone for a whole month. Saying good-bye wasn't easy but the reunions were lovely, and then he had two weeks off. It was a bit like the seaman's life, only he didn't have such long assignments away.

The mornings after he returned we would have breakfast in bed, and he would tell me stories about Egypt, or Pakistan, or the Dutch East Indies, like how the landing gear got stuck in the mud on the runway in Allahabad. On one occasion, he became a little too enthusiastic about a female passenger and I gave him a questioning look. "You're not jealous, are you?" he asked, smiling.

"Not a bit," I replied. "I just wanted to see your reaction. I'm not jealous."

"Are so."

"Am not," and before we knew it we were having a pillow fight in bed, followed by laughter, and judo holds. Breakfast hit the floor. We invariably ended up in each other's arms. The days, evenings, and nights flew by, and although we had been living together for almost two years, it still felt new. We promised to love each other forever and made plans for the future. It was 1936.

Rosie waiting at the airport for Wim, 1936

The morning when fate struck an unexpected blow began like any other. People cycled to work, the newspaper landed in the letter box, bread crumbs were brushed onto the floor. But Wim didn't return from his flight to Asia. Such flights could take weeks and were sometimes held up by the weather or for repairs, so at first I wasn't concerned when the flight didn't arrive on schedule. It happened often enough. But two days later, when I inquired at the airport, they informed me that his plane had crashed near Allahabad. Thirty-seven aboard died in the accident. Wim was one of them.

At first I didn't believe the report. It couldn't be happening. He'll be here later, he'll walk in the door, I reassured myself. But it slowly began to dawn on me that I was never going to see him again, not even his body. The throbbing awareness in my head that he was gone, gone forever, left me empty.

Rosie and Wim on a café terrace, 1933

Each morning when I woke my first thoughts were untroubled, and then I realized moments later that he was never coming back.

The feeling clung to me like a shadow and I couldn't shake it off. It refused to go away.

In bed at night I tried to imagine what his final moments were like, flying through a storm, so they told me, with a sputtering engine: The aircraft begins to tilt, they regain control, then the engine catches fire. They have to land right away, but there's zero visibility and they can't tell that the wind is driving them toward the side of a mountain. At the last instant they see a steep slope up ahead, scream, crash, and it's over. Other times I pictured Wim surviving the disaster but badly wounded and unable to move: I want to save him but he's beyond my reach. The same images returned time after time, until I fell asleep, exhausted.

ROSIE

Dancing with Leo and Kees

OUTSIDE, LIFE CONTINUED as usual. Inside, I felt empty. I didn't dance anymore, let alone go to dinner or the cinema. I still hadn't been back to see my parents, who still lived in Den Bosch. I'd never felt so miserable.

But after a long time I finally woke from my stupor. I wasn't in a social mood, but for the first time in ages I went dancing. The rhythm and the dance steps helped absorb some of my sadness.

One evening on a train trip to Amsterdam I bumped into Leo Crielaars, a dance teacher I'd briefly worked for when one of his instructors had fallen ill. He was a nice guy and visibly pleased to see me. "How are you?" he asked as he entered my compartment. My expression was somber, and while I didn't like to flaunt it, I told him about my grief. He turned out to be genuinely sympathetic. Then silence fell between us. The train trundled on its way, rocking monotonously from side to side. Was he thinking about my loss? He carefully turned the conversation to his dance schools in Eindhoven and Den Bosch. He could see that I was listening and told me all sorts of wonderful stories, getting more enthusiastic by the minute.

"You have a fantastic job," I said. "I really enjoyed filling in for your colleague last year."

"I've seen you dance," he replied. "Lovely style, fluid, good sense of rhythm. You're a good teacher too. You know how to kindle enthusiasm among the students, even the shy ones."

I smiled back.

He looked me in the eye and continued: "Why don't you come and work for me? I'm pretty sure teaching people to dance is more fun than working for a clothing manufacturer, and you'll earn more money."

The idea of making dancing my career was appealing, but I didn't let it show. I let the train roll on in silence for a moment and then responded, "Let me think about it." But he had such a kind expression on his face, and when I saw him frown a little I relented. "I'd love to try it out for an evening, to see if I enjoy it as much as I did a year ago."

We made a date, and that's how I ended up back in Leo's dance school. He eventually offered me a permanent position. In addition to teaching, I'd also be taking care of administrative matters and correspondence. Working for my father and the clothing manufacturer had given me some useful experience. Incidentally, I'd be working in Den Bosch, where my family lived. It was time to move, rent a room, and hand in my notice.

Dancing at Leo's school, taking part in national and international dance competitions, I began to think my surname didn't fit, that it was even a little common. So I changed the *s* to a *c*, added an accent to the *e*, and from then on my name was Glacér. It was much more elegant and international. The rhythm of my days also changed. The workday extended from midday to late night, and most of the time we stayed a couple of hours longer to enjoy life a little, knowing that we didn't have to start again until noon the next day. And so night became day.

It quickly became clear that Leo saw me as more than a coworker. And I liked him. He was kind and well groomed, and he helped me forget my great loss. When he pulled me close while we danced it felt pleasant and familiar, and I let it happen. We regularly stayed after class to chat, have a drink, talk about the day, and organize events. Meanwhile, we attended international meetings in Brussels, London, and Berlin to learn new dance steps and bring them back to the Netherlands. I became a member of the Union des Professeurs de Danse et Culture Physique in Brussels, the Syndicat National in Paris, and of course the Dutch Association of Dance Teachers and the Dutch Dance Union. Along the way we met lots of interesting and elegant people. Life regained some of the color it had lost.

Rosie and Leo, 1936

After a while, Leo and I began to look like a couple to the outside world. It happened so gradually I hardly even noticed. We danced together at the school, traveled abroad together, and at night, after the lessons, I stayed over at his place. I was feeling better and better, and when he asked me to move in and marry him I said yes, as simple as that. No big decision.

When we got engaged we didn't tell anyone. Even though my parents lived nearby, I had virtually no contact with them. They weren't very happy about the fact that their only daughter had run away from home, abandoning her father's business. And like the other people around us, they hadn't approved when I moved in with Wim, at least my mother hadn't. In hindsight, my sudden departure must have saddened them deeply, but at that age I wasn't aware of it. Just like me, Leo had little contact with his family, besides his brother. When we married in Den Bosch we had only a few friends as witnesses. Not even my parents and brother were in attendance. We celebrated with drinks and snacks. It was 1937 and I was twenty-three years old. The dance classes continued that evening as usual, but now I was dancing as Mrs. Crielaars.

Rosie and Leo

Since Leo's room was too small for both of us, we temporarily moved in with his brother and sister-in-law, Marinus and Betsy, in Waalwijk, where we had an entire floor to ourselves. We paid rent, and they made us extremely welcome.

On Sundays we went to mass at the local Catholic church. The atmosphere was quite convivial. Catholicism seemed to be a friendly, cheerful faith, marked by a sense of forgiveness and love of one's neighbor, and when things went wrong, there was confession to set things right again. In spite of the good start, however, the atmosphere at home quickly soured.

It appeared that Leo's brother was an enthusiastic admirer of the National Socialist wind that was blowing through Germany and gaining followers in the Netherlands. He talked about it often with Leo, attended meetings of the NSB (Nationaal Socialistische Beweging, the Dutch equivalent of the Nazi Party), read their weekly journal *Storm*, and was a member of the Nazi-affiliated Dutch Welfare Service and the Dutch Labor Front. Leo clearly admired his older brother, and Betsy always agreed with her husband. For them, the present government's endless compromises had led to nothing more than democratic clap-trap. We were living in a period of economic crisis, poverty, and widespread unemployment. Life for many was harsh and difficult. They thought National Socialism had a new perspective to offer.

I was not of the same mind. I had been living in Germany when the foreign minister Walther Rathenau was murdered and the Nazi movement started to gain strength. I was familiar with the party's economic productivity, but I also knew about their racist ideas. As I began to voice my opinion, tensions quickly developed at home. Marinus didn't like it when I participated in discussions, and Leo wasn't sure what to do or say. His brother was used to his obedient wife agreeing with his every word. The situation went from bad to worse. Leo was my husband, but he was also fond of his brother. He wouldn't break off relations with Marinus, and I wouldn't want him to, but I had to find a way out of the increasing tension. Minor irritations only complicated matters. I once got angry with Marinus for opening my mail.

"I do the same with my wife's mail," he snapped. "I'm the boss in this house."

When I saw him with it the following day I snatched it from him. "Keep your hands off my mail," I shouted. He immediately lunged at me to try to get it back. He was heavy and strong, but I managed to scratch his face and kick him in the crotch. At that he let me go, grabbed a breadknife from the kitchen, and chased after me: "I'll get you," he shouted. "I'll teach you who's boss in this house." I didn't wait for the knife. I ran out of the house and made my way to the dance school in Den Bosch, where I intended to stay the night. Leo came to get me, and we agreed to start looking for our own place, somewhere nearer the dance school.

But as Marinus continued to plague me, things only got worse. When I calmly asked him one day why he hated me so much he said, "You can go to church a hundred times, but you're a Jew and always will be. I'm a National Socialist, and you'll see: all Jews are destined for hell and we're going to help them get there. Just you wait, my time will come. Then we'll be done with all the corruption." Leo failed to intervene during these fights. And when I told him I wanted to leave, he persuaded me to stay. It was difficult making one compromise after another, and disheartening that my husband wasn't siding with me enough.

While these quarrels continued Leo and I decided to remodel the dance school. In the interim we rented a large hall at a nearby hotel/restaurant where we continued our classes. It was called the Lohengrin, a name that brought me back to my childhood in Ger-

Lohengrin

many. The Lohengrin saga, which inspired Wagner's opera, is set in Kleef, where I grew up.

One Wednesday afternoon while I was preparing for that evening's class a young man walked into the hall and immediately caught my eye. He introduced himself as Kees van Meteren, the son of Lohengrin's owner. His father's recent death had brought him back from abroad. Though he was only twenty and I was twenty-four, he seemed very mature for his age. He'd worked in renowned hotels in Frankfurt for almost a year and a half and spent a year after that in Hungary.

I soon discovered that he was quite at home in the world of important guests, dinner dances, and gala nights. He was charming and glamorous, moved with ease, and always found a way to turn a profit.

One evening while I was freshening up in the changing rooms, changing from my ball gown into something more simple, Kees walked in out of the blue, marched right up to me, and kissed me on the neck. Taken aback by his boldness I turned, and we kissed on the lips. I asked him to leave on the double because Leo might appear at any moment. We kissed again and he left. A couple of minutes later Leo threw open the door, making me jump. "Are you coming, sweetheart?" he asked. "The car's ready."

Kees van Meteren, 1940

On the way home, my thoughts strayed back to the kiss in the dressing room. Was it just a summer-evening whim or was it more? Was it because the atmosphere at home with

Leo and Marinus had become so unpleasant that I was susceptible to the kind attentions of a young man whom I happened to find more attractive than my husband?

Whatever spurred it, my desire for Kees persisted long after that first kiss. Though we saw each other regularly after the dance lessons, we were usually in the company of others. But sometimes, since I was responsible for administrative matters at the dance school, I managed to see him alone. He courted me unashamedly during those hours, and a couple of times we ended up in one of the hotel bedrooms. The better we got to know each other, the more infatuated we became. We always managed to think of a reason to meet. We had to be careful, of course, otherwise people would notice. Luckily, Leo tended to go to bed after the dance classes, so I would sometimes tell him I was going for a drink with a girlfriend, then meet up with Kees, before sneaking back home. Since we didn't have to get up until eleven the next day, Leo didn't catch on at first. But after a while he noticed Kees smiling at me a lot at work and began to suspect that he liked me. Jealousy took hold of him, and he started to keep a closer eye on me. I could see it in everything he did. He became stricter and bossier, the wrong approach as far as I was concerned, and the atmosphere only got worse. I was not the submissive type, that was all there was to it, and I was certainly not a financially dependent housewife like so many of my contemporaries.

What a difference with Kees. Leo was often tired, grumpy, and bossy. He never stopped ranting about National Socialism. Kees, on the other hand, was not only attentive but also much better in bed. There was never a dull moment when we were together. Though I often took his stories about the famous people he'd met with a grain of salt, there was still something magical about such tales. And he was always so kind to me, which was a welcome change from Leo's unpleasantness.

Six months later, Leo announced the good news. The people who rented the floor above the dance school in Den Bosch had decided to leave. I'd run away from his brother's place no fewer than three times in the last months, and the news came as an enormous relief. In less than two weeks we moved from Waalwijk to the empty apartment above the dance school, and I finally began to relax. Even Leo was pleased, not only because our arguments stopped but also because of the easy commute. He missed his brother, of course, but I was much more cheerful and calm. And although he was still uncertain about me, a pleasant atmosphere began to evolve between us. Our love life also took a turn for the better. With the dance school renovations complete, there was no longer any need to use the Lohengrin, and I saw Kees less and less. I decided it was time to sever the connection.

With two years of hard work behind us, our school began to thrive and grow. Our photo appeared regularly in the paper, and Leo began to slow down a little, smoke fat cigars, and behave like a man of means.

But just before the annual Bossche Revue, we had to relocate to a rehearsal room in the Lohengrin, and Kees appeared, flirting with me openly in front of the girls. Although my husband always came to collect me after practice, Kees refused to leave me alone. He showered me with flowers, letters, and even gave me a diamond ring.

When Leo got wind of it his old jealousy was rekindled. We argued more and more, not only about Kees but also about the division of labor at the dance school, and, of course, about the coming new order.

Nothing changed. Kees followed me everywhere, and the situation at home became increasingly difficult. It was obvious to Leo that my heart and my mind were no longer his. I spent more and more time with Kees, and Leo sensed that he was losing me. He

CASINO DANCING
ZONDAG 28 NOVEMBER 8—2 UUR
NIGHT OF SWING

L. J. CRIELAARS
EN
ROOSJE GLACER
DEMONSTREEREN
DE ORIGINEELE
AMERIKAANSCHE
SWING STEP

Het publiek leert in 10 minuten SWING DANCE.

Uitgebreid DANS-ORKEST onder leiding van GUUS VAN OPSTAL.

Entrée 50 cent

Newspaper announcement for a "Night of Swing"

tried to win me back, but I felt his hesitation. It was clear that his brother Marinus's convictions had become his own convictions, and that complicated things for him. He didn't persevere in his efforts to recapture my affections, and his brother cursed me constantly. "Because you're part of the Jewish question," he bellowed.

And if I bit back, insisting that I wasn't a question but a person, that I was Rosie, it was like a red rag to a bull. I think he hated me, that's all, just like some animals go for each other's throats out of pure instinct.

Leo joined his brother at every opportunity. They listened to Hitler's speeches on the radio. They talked about how intelligent he was, about his plans for the future: The old world with its corrupt ways would be overturned. The world of unemployment and poverty would disappear. A new order would be established, free of spineless democracy, free of corrupt Jews who conspired against hardworking citizens and laborers. Cars for everyone, Volkswagens! Who wouldn't want a Volkswagen?

The German people's enthusiasm for National Socialism didn't surprise me. When I lived in Kleef, I saw for myself what the humiliating defeat of the First World War had done to the population, not to mention the effects of the enormous war debt imposed by the French, the British, and the Americans. We Dutch may not have had to endure the same cheerless poverty as the Germans, but we shared the same longing for strong leadership and a better economy. More and more people had been joining the NSB of late, and more than 8 percent of the population voted for the party in the election. And then there was the Black Front, another political party with Nazi inclinations. They'd been picking up votes too, especially where we lived.

In this climate, Marinus continually advised Leo to leave me. A Jewish wife just wasn't right, he said. I could sense that Leo still cared for me, but I also sought regular comfort with Kees, and Leo didn't know what to do. The more he tried to hold on to me, the more I slipped away. During yet another of our arguments he asked: "Have you read *Mein Kampf*? The Jews are to be annihilated. Maybe you'll be lucky because you're married to me and they'll only deport you to Palestine, but the rest don't have a snowball's chance." What could I have said in response to such statements? Precious little. And so our life continued.

It was clear that Leo was no longer in control of me or of his anger, and at one point he also lost control of his hands, slapping me in the face during one of our arguments. After running out of the house and wandering around the city center in despair, I knocked on my parents' door. In spite of my not having seen or spoken to them in months, they welcomed me in and offered me a place to stay.

When I called Kees and told him what had happened, he advised me to file for divorce, which I did. But Leo refused. "If anyone's filing for divorce around here it's me," he said. He quickly consulted a lawyer. The sad thing was that all the children of his lawyer's family were taking dance classes with me. But the customer was always right. I continued to give private lessons while the lawyer started divorce proceedings.

What a dreadful experience. I stayed with my parents, yet every morning I went to work for my ex-husband and everyone still called me Mrs. Crielaars. It couldn't have been more unpleasant.

In April there was an enormous ball at the Casino for almost two thousand people, organized by our dance school. Leo and I demonstrated the latest steps. The applause was enthusiastic, and I was given three bouquets of flowers, one with thirty roses from Kees. Afterward, he sat in the bar waiting for me, and I went to thank him. It was wrong, I know, but I was drawn to Kees like a magnet. I couldn't help myself. When Leo spotted me he exploded. Our two thousand guests were struck dumb. When I got home that evening, I decided never to work with Leo again.

After I quit, I wrote up the menus for the Lohengrin, sketching the swan knight in the top left-hand corner as a sort of logo. If

Rosie and Leo demonstrating the Lambeth Walk

I wanted to go out, I traveled with Kees to another city. He often had money, and he liked to spend it. In the meantime, Leo and I got divorced. The evening it became official Kees surprised me with a bottle of champagne and a beautiful silver brooch to herald my new life. It seemed so thoughtful and sweet. But though I was determined to get back to my dance classes, Kees didn't like the idea. He preferred me to be with him and not spend my evenings elsewhere.

Then I learned that besides me, Kees was also seeing a Belgian girl. I was furious, overcome yet again with a sense of being alone.

PAUL

A Hidden Sign

IN 1974 MY wife Ria and I were expecting our first child. We told our family and friends, furnished a nursery, thought up baby names, and discussed whether we should have our child baptized. Both Ria and I were baptized and grew up in Catholic families, she as a farmer's daughter in the polders near The Hague, me at the foot of Mount Saint Peter near Maastricht. We both have pleasant memories of an agreeable and carefree youth. Ria is one of ten children and had trained as a kindergarten teacher with the nuns in The Hague. I spent my youth exploring the caves of Mount Saint Peter with friends, attending grammar school near Vrijthof Square in Maastricht, and swimming across the River Maas every day in the summer.

Life in a largely Protestant environment tended to reinforce the Catholic identity of Ria's family, but Maastricht was different. Everything in Maastricht was Catholic. It was part of life.

Every Sunday after mass, Saint Luke's Brass Band marched through the streets, followed by a procession that included the priest under a baldachin, a collection of altar boys, members of the church council, and other prominent citizens. Many people kept statues of Mother Mary in the window or had her image inset into the facades of their homes. Everyone was familiar with Saint Servatius's Well on the outskirts of Maastricht, said to have miraculously appeared in the fourth century when Saint Servatius arrived on foot from Asia. There were also persistent rumors about golden statues of the apostles that were hidden in the neighborhood. If a chaplain was spotted on his way to visit the sick carrying a little box in his hand with a consecrated host inside, cyclists would dismount, kneel on the street, and cross themselves. When the neighborhood founded the Saint Peter's Handball Club, no one questioned the addition of the words "Roman Catholic" to the name. The parish priest agreed and blessed our ball. He blessed not only balls, but also people, houses, even cars. Once a year, citizens assembled their vehicles on the square in front of the church, and the parish priest dipped a copper-handled brush into a gilded basin of holy water, swung it wildly, and, in Latin, blessed the cars with holy water to protect them from accidents. Everything was so steeped in Catholicism that even the non-Catholics were a little Catholic.

Since Catholicism was such a strong part of my family's identity—not just my immediate family but also my grandmother and grandfather, uncles, aunts, nieces, and nephews—Ria and I decided to have our child, the first child of the next generation, baptized. In the meantime, we ran through the names of family members in the hope of finding one that we might use. When it came to my father, John, Ria inquired about his middle initial, *S*.

"It's for Samuel," I said.

"Nice name. It sounds Jewish," she responded. But we didn't give it much thought. We had Christian friends who had given their children Jewish names—Judith, Sarah, Job—simply because they liked the names.

But seven years after our first child, Myra Barbara, was born, something happened that made us reconsider the origin of my father's middle name. I was celebrating my thirty-fifth birthday with my parents and my friends, and at a certain point the conversation turned to the Israeli–Palestinian conflict. One of my friends, who was a member of the Netherlands Palestine Committee and had visited the former Palestinian leader Yasser Arafat in exile, dominated the conversation, condemning Israeli politics, talking about criminal Jewish activities, and equating Zionism with racism. My father, who usually liked to participate in conversations with my friends, listened in silence until his nose started to bleed. Suddenly, he grabbed a handkerchief, left the group, and went upstairs to lie down in bed. He didn't return until my friends had left.

The next day Ria and I chatted about the party. "Annoying, your father's nosebleed," Ria remarked. "I noticed it started when they were talking about Zionism and racism. Do you think the conversation might have had something to do with it? His middle name is Samuel. Perhaps your father has a Jewish background."

"It's possible," I said, "but not likely. He was always the one who insisted we go to church. Everyone in the family is Catholic, and his first name is John, not Samuel. Anyway, I've had trouble with spontaneous nosebleeds myself. And on top of that, I think he would have told me."

Nevertheless, we explored the possibility further. My father's parents were long dead, and as far as we could tell they didn't have particularly Jewish first names. His mother's maiden name was Philips.

"Aren't the owners of the Philips factories Protestant?" I said. "My father has a sister, Rosie, in Sweden, but I know almost nothing about her. I remember she visited us at home when I was a child, but beyond that we weren't in touch with her."

My parents had taught me that it was important to be attuned to the people and circumstances around you and to play an active part in your environment. That's the way I was raised. But in spite of my natural curiosity, the idea of exploring my identity further—and with it my family's past—simply didn't occur to me. I didn't feel that I was missing anything.

ROSIE

The New Order

Rosie in front of the city hall in Vught on May 10, 1940, the day Germany invaded the Netherlands

ON MAY 10, 1940, three weeks after I had quit teaching, the Germans invaded the country, and Queen Wilhelmina fled to England. It was criminal and cowardly, if you asked me, an insult to the rest of the population who remained. And it didn't make sense. She was married to a German with National Socialist inclinations. Why did she run? Was her money more important than her people?

The arrival of the Germans signified the arrival of the new order that Marinus and Leo had often talked about. I became concerned and couldn't get their discussions about the Jewish question out of my head. Those were German ideas. Germans were now in control, and plenty of Dutch people had similar thoughts. I wasn't afraid for myself, but it was going to be a particularly hard time for my parents.

Meanwhile, Kees was very excited to tell me that he had been conscripted, and he asked me to look after a number of valuable belongings for him. But a few days later, with equal enthusiasm, he said that he was off the hook, that they needed him at the Lohengrin, which was going to become the city's *Wehrmachtheim*—the army's home away from home. Kees, who spoke fluent German, was exceptionally friendly toward the Germans from the outset. He attributed it to the time he worked in Frankfurt, where he had joined the *Ausländische Hitlerjugend*—Foreign Hitler Youth. On the first day of the occupation he had made sure that German menus were placed on the tables for his new guests.

At that time my younger brother John no longer lived at home. As a young man of nineteen, he had been called up for military service and had mobilized before the war broke out. When the Germans invaded the country, he was there to defend it in some hastily dug trenches in The Hague, first at the Binnenhof—where the Dutch parliament had its seat—and then at the entrance to the Government Printing Office. Soon he would be face to face with the invading Germans. I hoped nothing would happen to him. Maybe he would be lucky. I heard through the grapevine that the Germans were being held back in heavy fighting near Grebbeberg in the Dutch midlands and that they hadn't yet been able to reach The Hague.

My brother told me later that it was fairly calm in The Hague at first, but that it was a miracle he was still alive. When he had been standing guard on that first day near the Printing Office, someone had started shooting at him from the building opposite. There was no one in sight, and the Germans still hadn't taken the city. It had to have been a Dutchman. It was probably an NSB supporter. My brother was lucky. The bullet hit his glasses and knocked them from his face. Half an inch farther and the shot would have been fatal. He was forced to take cover in a doorway and managed to escape only after nightfall. It made me wonder what kind of country ours was, when your own people shot at you while you were defending them from German invasion. There was no time to answer that question, but it shocked me nonetheless.

After five days of fighting that culminated in the bombing of Rotterdam, the Netherlands capitulated, and the Germans entered The Hague. My brother was taken prisoner and sent to Rotterdam to clear rubble. From the provisional camp that had been set up in a park for prisoners of war, he could see the bombed city smolder, and in some places it still burned. One night he left his friends to go to the bathroom and smoke a cigarette. It was dark when he got back, and he couldn't find his own group. When he caught sight of a number of men under blankets he thought he'd found the right spot and got in beside them. His neighbor felt cold, and even in the pitch dark he understood that he was lying next to a corpse. The war became tangible for him in that moment.

In those first days after the German invasion I heard all sorts of rumors. I didn't know what to believe, but I took one particular rumor very seriously: that the prisoners of war were going to be taken to Germany. I wasn't sure if my brother had heard, so I decided to go and get him just to be on the safe side. Information was very confused and public services were in complete chaos, but this could also be an advantage if you wanted to get to someone.

The next morning I headed for Rotterdam on my bicycle with extra provisions: a camera and extra women's clothing. It was roughly fifty miles to Rotterdam, and I passed German soldiers on foot and in cars along the way. In the villages I cycled through,

Rosie's photographs of Rotterdam after the bombing

Rosie and John in front of the railway station, October 1940

life continued as normal: mothers pushed strollers, children played on the street, a queue formed at the baker's. The usual routine. But as I got closer to Rotterdam things changed. The city center had been flattened. I quickly took a few photos and went in search of my brother.

After asking around, I arrived at the park where he was stationed. There wasn't much security, and the people were just like those I'd passed on my way there: calm, expectant, and obedient. When John saw me he couldn't believe his eyes. He was clearly delighted. I told him to come with me. He tried to object, but I cut him short and took his arm. Arm in arm we walked toward the gate. When a German soldier asked where we were going, I replied in fluent German: "Home. The children are waiting," and we continued on our way. The soldier didn't stop us. With the Dutch roads now awash with German soldiers, as soon as we were outside the city I gave my brother the women's clothing I had brought with me, and we cycled back to Den Bosch disguised as a couple of girls. No one stopped us, and the journey passed without incident. We arrived home late that evening, both of us exhausted.

Kees wasn't the only one who was kind and obliging toward the Germans. Most of the population was the same. Everyone just wanted to get on with their everyday lives. The German soldiers behaved themselves, and many newspapers wrote positively about them, calling on their readers to accept the new authorities. In the women's weekly *Libelle* I read a sympathetic article about the poor German soldiers who were away from home. Months and months away from their country, far from their wives and children. They were serving their fatherland with dedication, and we should respect them, the editors told us, only two weeks after they had invaded the Netherlands. Obedience and resignation characterized the general tone among the Dutch, but also admiration and desire to be part of the new order and the Great German Empire. The newly appointed Reich Commissioner was the Austrian Arthur Seyss-Inquart, whom Hitler had apparently tasked with befriending the Dutch. He was intelligent, sensitive, and churchgoing, played the piano, and was a moderate National Socialist. He insisted that the Dutch were also German, that the Germans and the Dutch were kin. Many of the Dutch agreed.

As a result of new German orders, the industrial sector flourished. Unemployment fell fast, and many were quite happy with the situation. There had been little, if any, resistance. Von

Falkenhausen, the commander of the German forces, wrote the following to Seyss-Inquart: "The attitude of the population was flawless and surprisingly obliging. There is no sign of hatred or inner rejection. The brevity of the war appears to have averted embitterment." I encountered the same attitude everywhere and didn't know what to think. Reports from German Jews hadn't exactly been good the last few years, and a number of them had fled to the Netherlands. My cousin Joost had warned our family about the Nazis. He advised us to leave before the occupation. He himself had left for the Dutch East Indies with his family. But I myself had nothing to do with Judaism. I was too busy with other matters, and the Germans had behaved respectably so far. But all those reports made me a little uneasy.

One day Kees came into the Lohengrin waving some documents stamped by the Germans under my nose and telling me he had interesting business to do in Cologne and Antwerp. He was enthusiastic and full of energy. I heard from a friend shortly after that she had seen him in an intimate embrace with a German girl at the Luxor Theatre. And a waiter from the Lohengrin told me that Kees had driven with a German woman to the Hotel Bosch and Ven in Oisterwijk, where they stayed the night and spent a lot of money.

For a few days I feigned ignorance. He was kind and sweet, as he always was. But I finally exploded and confronted him with everything I knew. He couldn't deny any of it. Then he claimed he had taken on an important diplomatic role since the Lohengrin had become the *Wehrmachtheim*. Senior German officers used the hotel to negotiate, so I imagined it might be true, but I had lost my faith in him by that point and severed our connection.

After a while I heard that a German woman staying at the *Wehrmachtheim* was his new girlfriend. I heard she was a member of the Gestapo who was working as a translator. They were regularly seen together in public. I spotted her one evening through the window of the Lohengrin where she was standing with Kees and his entire family. I felt miserable. After divorcing Leo I had sought support with Kees, but now he was off with someone else. I could no longer give dance classes. I had no income. I was once again living with my parents. I was twenty-five years old and penniless. I had to laugh at myself when I thought of how I rushed out the door in Nijmegen. A good income, a marriage, a dance school, and now I had nothing, I was back to square one. Was I just unlucky? Did I want too much all at once? Or had I been stupid? I didn't know the answer, and even if I did it wouldn't help. I had to do something. I missed dancing and I missed having a boyfriend, so I set to work.

Intent on restarting my career as a dance teacher, I contacted Leo to collect my diplomas and certificates. But my ex-husband refused and told me I was no longer authorized to teach dance. "Surely you don't think I would dig my own grave by letting you set up competition? I will do whatever it takes, and I mean whatever it takes, to ruin you if you ever even think of giving classes again." I was furious. His keeping my papers was little short of theft. He had no right, but I had nowhere to turn. It would take forever if I went to the courts. But I was determined. I would teach again come what may.

In those days dance teachers had to register with the newly established Dutch Society of Dance Teachers, which was part of the *Kulturkammer* set up by the Germans. Jews weren't allowed membership, but I managed to circumvent the ban with the help of a colleague who was well known in the dance world. Once I was authorized to give dance classes, I rented locations in different cities and started a publicity campaign. When Leo and I had split up I had taken the student records with me. Now, I sent each one of them a letter, giving them a chance to decide between

Magazine advertisements for Rosie's dance school

Leo and myself. I also advertised in the regional newspapers and hung posters around the city. I even had a poster hung at Leo's dance school. It made me feel good, although I later heard that it was removed the following day. I wrote and designed all the posters myself. "Stock Up on Joie de Vivre." The text spoke to people in those increasingly distressing times. I always varied the message: "Don't let the darkness prevent you from sending your children to dance classes"; "Rosie Glacér looks forward to adding your name to the list of tomorrow's top dancers"; "The dance school where good company meets"; "The school for the upper crust"; "Rosie Glacér for style and standing." In addition to my ads, I also wrote a book on dance and etiquette entitled *Zoo danst u correct* (*That's How to Dance*). I published it myself and gave copies to all my students.

Classes began first in Den Bosch, and soon afterward in Tilburg, Helmond, and Eindhoven. My publicity campaign seemed to have worked. In that first year, I had only fourteen students in Den Bosch—Leo caused a great deal of commotion there—but I had five hundred students combined in the other three locations. I was delighted to see a few former colleagues from the clothing manufacturer in Eindhoven. They hadn't forgotten me, and that did me a world of good.

The dances I taught varied from group to group, ranging from American tap and the new rhythm step to ballet and ballroom—including waltz, rumba, tango, and foxtrot. Sometimes I organized special evenings for my students that included a band. I couldn't imagine having a more wonderful job, and one that paid well too.

dansinstituut roosje glacer

eindhoven - tilburg - 'shertogenbosch - helmond

lesbewijs no. ....

uitgereikt aan den heer / mejuffr. ....

adres: ....

inschrijv.	1e les	4e les	8e les

cursus .... te ....

op ....

Registration slip for Rosie's dance school

Leo had made it clear that I was not welcome near him: "No one invades my territory," he had insisted. But my students were satisfied, and in February 1941 no fewer than forty signed up for my spring classes in Den Bosch.

Rosie surrounded by one of her groups of dance students in Eindhoven, 1941

With my professional life in order, I no longer wanted to be alone, so I set out to look for a companion. But where would I begin? I thought about the men I already knew. Which of them did I find attractive? Were they reliable? Did they have a decent job? I then remembered a kind and respectable man I had met at a previous dance course. He had wanted to get to know me better and had even suggested a date, but I had brushed him off. His name was Ernst Wettstein. If I remembered correctly, he worked for a Swiss company that designed, exported, and installed new industrial looms for the textile industry. He was in the Netherlands at the time, living in Eindhoven.

Establishing contact was easy enough. I knew where he usually went to eat, and one day I made sure I was there before he arrived. He spotted me by the window with a cup of coffee. We had dinner together that evening, and he turned out to be even nicer than I remembered.

Before long we were seeing each other regularly, and in no time at all I was spending the night at his flat in Eindhoven, sprucing up the place with things of my own. Being with Ernst did me a world of good, and I began to feel human again. We enjoyed regular weekends away, in Scheveningen, Brussels, and Knokke. I had a great time, although I was reminded of Wim and the trips we had made together. But gradually the tensions of the past and the pressures of starting my own dance school faded into the background. Ernst was very attentive, much more than Leo ever was, and he was a lot more reliable than Kees. Precise and dependable, like a Swiss watch.

Rosie playing cards with Ernst

The dance school kept me busy. I looked after the accounts, kept track of enrollment, and took care of advertising. In fact I did everything myself. To get around, I bought a little car, a Fiat. In addition to teaching classes, I gave private lessons and made sure I trained as much as I could. Together with Tommy

Mullink, my new dance partner from Amsterdam, I introduced new dances from London, Brussels, and Paris. I had done the same when I was with Leo and still had connections from those days.

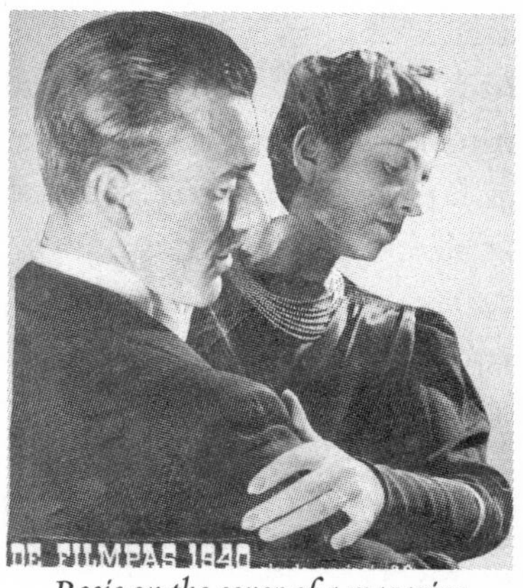

Rosie on the cover of a magazine

It was a shame we could no longer travel to London. It prevented me from seeing Alex Moore and Pat Kilpatrick from the School of Dance near Kingston-on-Thames. Alex and his wife Pat were an exceptionally nice English couple who were featured on the BBC. I had learned a great deal from them about performing in public. Fortunately I had managed to visit them at the beginning of 1940. Since the German invasion we had to keep in touch by post. Alexander sent news on a regular basis and sometimes included step charts and photos for new dances.

Stills from the Polygon Newsreels' 1940–41 season

Visits to Brussels and Paris, which were still accessible, were a continued source of new ideas. Tommy and I gave performances in Amsterdam (Krasnapolski and Bellevue), The Hague (Tabaris), and Utrecht (Tivoli). We danced the Filmpas 1940, which was all the rage, and demonstrated other new dances such as the Sherlockinette, the "motor" polka, and the quadrille. The Polygon Newsreel people had filmed one of our performances, and it was playing throughout the Netherlands—including the Luxor Theatre in Den Bosch. Things couldn't have been better. My picture appeared all over the place in magazines and news-

A still of Rosie demonstrating a new dance from the Polygon Newsreel, 1940

papers. No matter where Leo turned he couldn't avoid my successes. And in the meantime his school was deteriorating badly. One respectable Den Bosch resident had told me, "You can't go to Leo Crielaars anymore. He has a fine school, but the people who attend are such a mixed bag." Music to my ears!

Then things started to shift. Slowly but surely new restrictions were imposed on Dutch Jews—those designated Jewish according to German racial theories, that is. This was a surprise. Even if you didn't practice your faith and your ancestors had always been Dutch, you suddenly didn't belong anymore. Even though you weren't registered in a Jewish community, had never seen the inside of a synagogue, and had fought for your country in the army—like my brother John—you no longer counted and that was that. It was such a strange notion to me, but according to the German race laws I was a Jew. Rotten luck! Jews weren't allowed to own a radio, no longer had access to the stock exchange, and were obliged to send their children to Jewish schools. I wasn't allowed to eat out at restaurants, visit hotels, go to the cinema, walk along the beach, take a stroll in the park. "No Jews Allowed" signs appeared everywhere. I was also not allowed to travel.

What did one do in such circumstances? Life was restricted in unprecedented ways, and the people who weren't affected didn't seem to care. There was almost no one I could talk to about it, no one who could do anything about it. The government had taken my rights, but most people didn't seem to be bothered. For them, life went on. What if I couldn't rent locations for my flourishing dance school? What if I couldn't travel to them? Impossible!

I decided not to wait for my own funeral and resolved to ignore all the new rules and regulations, in spite of the serious penalties that had been threatened. I drank tea at café terraces under a huge "No Jews Allowed" sign. I even asked someone to take a photograph of me smiling from ear to ear under the sign. On one occasion I got into a conversation with a German officer, who was very polite, then asked him to take my picture with the same text in the background. I kept my spirits up, although it gradually became more difficult.

Things were good between Ernst and me. Late in the evening, after the lessons were over, I would drive to his flat in Eindhoven in my Fiat. Sometimes he was already asleep, especially if he had to get up early the next day, but most of the time he waited up. Our love grew and grew. One Sunday when we returned to his living room after a nice summer walk, he produced a box with an engagement ring inside, gold with two small sapphires. I was dumbfounded. We had been living together for a while, so it

Rosie on a café terrace with a German officer

seemed unnecessary to get engaged all of a sudden, but at the same time I thought it was fantastic, and before I gave myself a chance to think about it further I said yes. He produced a bottle of champagne and we sipped it together as the wonderful summer evening drew to a close.

Ernst's work in the Netherlands was only temporary, and I wondered what would happen when it ended. But we postponed the discussion until one evening in September when he announced that his Swiss employer has already lined up his next assignment. He was expected in Spain in March to oversee the

Rosie and one of her students riding a bike in The Hague, 1941

Rosie and Ernst at the beach in The Hague, 1941

modernization of a couple of textile factories. Now that we were engaged he wanted me to join him in Switzerland and afterward in Spain. I didn't know what to think. I had known he would want to return to Switzerland someday, but that day had arrived sooner than I expected. What about my dance school? It was going so fantastically well. But Ernst was eager for me to go to Switzerland and meet his family. "We can get married, and then you can come along to Spain." When I protested, Ernst understood. "I know it's difficult," he said, "but I desperately want you to come with me. It'll also be safer for you. You don't know what the Nazis are planning and my country is neutral in this war." We agreed that I would take a week to think things over before I gave him my answer. I lay awake at night worrying: Switzerland and Spain would be such a pleasure; leaving my dance school, my friends, and my students would be a punishment.

A week later I announced my decision over dinner. I'd thought it through. I wanted to go with him to Switzerland, get married, meet his family. But to make that possible I'd need to stay in the Netherlands for a while to tie up all the loose ends and find someone to take over the dance school.

Ernst beamed with delight. "Of course you should tie up loose ends."

I continued. "I should finish the present season. I owe it to my students. And then there's my parents, of course. It'll be difficult for them if I go to Switzerland. They rely on me for so much." My father had been forced to give up his job at Venmans because of the anti-Jewish regulations, and they no longer had an income. We lived on what I earned from teaching dance, and I wasn't sure what they'd do if I left. "I have to work something out," I said.

I was relieved when Ernst said that he would respect my desire to stay for a while to make arrangements for the school and my parents. That evening we fell asleep in each other's arms, content and brimming with plans for the future.

A photo of Rosie on her balcony, taken by Ernst

A month later Ernst left and we promised to see each other soon.

And then something rather annoying happened. I soon received notification from the *Kulturkammer*, which I had managed to join, that I was no longer allowed to give dance classes in public. Someone had apparently informed them of my Jewish background, and I was forced to close my dance schools in Eindhoven, Den Bosch, Tilburg, and Helmond. I said good-bye to my students and my income in one fell swoop.

When my parents suggested refurbishing their empty attic and installing a dance floor I was moved by the gesture and wasted no time. I didn't really have an alternative. The demand for my classes hadn't ceased.

So I started a little dance school in my parents' attic, which was just big enough to accommodate forty students at a time. The fact that people were bored in those dark days explained my popularity, as did the reputation I had established. Also, people weren't interested in going to places like the Iron Man anymore because it was full of NSB members and Nazis. The Dutch girls found it hard to refuse if they got asked to dance. And so the young people of Den Bosch came to me.

Fortunately, my parents didn't seem to mind all the commotion. My mother and I now spoke daily, my father was out most of the day, and my brother was attending a sort of business college. He had wanted to go to the university in Tilburg but was denied admission because he was registered as Jewish. The college he attended instead wasn't officially recognized and he didn't say much about it, but from what I could gather it was just a small group of students who met for class at someone's house. I also stuck to the new teaching regulations that required segregation between Jewish and non-Jewish students. I found the distinction irrelevant, but my students preferred it that way. As a result, one of the groups was made up entirely of Jewish students. Almost all the others were Catholic.

Before classes I joined my parents for dinner, which made me feel at home again. My mother visibly enjoyed the situation. I saw it in everything she said and did. She laughed at the smallest opportunity, provided me with snacks, and paid frequent visits to the attic to see what was going on. When I was busy teaching she answered the phone with enthusiasm, and she often chatted with the students. One night she almost fell over a couple cuddling in a corridor, but she said nothing, in spite of the fact that she was quite prudish. And it wasn't the only time. She spent a lot of time in the dark corridors of the house, looking out the window at the blacked-out city and the huge spotlights combing the sky for enemy aircraft. The corridors had to be dark because of the blackout, but in my attic the dance school was cozy with light and music.

Rosie's illegal dance school, 1942

Ernst and I wrote each other every week. In spite of my busy schedule I missed him. He said his mother was looking forward to meeting me, and I told him how the dance season was progressing. I celebrated the Feast of Saint Nicolas at home with the students. At Christmas we danced under the mistletoe in evening attire. Neighbors had to lend us chairs so that we had adequate

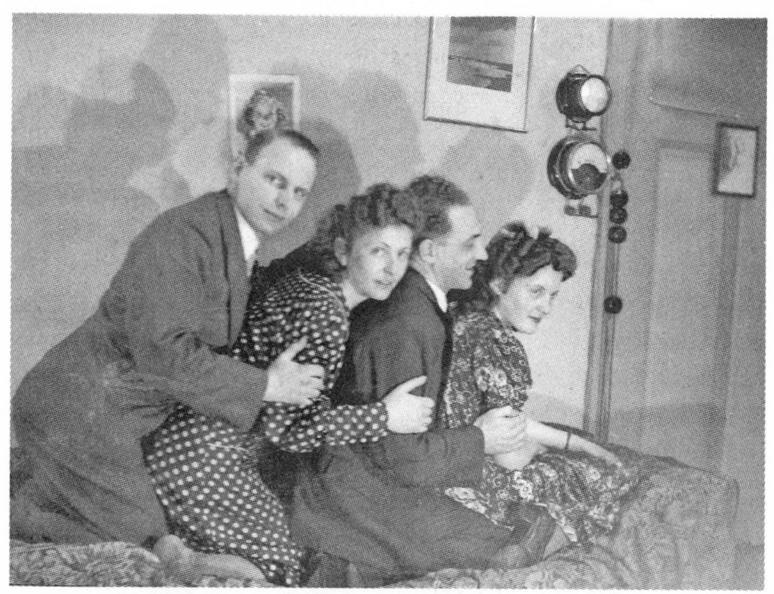

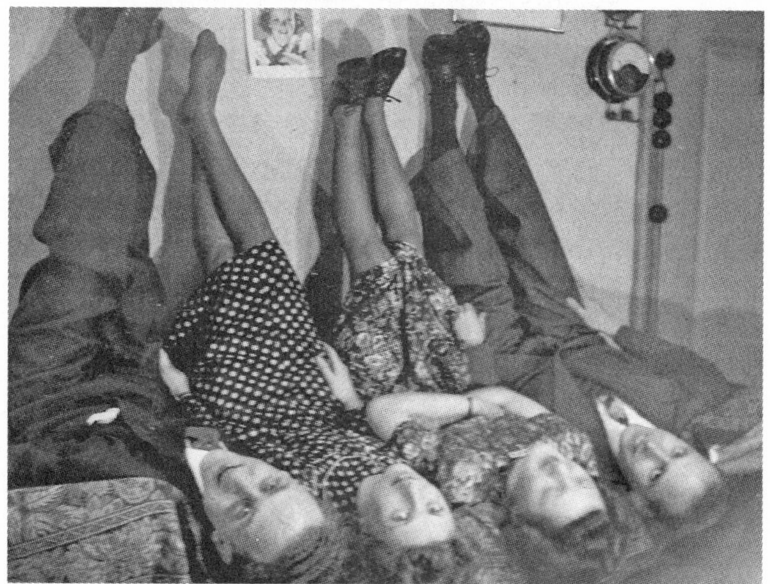

A party at the home of one of Rosie's students in Eindhoven, 1941

seating. At the end of February 1942, I invited the mayor of Oeteldonk—the name bestowed on Den Bosch during carnival—and the carnival prince to visit our little attic, and they accepted the invitation, much to my surprise. It must have been the only place in Den Bosch to be visited by both of them at the same time. The students were elated and still talked about it weeks later.

But eventually Leo got wind of it. And my rival was jealous.

Carnival in Rosie's illegal dance school, 1942

PAUL

The Discovery

ONE EVENING WHILE I was chatting with a colleague from Austria, he told me that Glaser was a common name in Vienna before the war. My father had told us that our distant ancestors came from the German-speaking region of the Czech Republic, which used to be part of the Habsburg Empire, so it didn't surprise me that there were Glasers in Vienna.

"It's a typical Jewish name," my friend said.

"But I'm Catholic," I exclaimed. Immediately I was reminded of Ria's words: "Perhaps your father has a Jewish background."

Later on, I continued to think about the conversation. If my father had Jewish roots then so did his parents, but they died before I was born and I never met them. Was it possible that they didn't survive the war, just like the millions of other Jews? The idea startled me.

I decided to contact my father, but what would I ask him? Whether he was Jewish? To question him about such a critical omission seemed too confrontational, too direct. It might be better if I asked him something about his parents. I would call him that evening.

Normally I wouldn't ask such an important question over the phone. But it seemed better at that juncture to give him the opportunity to conceal his expression. Or maybe I was just too impatient to wait until I could visit. I don't know.

When he picked up the phone I told him about the conversation I'd had that day with my Austrian colleague. I asked if the death of his parents had anything to do with the war, and he told me that they both died of old age. His responses were clear enough, so I moved on to other less serious topics. But I still wasn't completely satisfied. Something about his voice—so flat, so emotionless, so detached—sounded off. Something wasn't right.

After the phone call, instead of fewer questions, I was plagued with even more. Did my grandparents really die of old age? Why was my father's family so small, just one distant aunt, just Rosie? Did my parents consciously decide to say nothing to their children? Or was I off the mark? Pressing my parents further wasn't an option. For one thing, I wanted to respect their wishes. But also, if they had consciously decided to conceal the past from their children there was no sense in pushing them; nothing was going to come of it.

But there was someone else who might be able to help: my maternal grandmother, Jo de Bats. I decided to pay her a visit. I was her first grandchild, and we had always had a strong relationship.

On the winter evening that I visited, we sat together in a pair of armchairs that had seen better days, in front of her coal-fired stove. It was dim, the stove's little windows were ablaze with warmth, and the wind whistled through the chimney. We drank cognac and made small talk. Every now and then I got to my feet and tossed some coals on the fire. When the conversation turned to my parents, I took a risk. I told her that I knew about my father's Jewish background. She didn't deny it. We talked about the war, and without her even realizing it, my suspicion was confirmed. Now I knew for sure. It may not have been the best way to go about it, but how else could I have wrested a family secret from the ones I loved without making it difficult for them?

In spite of my hunch I was still rattled, and in a moment of paralysis I forgot to continue the conversation, to ask about my father's parents, what kind of people they were, and, of course, about my aunt Rosie. I remembered my grandmother saying, "I can see them now, the poor creatures. They came here before they left. It was a sad get-together." I stared at the glowing embers in the stove and listened to the ticking clock. I couldn't bring myself to ask why everything had been kept from me. I'd said what I had planned to say, so I finished my cognac, told my grandmother that I had to get up early the next day, and went to bed.

Discovering the truth didn't exactly fill me with joy; on the contrary, it upset me. I didn't know what to do with this information. I still wasn't sure what happened to the family during the war—we hadn't talked about it—but knowing that they were Jewish made me fear the worst. Almost 73 percent of Dutch Jews did not survive. Though I could have asked for individual stories and details, that statistic alone—and the revelation that I was somehow connected to it—overwhelmed me. If I let the news sink in any further, it would drive me crazy.

But the questions persisted. As I drove away the following morning, I dwelled on my grandmother's words. If my family was Jewish, did that make me Jewish? I knew next to nothing about Judaism. The only mental association I had was the frequent news reports about attacks on Jewish sites and institutions. Jews had to organize extra security for themselves, and in many countries they were under threat. Even in the Netherlands, I'd been part of many discussions in which Jews were spoken of negatively. My friend, after all, was convinced that Zionism was racism. When I was young, people in the Catholic Church had promoted the idea, albeit in hushed terms, that the Jews killed Jesus. Even the Vatican refused to recognize the State of Israel until 1993.

Wouldn't it be better to just leave things be, to forget my discovery? Should I tell my brothers and sisters? My parents had concealed our Jewish background for a reason.

I finally concluded that acknowledging the information further would only cause a fuss. And with that, I pushed it out of my life.

ROSIE

Caught!

THE STAR OF DAVID was introduced in the Netherlands on May 2, 1942. My brother and I decided not to participate and refused to sew a star on our clothing as every Dutch Jew was required to do. We also removed the large letter *J* that had been stamped on our identity papers, which we were required to show during the constant street inspections. I traveled, ate out at restaurants, went to the cinema, and basically did whatever I wanted, although I sometimes wore glasses or a hat to camouflage my face. Still, there was nothing about my appearance that made me look Jewish, at least not like the Jewish caricatures that were displayed on posters and in movies.

Though I didn't wear a yellow star, I instinctively opted to wear a yellow sports coat. I ended up wearing it so often that some of my friends asked whether I had anything else to wear.

Everything was going swimmingly until one day when I found an official letter in the mailbox: "You are expected for questioning at the police station, detective investigations department, at 6 this evening. W.G. Verstappen."

Boy, oh boy! I thought. Now I'm in for it. I said nothing to my mother, carefully sewed a yellow star onto my coat, inscribed my identity papers with a handsome blue *J*, which I had erased because I traveled a lot to other cities, and headed off to meet Mr. Verstappen.

The officer was very polite at first, asked my name by way of formality, and invited me to take a seat. He started to read from a letter in which I was accused of having Jewish blood (I couldn't help that), of not wearing a star, of visiting restaurants, sports clubs, cinemas, and so forth, of being out after eight at night, of traveling without a permit . . . more or less everything I was prohibited from doing.

"Do you admit it?" Mr. Verstappen asked.

"No," I replied. "I wear a star, look," and I lifted my handbag out of the way. "I admit I always carry my bag that way, but I never go out without a star." I spoke without batting an eye. It was make-or-break time—to be or not to be.

"So," he said. "But I have here an incriminating document about you," and he held up a sheet of paper for me to see. It was stationery from the Crielaars dance school. A letter written on my own typewriter, which Leo had kept at his place, in which my ex-husband was pressing serious charges against me.

"This is from Crielaars," I said.

I should have suspected it. A few weeks prior a policeman had come to my door asking if I was operating a dance school. I denied the allegation and said that I simply had friends who sometimes came over to dance. When the policeman persisted I became aggravated, and then when he tried to intimidate me I ended up slamming the door in his face. Now I wondered if Leo had been behind that incident too.

The officer answered curtly, "You're not stupid." His politeness then deserted him and he started to lecture me: I had broken the law. I should obey the law and respect National Socialism. Did I actually know my place as a Jew? Why was I so foolish? As he ranted and raved, his face turned bright red. After he finished I stared at him unruffled. He asked what the matter was. I said nothing and continued to stare at him. At that point he was clearly agitated. He typed out a charge sheet and made me sign it. Then he took me in the company of another detective to the police building on Orthen Street. The police officers there were surprised. They apparently weren't expecting me, but it was clear that I had to stay.

To pass the time that evening I played chess with one of the officers and we enjoyed a pleasant chat. Did I want to call my parents? I declined. They were used to my staying out at night, and I didn't want to worry them unnecessarily. I would see what happened tomorrow. I slept that night on a table in the holding room.

The next day the guards planned to transfer me at noon to Wolvenhoek, where the SS kept their offices and a prison. As soon as I heard mention of the SS, I got scared. This was more serious than I had thought, and I asked permission to give my parents a quick call after all. They refused. Determined, I told them I was having a heavy period and was badly in need of a change of underwear. At last, one of the police officers called my parents, told them I was in custody, and asked them to bring some toiletries and a change of underwear to get me through the next few days. My mother arrived a half hour later, and I was allowed to talk to her. I had no idea how long they planned to hold me, of course, so I told her not to worry and that I'd be all right. We arranged for her to call the dance school students and cancel classes for the next few days, and then we had to go. My mother put on a brave face, but I saw tears when we said good-bye. It was sad to see my mother forced to leave just because of Leo whining about the star on my jacket.

When it was time to leave I asked if I could walk, and they said yes. With the exception of Mr. Verstappen, I had nothing but praise, a lot of praise, for the Den Bosch police corps. They were friendly and behaved professionally.

When we arrived at Wolvenhoek I started to go inside, but one of the officers stopped me and said I had to go to the prison. The SS took over at that point, and I was immediately locked up. On Tuesday I was brought in for questioning, and the SS police officer realized that this arrest, my first, was the result of a competitive rivalry between my ex-husband and me. He was reasonably civil, although he did blow cigarette smoke in my face a few times and slipped a couple of bottles of cognac in his briefcase while he talked to me.

Afterward, I was put into solitary confinement. I was kept away from the other prisoners and was not allowed to have contact with the outside world, certainly not with my parents, friends, and students. It was a load of bullshit. I was not concerned for myself, but for the people outside who would be worried about me. I was also not allowed to receive letters from Ernst, or reply to them. What was he going to think if this wasn't over in a few days? Such nonsense made me so angry. The only contact I had was with the prison guards when they brought food or came to empty the bucket. Once in a while we exchanged a few words. I was not allowed to speak to them, but that was not my style and the guards were friendly enough. Beyond that I was alone. I had plenty of time to think.

It was strange to be in prison without having been put there by a judge. I was there because of who I was and nothing more, because of my serious "crimes" such as traveling, going to the cinema, and such. But at the same time it was understandable. After all, there was a Jewish problem, at least that's what everyone believed, and problems called for solutions, didn't they? So Dutch Jews were being pushed to the margins of society, subjected to stricter rules, and betrayed. My ex-husband Leo wasn't the only one. Neighbors, policemen, NSB members, even the mayor, were actively involved, many without being asked by the Germans for their help. It was their way of contributing to the solution, of trying to ingratiate themselves with the new rulers. Arrests were increasingly normal. Few if any questions were asked when children disappeared from schools.

The Nazis were running the show in the Netherlands, while the Dutch queen and her ministers—living in relative luxury in London—hypocritically urged resistance and heroism over the radio. More and more Dutch people were benefiting from the new order. Unemployment had declined, trade was better than ever, and the indecision of democracy had been replaced by something more effective. New social laws had been implemented. Everyone had health insurance. Labor conditions had improved in the factories. The much-loathed bicycle tax had been abolished, a family allowance was introduced, and benefits for the elderly, widows, orphans, and invalids had been increased. Union leaders were eager to visit Germany for educational purposes. Because the Jewish problem called for a solution, the majority of Dutch people didn't think it strange that measures had been taken. Some were even enthusiastic. They were proud of the new order that had brought prosperity and disabled competition. Though being in prison without a conviction was clearly wrong, it didn't seem that strange. It was quite congruent with the sentiment of many Dutch citizens.

I started each morning with an hour of exercise to stay flexible. A cell was not large, but it was big enough for a ballet step or two. When the female guards saw what I was doing, one of them told me she used to take ballet lessons and wanted to know more about my dance school. It was the only contact I had with the outside world. The same guard later gave me a small notebook and a pen when I asked, so that I could keep a diary, or really a book about my life. Nothing of interest happened in the prison, but I wanted to write about my experiences and adventures from my early childhood until then. I was lucky to have the time to write. Without the prison I never would have gotten around to it. My writing also helped me escape from my lonely cell.

I thought back to the time when I lived in Germany, beginning when I was a toddler. It was immediately after the First World War, and the country was in a difficult, miserable period. I thought back to the schools I went to, to my first experience of discrimination. I was only a child, but it left a deep and permanent impression. And of course I thought back to my first crushes and infatuations, especially to my first kiss. Sifting for events that were particularly formative, I began with the first years of my life:

> I was born in 1914, when international political tensions reached their peak. The dark clouds that had been hanging over Europe for months finally collided and a bolt of lightning struck the heart of Europe, igniting a fire that seemed inextinguishable. The First World War had begun.
>
> My father, Falk, was called up for military service in the Dutch army. My mother, Josephine, was at her wit's end, and not surprisingly. She was expecting her first child in four weeks and was living on German soil in Kleef. In addition to being eight months pregnant, she had to manage her family's move back to the Netherlands. It happened all at once. Two weeks later, in her new home in Nijmegen, Josephine set about carefully unpacking her precious crystal and her Meissner porcelain with the help of her new Dutch housekeeper.

In spite of the country's neutrality, the tragic war unfolding across the rest of Europe also had a serious effect on Dutch life. While some things were freely available, the black market flourished. People with money or important commodities to exchange lived as freely as before, but the poor were forced to stand in line for hours for a liter of milk, a half pound of meat, or a bag of coal. In the meantime, defense preparations were being made should the enemy invade. The enemy? We didn't have an enemy. The Netherlands was a small country and popular with its neighbors. Import and export trade with both Germany and England had only reinforced the ancient bonds of friendship between us.

Nevertheless, the station in Nijmegen was barricaded with sandbags, as were all the other strategic buildings. Large numbers of soldiers trooped through the streets, packed up and ready, singing songs like "Puppchen, du bist mein Augenstern!," "K-K-K-Katie," and "Tipperary." Bridges were loaded with explosives, and trains moved over the broad river crossings at a crawl, their windows closed. This was the atmosphere in which I was born and grew up as a toddler.

Rosie at age two, 1916

When Falk came home he lifted me into his arms, and I tousled his black curls. But as sunny as life was at home during my first years, outside it was dark, and the consequences of the war were becoming more pronounced. Great hordes of Belgians, starving and dressed in rags, sought refuge in the Netherlands. After the assault on Antwerp, many passed through the Dutch cities, including Nijmegen. In the meantime I celebrated my fourth birthday with the neighborhood children with lemonade and whipped cream pie.

One dark November day, peace unexpectedly arrived. The German kaiser fled to the Netherlands and the war was over. "*Nie wieder Krieg* (No More War)" was the slogan in the newspapers and on everyone's lips. The millions of little white crosses that dotted the military cemeteries testified to this deep desire. "Peace on earth for all."

Rosie at age three, 1917

Christmas, New Year, carnival, Lent, and Easter glided past, and life in the Netherlands returned to normal slowly but surely. There were still masses of refugees. They talked about how fortunate they were to have escaped with their lives. The Netherlands was popular, and being Dutch had great privileges. The Germans sometimes sneered at the *reiche Holländer* (rich Hollanders). In those days they meant the ordinary Dutch folk.

The large margarine factory in Kleef gradually resumed operations, and many Dutch workers moved to the German border town for work. Germany needed manpower. Too many of its citizens had been used as cannon fodder or were maimed and crippled. Poor Germans! They fought so hard for their alleged rights, and now they'd lost everything: their best men, their great army, and their honor.

After the war we followed my father back to Kleef, where he was working to get the factory up and running again. We took up residence at the Hotel Bollinger, the spa town's most prominent hotel, and looked forward to an extended stay. The hotel also housed a number of Belgian officers, part of the army unit that was occupying Kleef.

The Hotel Bollinger in Kleef, 1918

In the wake of the war, the old spa town was a sorry sight. The once lively streets were dull and gray, and the once exuberant Lower-Rhineland population was quiet and introverted. The dominant color was black, the color of mourning: mourning for those who fell *Für den Kaiser und das Vaterland* (for kaiser and fatherland). Interned in a fine castle in the hospitable Netherlands, the kaiser wasn't particularly interested in the profound misery plaguing *das Vaterland*.

The Belgian soldiers occupying Kleef were the only cheerful people in the depressed town. But though the inhabitants treated them kindly on the outside, their real feelings were quite the opposite. Envy and hatred glowed in the hearts of the imperious Germans as they watched the Belgians usurp their rule.

I had warm memories of the Belgian officers who lived with us at the hotel, though I was only a small child at the time. Almost all of them had mustaches and spoke with a strange accent. They were always nice to me, gave me sweets, stroked my hair, and sometimes lifted me onto their laps. My mother told me later that they paid far too much attention to me. She was especially fond of one anecdote:

> One day I was sitting in the hotel conservatory when Lieutenant Ditché, General Motti's adjutant, walked in, saluted me, and asked where you were. I suggested we look. As Lieutenant Ditché opened the glass folding doors into the enormous dining room cum dance hall we both started laughing. General Motti, his monocle dangling over his medals and his portly frame stuffed into a too-tight khaki uniform, was sitting at the grand piano on a small stage, with you on his lap. He said to you in Flemish: "If you do it again, I'll give you a chocolate bar," and he indicated a candy so large it would have certainly left you with an upset tummy. You slipped from his knee, nimble as a cat, ringlets dancing alongside your face, and played the popular Belgian soldiers' song "Madelon" with one finger on the piano, followed by the Belgian national anthem, "La Brabançonne." A few of the officers came to take a closer look and gazed intently at the little girl who reminded

> them of home. They too had wives and daughters far off in their Belgian homeland. When you had finished playing, one of the officers lifted you high above his head and planted a kiss on both your chubby cheeks. At that moment you saw me and started to scream and struggle to break free from his embrace. "Mummy, mummy," you said, "he wants to kiss me! Strange men aren't allowed to kiss me, only Daddy," to which General Motti replied, "You won't be saying that in fifteen years." The entire room exploded with laughter and you flew into my arms.

My early childhood was a wonderful period, but after that I had to take piano lessons and go to school. I wasn't impressed; I had no girlfriends and felt lonely. I also encountered discrimination for the first time because of my Jewish heritage. It left a deep impression on me as a child and has stayed with me ever since.

In 1919, after almost a year, my father managed to find an old villa on the edge of the city, and we left the Hotel Bollinger, the Belgian soldiers, and, to my great sadness, the dance teacher Liselotte Benfer. A new era dawned for me: a different house, a girl next door who refused to play with me, a mother who seemed interested in nothing beyond the baby that was on its way, and a father who had no time for me. I took piano lessons with Herr Bister, who had previously conducted a renowned military orchestra from Strasbourg that was disbanded after the war. He was extremely strict, swatting my hands with a ruler each time I made the slightest mistake. With tears in my eyes I was left to practice my waltzes and sonatas. Two older cousins who also lived in Kleef were always asking about my mother and father, and they giggled and talked to one another in English, which I didn't understand. Several aunts and my grandparents invited me to live with them, but I didn't care for the idea. Most of the time I just sat in a corner and stared.

I was not happy. I thought a lot about what the girl next door had said to me: "I'm not allowed to play with you anymore. My mummy says you're a Jew." Her words hurt, and I couldn't get them out of my mind.

When my little brother John arrived my parents were over the moon. A crown prince, an heir, a boy. Family and friends came to visit, and there was a party—good company, flowers, good food and drink. I felt miserable and even more excluded.

A few weeks later my life changed yet again. I had reached my sixth birthday, and I had to go to primary school. There were two schools in Kleef, one Catholic and one Protestant. Next to the synagogue there was a classroom where the six-year-old Jewish children were expected to go to school. There was only one teacher, Siegfried Löwenstein, who taught arithmetic, language, and religion in German. They called him "Pietsje." An unappetizing man of about fifty-five years, Pietsje had a big belly, a bald head, a reddish face dotted with tiny blue veins (betraying his heart problem), a greasy jacket, a gold pince-nez perched halfway up his nose, several gaudy gold teeth between his round chubby lips, and a ruler eternally in his hand. The ruler was supposed to add the finishing touch to our German education.

Behind the school there was a playground with an excellent view of the *Schwanenburcht*, or Swan Castle, renowned from the Lohengrin saga as the castle where the princess Elsa was liberated by the swan knight, and a panoramic view of the Rhine twisting like a silver ribbon in the summer heat. All the children in Kleef knew about the legend, and I often thought about it.

I remember once being interrupted in the middle of just such a daydream. "Rosie, Rosie!" the boys in the playground yelled in unison. "Come and join us." The entire class, all boys, had gathered around me. "Fine," I said, "but I'm the *baas*." At that moment Pietsje, munching on a green apple, came around the corner. He saw me giving orders and was clearly aggravated. A couple of weeks later when my mother was visiting the school he asked, "Can you tell me, madam, what the Dutch word '*baas*' means?"

One day Pietsje was teaching religion class, talking about the first human couple. When he got to the story of Cain and Abel I stuck my finger in the air and asked, "But Adam and Eve had two sons, the one killed the other, so there was only one left. How did he manage to populate the world? Fables, sir, all fables." Pietsje was speechless. He had taken a serious dislike to me, and it was getting worse. I could see it in everything he did, even the way he looked at me.

Early one morning I had a fight with my little brother, John. He had broken the arm off my favorite doll. I was angry and sad and had cried. My mother tried to comfort me by saying, "A big girl like you shouldn't be playing with dolls. You have homework and girlfriends."

"Girlfriends?" I thought with a sneer. "Not me." On my way to school I recalled my mother's words. Who would want me as a friend? Not far from the school three girls jeered at me on the street: "Jew, Jew, stinks like pooh," to which I jeered back: "Christ, Christ, stinks like *scheiss*." They started pelting me with stones, and I quickly ran inside the school building.

That day Pietsje was teaching arithmetic. As usual I

hadn't learned my tables. Half mad at the world and half mad at Pietsje, I wakened from my daydream with a start. Pietsje had called me to the front of the class, and before I got the chance to react he snarled, "Why don't you stand up when I speak to you?"

I began to get angry. "Leave me be," I snapped. Did someone dare stand up to Pietsje? The boys were quiet as mice.

"What's all this, you cheese head, you stupid Hollander," Pietsje hissed in German, his tiny eyeballs glistening behind the lenses of his pince-nez. "Come here, I say, or shall I come and get you." He lunged toward me and grabbed my earlobe. *Smack, smack, smack.* The ruler whistled through the air and left my hands red. Without shedding a single tear, but with a lump in my throat, I endured the torture. "Thank you," I said curtly when he had finished. "This is the last time you'll see me here." And without looking at him or my classmates I got to my feet and walked out of the classroom and out of the school.

Strolling along the streets, I explored the shop windows. Kleef was known for its veneration of Mary, and they were preparing for the annual Holy Blood procession. There were statues of the Virgin all over the place. I remembered last year's procession, when I held our maid's hand as I stood watching at the side of the road surrounded by a crowd of thousands. A strange feeling had come over me when the Blessed Sacrament—as my escort called it—passed by to the sound of the bells. Everyone fell to their knees except me. "Kneeling is forbidden in Jewish law. We stand and look God in the eye. We don't have to kneel or bow our heads," my father had taught me. "We Jews," he said, "we are the chosen people," and as I wandered the beautifully decorated streets I thought to myself that you first have to be rejected before you can be chosen. *Jew, Jew, stinks like pooh . . . I'm not allowed to play with you, you're Jewish . . . cheese head, stupid Hollander.* One insult after the other rattled through my head, and when I got home I burst into a flood of tears in my mother's protective arms.

That night I tossed and turned in bed and couldn't get to sleep. I felt oppressed, rejected. One sentence had lodged itself in my mind and kept repeating itself: "You first have to be rejected before you can be chosen." Then I reached a conclusion: I *will* be chosen. If no one wants me, then I'll want no one, only myself. And from then on I vowed to not let anyone or anything upset me. I'd be hard on John, and if I had to I'd be hard on my father and mother too. I turned in bed countless times that night, and it took an age before I finally fell asleep.

A week later my mother took me to the Evangelical School for Girls in Haagsche Strasse, a very formal German establishment where I quickly made friends with a lanky blond girl named Else Dahmen. We played together during the short recess and got on extremely well.

My parents were relieved that I was more content with my new school. Every day I talked enthusiastically about my new friend Else. I didn't say much about the lessons. One day my mother allowed me to invite Else over to play. When she appeared at the door my mother seemed startled. Later, when Else took her leave with a grateful curtsy, my mother took my hand, and we went to the living room.

"Tell me," she said, "what sort of child is that?" I didn't understand what she meant. "Where does she live?"

"Braunengasse," I answered.

"I thought as much," said my mother. "Her father worked for Daddy at the factory. He's a common laborer. Don't bring her to the house again. She's not your kind of friend." After a few days they moved me to another desk at school. I didn't talk to Else anymore, and I no longer dared to look at her.

The arithmetic at school was difficult to understand. Irmela Schwarz, my new desk mate, helped me out now and then, and I told my parents about it at home. "What does Irmela's father do?" my mother asked.

"He's a lawyer," I said cautiously, her remarks about Else still fresh in my mind.

"Oh, that's good," my mother said. "Feel free to play with her." But when I invited Irmela home, the lawyer's daughter kept me waiting in vain all afternoon. Another illusion shattered.

It didn't take long before I lost interest in school again. The teachers and the headmistress were so strict. I could no longer behave like I used to with Pietsje. At some point I started going to the woods opposite our villa instead of school. Then I made my way to Aunt Janny's, my mother's sister. The first time I used the kitchen door and told Tilla, the housekeeper, that the senior classes at the lyceum were having exams that day and the junior class was free. I asked if I could play with my cousins' toys, and Tilla had no objection. I kept this up for a good couple of weeks, until one sunny spring afternoon when I arrived home after my visit to Aunt Janny's to find my father, my mother, and my teacher lined up in the living room. There was nothing to say. The teacher had come to ask my parents whether I was on the mend, and their surprised faces were answer enough. I'd never seen my father so angry. I was given a firm spanking, no dinner, and no pocket money and was locked in the attic. I was furious. I screamed and kicked the door, turned the attic upside down, sobbed and wailed as loud as I could. The next morning they found me asleep on the floor, exhausted, and exchanged a look of despair. How were they ever going to raise this child?

I was stiff from sitting still in my cell for so long. I took a break and did some dance exercises for a change of pace, thinking about the Lohengrin saga, about Elsa and her swan knight. Elsa was stricken with misfortune after ignoring every warning and insisting that the swan knight reveal his true identity. Now that Leo had revealed my true identity to the police, I was stuck in prison. The Lohengrin saga had haunted me all my life, and now it had become a reality. After a while I continued writing:

> With the rise of National Socialism, anti-Semitism in Germany grew rapidly, and in 1925 my father's work situation became increasingly unpleasant. Germans could not stomach the idea of having a Jew as their boss, especially a Jew who had more money than they did, even if he had acquired his wealth through hard work. His new villa and the knowledge that he had a steadily maturing nest egg tucked away in the Netherlands simply reinforced the jealousy.
>
> In spite of the number of times he'd saved the factory from serious danger, including a major fire at the oil refinery, and used levelheaded negotiations to get the workers back to work after a strike, the board had become increasingly reserved toward him. They had recently appointed a German as his supervisor who knew literally nothing about the business. The situation annoyed and depressed him, so much so that he eventually resigned and sold the villa.
>
> We were driven back to the Netherlands by the factory owner's chauffeur, who delivered us to an eighteen-room

house in Nijmegen. The moving van arrived shortly thereafter, and the movers carried everything inside. A newly hired Dutch maid helped unpack the porcelain. I spent most of the day standing at the window watching the people outside. Almost everyone had a bicycle. Young and old, rich and poor, they all cycled everywhere.

Rosie and John in Nijmegen

Only thirty feet from our door was a huge and beautiful Catholic church. Farther up the road were the barracks for the Colonial Reserve, which dispatched soldiers to the Dutch East Indies on a monthly basis. A convoy marched past the window one day with a brass band at the helm. The blue braids and wide navy blue capes gave them a martial air. Crowds of errand boys and children on funny Dutch scooters brought up the rear. Everything was new to me. The following day I explored the streets of Nijmegen hand in hand with my brother.

And that was how I described my youth. I had no idea how long they planned to hold me in solitary confinement, and the guards I asked either didn't know or weren't allowed to say. It was a little boring, but I had so much more to write about my early years that I made up my mind to continue writing. I decorated the text with drawings and sketches.

After six weeks, on July 11, 1942, and to my great surprise, I was set free. The SS had interrogated me several times during my incarceration, but without violence. I was treated nicely and had nothing but praise for the director and the guards. Because they released me without notice, I walked to my parents' house with my toilet bag and diary clutched under my arm. I popped the key in the lock, pushed open the door, and shouted, "I'm home." My brother flew into the hallway and threw his arms around my neck. My mother's eyes were full of tears and joy. The three of us hugged until my father interrupted. "Are you coming into the living room?"

We sat at the table with a pot of coffee, and I told them about my dull adventures in the cell. "I went to the SS twice to ask if I could visit you," my mother said. "They refused, and the second time they threatened to lock me up too if I persisted. Your father and brother didn't come with me because they were afraid they might be arrested. There are so many nasty rumors. We heard nothing from you and were so worried."

"Thank goodness they treated you well," my father added. We talked about it all night.

The following day some friends and students treated me to a delightful visit. I had a photo taken of myself surrounded by all the flowers they brought and sent it as a thank-you to everyone I knew in the city. Now they knew I was back. Leo's deed was unsuccessful. My students were far from impressed with what he had done and talked about it with friends and family. Now his own school was in disrepute. The entire city was abuzz with warnings to avoid Crielaars's dance school. It was music to my ears.

After a few days I was already accustomed again to normal life, eager to get back to the world after six weeks of being locked up in solitary confinement with no one to talk to. I hid my diary in my desk and reopened the dance school. Nothing had been happening for six weeks, and I needed to catch up on the missed lessons. My students wanted to get back to business. They had paid for it, after all. The holiday period was about to start, but few people planned to go away during the occupation so it made little difference. Now that everyone knew what had happened to me, even more students signed up for lessons, even some from Leo's dance school. It was a busy and hectic time.

Rosie after her imprisonment

I wrote to Ernst and told him what had happened, that I needed an extra six weeks to catch up on my commitments at the school. He was not happy with the idea and insisted that I come to Switzerland immediately. But leaving then would mean abandoning my students and my parents, who had no income, and that wasn't what I wanted.

Shortly after my release I received a letter Kees sent from the Hotel De Witte Brug in Amersfoort. He told me what I already knew, that he had been engaged to a girl from The Hague. The relationship was over, and now he realized what I meant to him. He'd heard about Leo's betrayal and said he would do anything he could to help me. He also wrote that his mother and sister no longer lived in the Lohengrin, that he was working as head barman at Hotel Het Bosch van Bredius in Naarden, and that he desperately wanted to see me. It was his birthday on July 22, and he invited me to a party with friends in The Hague.

I was in no mood for a party and didn't attend. Days later a veritable flood of letters and telegrams arrived. I wrote back, telling him that he was free to visit me at home with my parents if it was so important, and if not he should leave me alone. He wrote back that he didn't dare show himself to my parents.

The following week I was expected at a meeting of dance teachers in Utrecht. Kees heard about it and said he needed to talk with me urgently. Curiosity finally got the better of me, and we arranged to get together after the meeting. We had dinner at the Jaarbeurs restaurant. Common sense said no, but I still found him attractive. It was stupid, I know, but I couldn't help myself, and after dinner we took the train to Hilversum and checked into the Grand Hotel Gooiland. Kees threw a lot of money around and told me about his broken engagement. He warned me about Leo, that I should be careful and that Leo would certainly try to have me arrested again.

At that point I knew that Leo was just one in a growing movement. Everywhere you read and heard about the Jewish problem, and restrictions intensified. Dutch Jews were ordered to hand their money and jewelry to Lippmann, Rosenthal & Co. in Amsterdam, a bank under the control of the Germans. Heads of families were required to register for forced labor camps. It was getting scarier by the minute, but what struck me most was the fact that everyone either seemed to find it normal or wasn't interested. Daily life continued as usual for the majority of people: school, work, birthdays, lazy Sundays, swimming in the IJzeren Man, the big lake that bordered Vught. But for us Jews it became increasingly difficult.

In accordance with the new laws, my father had to hand over his money and jewelry to the Nazi bank, but he managed to hold some back and hide it. He also had to register for a labor camp. He complied with the requirement, assuming it meant his family would be left alone, as the authorities had promised. When he left for Schaarshoek, a state-run labor camp in Heino, he insisted there should be no tears.

I didn't feel completely safe in Den Bosch. Too many people knew me and now, thanks to Leo, they also knew about my Jewish background. On top of that, my friend Fran and I had been taking a risk by helping Dutch Jews like my father who were required to register for the labor camps. In the shed behind our house, we let them stay for a day or two, removed the Stars of David from their clothing, made sure they had food and blankets, and, when possible, arranged for new papers through Fran's brother. Then we brought them to another address, where they went into hiding. It was a risky business. People were stopped and searched all the time, and one of our neighbors was an NSB member. For safety's sake I slept at Fran's place, and she slept in my parents' house. That way, if there was a raid in the middle of the night both of us were out of harm's way. Fran was Catholic and her papers were in order.

We had managed to help about fourteen people go into hiding, but things didn't always run according to plan. One day we were bringing two men to the train station, and Fran had gone ahead to see if the coast was clear. We had arranged a signal to use if the officers were stopping people and checking papers: she would walk back in our direction with her handbag on her belly instead of over her shoulder. That day I spotted Fran's signal in good time, and I told the men at my side that they should turn back and let me walk on alone. I continued walking right up to the Dutch inspectors and greeted them with a smile. They tapped their hats and I passed. But to my surprise, one of the men who had come with us was walking about ten yards behind me. They stopped him, and because he couldn't provide the right papers he was arrested. Why he didn't turn back I'll never know. Was he too slow to react? Overconfident? Did he trust the Dutch inspectors more than he should have? I can only speculate. I never saw him after that.

A short while later, Fran told me she'd had a fight with her brother. She had thought that he was in the Resistance because he was able to provide false papers, but when she asked him about it he demanded that she stop smuggling people into hiding immediately. He was worried about his youngest sister, but she didn't care

Meanwhile, I was worried about how my mother and I would escape. One evening I noticed that a student of mine, Corry Donkers, had left her identity card. She looked my age, twenty-seven. I took it, well aware that it was theft, but I didn't know where else to get hold of a real identity card. I saw no other option. The papers Fran's brother provided were false and risky to use. That wasn't good enough for me. I tampered with the stolen identity card, replaced the photo with one of my own, and from that moment on I was officially Cornelia Donkers, at least outside of Den Bosch. No one knew about it, not even my parents. Meanwhile, Corry realized she'd lost her card, reported it to the police, and received a duplicate. For her the matter was settled. Since Cornelia usually referred to herself as Corry, I decided to call myself Lya, another diminutive, to reduce the chances of anyone connecting the two of us.

Finally, the end of the dance season was in view. In a little more than a month I would be traveling to Switzerland and then, in all likelihood, to Spain. How would I break the news to my mother?

I decided to throw one final party, a gala ball for all my students. It was a shame that I couldn't rent a space large enough to accommodate everyone. As a Jew I was no longer allowed to. Instead I organized a day out at the Drunen Dunes, and we had a fantastic time with dancing, picnics, ball games, and music. Despite the cheerful atmosphere, I still felt sad, and I was constantly aware of my imminent departure. I filmed the day as a memento.

Rosie on the dunes with her dance students

Early on the morning of August 26, 1942, my mother, my brother John, and I received a summons saying we had to report to Westerbork, where we would be transported to Germany for forced labor. It said that the police were going to bring train tickets for Westerbork the following morning. Under their protection, it said, we would be brought to the station. What now?

My mother was stunned. The authorities had promised we would be left alone after my father had volunteered for the labor camp. They told us more than once. But it had been a long time since I trusted the Germans or the Dutch, and their words meant only one thing: It was time to get the hell out.

My brother said little and was the first to act, disappearing while we were upstairs packing our bags. He left a note on the table: "Rot in hell, *Kraut*!"

"Why didn't he say good-bye?" my mother exclaimed. I thought he just found it too difficult, but I didn't have time to worry about it.

I could try to escape to Switzerland, where Ernst was waiting for me. I could travel unimpeded with my new identity, and I was sure he'd come to meet me at the Swiss border. But under these circumstances I couldn't abandon my mother. In much the same way that I had falsified my own identity, I quickly arranged a new set of "genuine" papers for my mother in the name of a certain Mrs. Van Moorsel, who rented me a room before I moved in with Leo. She was a nice lady, and we used to talk a lot. I knew where she kept her papers and stopped by for a coffee. She was not at home, but I still had the key so I went inside and removed her identity card. I knew it wasn't right, but I didn't have time to think about it. It was a matter of life and death. Quickly I walked home and changed the photo, making sure the stamp ran across the corner. I buried my photo albums and film in the garden, brought my gramophone and records to a friend, locked up the house, and left for Eindhoven with my mother that same evening. Our neighbor, Mr. Pijnenburg, saw us off. In one fell swoop I left behind my home, my belongings, and my dance school. The dance school was the hardest.

We spent the night with friends and traveled the following day to Tilburg, where other acquaintances put us up for a week. I was determined to find a place where we could go into hiding. Money wasn't a problem—my father had left behind a lockbox containing approximately 10,000 guilders in cash with a company he used to represent, Venmans Bros., a clothing manufacturer in Tilburg, and my mother, my brother, and I had access to it—but safety was our crucial concern.

I knew how difficult it was to find a hiding spot. People often thought they were safe, only to be handed over to the police by their Dutch neighbors. They either got paid for it or used it to get into the good graces of the Germans. I racked my brain and suddenly remembered what Kees had said to me the last time we met: "If you're ever in trouble, I'll always be ready to help."

I traveled by train to Naarden, then took a taxi to the address where Kees was living. The house was just outside the town center and regularly welcomed boarders. I had met the people he was staying with before a number of times. Henk Coljee was Dutch, and his wife, Magda, was German, although she spoke excellent Dutch.

I rang the doorbell, and Mrs. Coljee greeted me kindly. I asked after Kees, and she told me he was in the hospital in Naarden with a kidney stone. With a borrowed bicycle, I set off to visit him. At the hospital I knocked on the door of his room, but he didn't open it. I accosted a nurse in the hallway, who told me to try again, and after I thumped and thumped again a black-haired young woman with a flushed face opened the door. I was allowed inside, where I found Kees lying in bed. The girl left, and when I asked who she was he said he knew her from the bar at Hotel Bosch van Bredius, that she was a customer. When he had taken ill unexpectedly, he had borrowed 350 guilders from her because he had to pay his hospital fees in advance. He asked me if I could lend him 350 to pay her back because he didn't like borrowing from strangers. I told him about my problems, and he was immediately ready to help. He advised me to move in with the Coljee family. I gave him the 350 guilders and returned to Mrs. Coljee.

I once heard that it was better to dwell in the belly of the beast. Theirs was a house that would not be searched: Mrs. Coljee was German, and Mr. Coljee was a member of the NSB. I told the Coljees nothing about my Jewish background and pretended that my father had been taken hostage and locked up in Camp Haren. My mother and I were on the run because they wanted to arrest us too. Would it be possible to rent a couple of rooms? Everything was settled in no time. I headed back to Tilburg. With my new identity papers and the smile on my face, everything ran smoothly, in spite of the increasingly rigorous identity checks.

My brother's girlfriend, Elisabeth de Bats, also lived in Tilburg with her parents and two younger sisters, and I presumed John was staying with them. John and Elisabeth had been seeing each other for a couple of years, and she was a nice girl. I found her address and John was indeed there, staying in the attic.

We arranged to meet one more time. The next day I brought my mother along. The entire de Bats family was kindness itself. They provided tea, coffee, and biscuits. Yet the atmosphere was tense, and everyone seemed troubled. With the exception of the cuckoo in the cuckoo clock, there was not much joy. Around the table we talked about practical things: where to find money and where to go into hiding. I divulged where my mother and I were planning to go and asked my brother if he had found a place. Just as he was about to speak, I noticed that his girlfriend kicked him under the table. He stopped, then said something about De Peel, a rural region where Elisabeth's father had family. They had found a residence they could trust on a farm, and John could stay there if he paid his way. It was reasonably safe because the Germans rarely visited De Peel. The farm was remote and surrounded by marshes. An ideal place to hide.

In addition to practical matters we also talked about the miserable situation. Would Father be all right? What was likely to happen to us? When would all this business come to an end? Always a mama's boy, John held his tongue. Suddenly he got up and sat on her lap. A soldier who had recently fought in defense of queen and country sitting on his mother's lap. And she caressed him. No one spoke. Silent, almost petrified, we sat around the table. The outside world was far away, until the cuckoo popped out of the clock. As if we were in a film that had been momentarily paused, everyone started to move again all at once. We said our good-byes, since we'd be heading our separate ways early the next morning. We slept that night on extra mattresses in the attic, between stocks of apples and red cabbage.

My mother and I left the next morning for Naarden, where we lived a quiet life on the outskirts of the city. Elisabeth's father and her uncle brought John to a safe house. My friend Fran told me a couple of weeks later that the police had been at our door in Den Bosch the morning we left and that they had searched for us. Fran herself had to go to the police station no fewer than three times. They wanted to know where we were. They put her under pressure and even locked her up for two days, but she told them nothing. How could she? I hadn't told her my new address.

The Coljee residence in Naarden

They never found John's address either. An SS officer had inquired at Elisabeth's door more than once about his whereabouts, but she insisted they were no longer in contact. "I dumped that Jew-boy long ago. I'm not crazy!" In the meantime, Elisabeth secretly visited the safe house in De Peel on her bicycle, and they were able to stay in touch. The difficult circumstances strengthened their love and determination. He was safe where he was, and when the money ran out he could stay if he helped on the farm. He had already offered his services. Doing nothing all day wasn't his style. The people were kind, and a diligent farmhand like John was more than welcome. Because he wasn't a real farmhand they nicknamed him John Surrogate. John didn't mind, as long as he was safe.

There was a windmill not far from the farm, high up on the side of the road and visible for miles. If the Germans or an NSB member was spotted, the miller would set the sails in a prearranged position, giving the people in hiding a chance to take refuge in the nearby woods. As soon as the coast was clear, the miller would return the sails to normal, and everyone would get back to work.

Things almost went wrong at one point. John came down with such a serious ear infection that they feared meningitis. He desperately needed treatment and an operation. With the help of the resistance he was admitted to Saint Joseph's Hospital in Eindhoven. He had to use false papers, of course. Only the head sister, a nun, knew the real story, and she arranged everything. The doctors and nurses did what was necessary without asking questions. Everyone was on edge, because the local government and the Germans checked the hospitals from time to time, and the occasional traitor had surfaced among the hospital staff. Two days before being admitted to Saint Joseph's, John had to cancel an appointment at the hospital in Den Bosch at the last minute when he found out that the doctor had betrayed a patient in hiding. He cycled back to De Peel with a bandage over his ear.

Just to be careful, he moved to a temporary safe house because people talked to one another, and you could never be sure. Two weeks later, when the coast was clear, he returned to his regular safe house.

Life in Naarden was fine. My mother usually stayed home, but I often went out into town or somewhere else. As Lya Donkers it was easy. I played tennis at a local court with a racket I had picked up from Elisabeth's place in Tilburg. I was also able to retrieve the money my father had stashed away at the clothing factory. I was sure my father had no need of it at the labor camp, nor did my brother, who worked on a farm for bed and board. I figured my mother and I could put it to good use. Time passed undisturbed. I didn't celebrate my twenty-eighth birthday. What was there to celebrate when my father and John were away from home and my friends were in Den Bosch? Anyway, my identity papers said I was Lya Donkers, and her birthday was on another day. My mother and I enjoyed a drink together instead. I didn't know what would become of Ernst and me. I wrote to him to explain the situation and told him I had to take care of my mother. As soon as I could make arrangements for her I would leave for Switzerland.

Kees was discharged from the hospital after a week. He told us he was fired from his job at Hotel Het Bosch van Bredius because he was sick, and though we found it hard to believe, we accepted him at his word. He said he had paid back the 350 guilders he had borrowed from the girl I saw at the hospital, but now he had run up a debt with Mrs. Coljee for lodgings and happened to be short of cash. He asked if he could borrow another 350 guilders, told me he would do some "business," and promised to pay me back within two weeks. So I lent him another 350 guilders. Then he disappeared to Soestdijk, to friends of his mother's, to recover for a week.

Ten days later an official from the tax office knocked at the

Coljees' door asking for Kees. In spite of repeated reminders, he still hadn't paid his taxes. The man made an enormous fuss and threatened to sell off Kees's possessions. I gritted my teeth and telephoned the family in Soestdijk. They told me that they hadn't seen him. When I mentioned this to Mr. Coljee, he told me that Kees had moved into Hotel Jan Tabak in Bussum ten days earlier. I couldn't contain my rage. At lunchtime I made my way to the hotel, where I had a long conversation with one of the waitresses, who told me he had borrowed 100 guilders from her too. The week before she'd had an urgent bill to pay and when she asked Kees to repay her, he palmed off some excuse on her. The girl sat at my side and had a good cry. Kees spent a lot of time at Café Rutten in Bussum, she said, where the black marketeers regularly met to gamble and drink. He'd also paid for a seriously expensive dinner a couple of evenings earlier for the four nurses who had taken care of him in the hospital. On another occasion, he took a taxi to Amsterdam with a black-haired girl and spent the night there.

After that, I went over to Hotel Het Bosch van Bredius, where Kees used to work, ordered a coffee on the terrace, and struck up a conversation with one of the waiters. "Is that nice bartender still working here?" I asked.

"No ma'am, he's staying at Hotel Jan Tabak."

"Oh, why did he move?"

"He had to, ma'am, he stole money from the boss."

I finished my coffee and returned to my mother. Now I was in a bind. Did I add to my mother's worries and tell her about Kees? Certainly not. I kept it all to myself.

After a week Kees resurfaced, sweet and friendly as ever. He'd run out of money, he said, and couldn't pay me back. He promised to settle things in a couple of weeks. I told him nothing and reacted coolly.

Around this time, we received a letter from my father from the labor camp in Heino. For security reasons it was addressed to the Coljee home, but in the name of a certain "Mr. De Wit." It was his first letter, and he used the names I'd passed on to him, the names that concealed our identities. He wrote:

> Dear Sir,
>
> You probably have heard that I am here. I hope to receive provisions by return, express delivery. I'm also in urgent need of a large backpack if you can arrange it. I hope I can stay here for a while longer. Write me a letter when you can. How are Mrs. Van Moorsel, Lya and Jan keeping? I keep my chin up, since I'm determined to come back.
>
> Kind regards

I made my way to the camp in Heino under the name Lya Donkers. As an Aryan, I had no difficulty visiting my "former colleague at Venmans." I showed my identity papers to the sentry at the gate, and he let me in. Inside the office, a number of guards were gathered drinking coffee. All of them were Dutch, and they immediately grabbed a chair and offered me coffee. I made small talk, and it was actually fun.

My father had been working on a nearby farm, one of many that had joined the NSB, hoping to increase their income by using prisoners as cheap labor. As I chatted with the guards I told them that my colleague was actually an excellent bookkeeper, that it was his profession. I also told them that his health wasn't up to the heavy work he was expected to do in the fields and that they'd be better off using him for administrative work. That way you'll get more out of him, I said, hoping, of course, that it would make life a little easier for him. An SS officer listened attentively, nodding and muttering "good idea."

Then someone from the military police arrived to tell me that my colleague was on his way. I said good-bye and followed him. He politely held the door. Outside I saw my father, and before anyone had the chance to speak, I said, "Ah, there's my colleague." I made sure I said it loud enough for my father to hear. He greeted me as Lya Donkers and offered me his hand. And so we played the game, leaving out the usual hugs and kisses. He wanted to show affection, but I squeezed his hand and kept him at a distance. It was too dangerous. "How nice of you to come. How are things at work?" he asked.

"Excellent. We've just received a huge order from Germany. Mrs. Van Moorsel and Jan send their regards."

After that initial exchange I told the military policeman that I would like to go for a walk in the camp with my colleague, that I had been sitting long enough. He pointed to a path that led to the fields and told me to notify the sentry when we were done. Then he turned and sauntered off. We were now alone, and halfway along the path we stopped and sat. We didn't touch each other, not sure if anyone could see us in the open field, but we were free to talk. I quickly told him about Mother and John. My father was clearly tired, and when I asked him about life in the camp he said, "The work is hard, and the hours are long. The food is sufficient, but it's tasteless. I don't know how long this is going to last. I hear there are plans to send us to Poland, and reports from there are bad."

I felt sad but didn't let it show. "This is hopeless," I said. "I don't trust the Germans or the Dutch anymore. For them we're just a Jewish problem. Is there anything to hope for?"

My father shook his head. "I don't know what to do, and at

night I'm so tired I don't have the energy to think. It was stupid to volunteer for the camp. The authorities assured me that nothing would happen to you. Empty promises."

I interrupted him; complaining got one nowhere. "They betrayed our confidence before and they'll do it again. That means there's only one solution: we have to get you out of here, you have to escape."

He looked at me, surprised. "I can't just walk out of the camp . . . I wouldn't know how."

"True," I replied, "but this camp isn't heavily guarded and you work on the outside, on someone's farm. There has to be a way. You have to escape. I'll help you. I'll work out a plan. I promise."

My father thought long and hard and finally agreed. We wasted no time, and started to analyze the possibilities and potential risks. We tried to work out why some earlier escape attempts had failed.

After an hour we said our good-byes, and I shook his hand. He walked back to his barracks, and I reported to the sentry. I asked for the shortest way back to the village, where I rented a bicycle and explored the area, which was necessary if my escape plan was to work. When I cycled toward the land where my father worked I discovered that it lay on the edge of a forest. Excellent, I thought to myself. He could easily disappear into the trees at the end of the day, and no one would notice. He could tell them he was going to relieve himself. My father told me that their guard was armed but didn't have a dog. So by the time they realized he was gone it would be dark, and without a dog they wouldn't be able to do much about it. I now had the first step of my escape plan, but what next? A little stream cut into the forest on the north side of the field and then ran under a narrow bridge. If my father made his way through the forest to the bridge, I could arrange for a car to pick him up. With a clean suit, polished shoes, and a new set of papers for him we could just drive away.

My plan still needed fine-tuning. All sorts of things could go wrong, and my worst fear was the tracking dogs. According to my father, they didn't send dogs out in the dark but waited until daylight the following day. You also had to be on the lookout for the farmers. Earlier escape attempts had gone awry because a prisoner would simply appear on a farmer's property asking for shelter. The farmer would then call the military police, who returned the prisoner to the camp. As punishment he would be sent immediately to Poland, to set an example for those who remained. Three such attempts had already failed. It was thus important to avoid the farmers and throw the dogs off the scent. The best way to do that was to run through the stream. Your feet would get wet, but you would stay out of sight, and the dogs would be unable to follow your scent. My father could then hide under the little bridge. In order to frighten off the dogs even more I would get hold of some wolf droppings, which my father could scatter behind him. I read somewhere that it made dogs nervous and that they ran away when they smelled it. One of my students worked at the zoo in Tilburg, so it would be easy enough to obtain. But new identity papers were another question altogether. I'd have to give that more thought. At an arranged time I'd arrive at the bridge by car. Since unexpected obstacles were always a possibility, I refined my plan further. I'd visit him on Sunday when he was off work, and when we were out for a walk I'd give him money, a detailed map, wolf droppings, and identity papers. I'd pack an extra sweater for the cold night air and some extra food. That Sunday I'd spend the night in a nearby hotel in Zwolle, and on Monday night I'd pick him up. It had to work.

When Kees arrived home that afternoon and saw me deep in thought, he asked me what was wrong, and I told him about my plan. He immediately offered to help. "I'll organize identity papers for your father. I know a coach driver who's willing to sell his papers for three hundred guilders. I'm terribly in need of money right now, so fifty guilders for the inconvenience would be much appreciated."

My mother gave him the 350 guilders, and he returned that evening with papers for my father. He also offered to drive the car we planned to use to pick up my father, and I was pleased—it would be less conspicuous with a man at the wheel. Kees and I visited the camp on October 1, 1942, and went through the escape plan with my father down to the last detail.

Then fate dealt an unfortunate blow. My father's birthday was on October 4, and Mother and I sent him a birthday telegram. To our horror, the telegram returned unopened the same evening: "Addressee departed, destination unknown."

Kees offered to size up the situation the following morning. He left for Heino on Monday, October 5, with another 200 guilders from my mother. He also had my father's identity papers.

Falk Glaser, far left, at labor camp in Heino

PAUL

A New Cousin

FOUR YEARS AFTER my conversation with my grandmother, I parked my car in Brussels and walked into the main building of the European Commission, the heart of the European Union. The foundation that I directed had applied for a grant, and I had been invited to present the project. I had also made an appointment with the office of the relevant commissioner in hopes of acquiring political support.

The meeting with the director went well, and I was then met by someone from the office of the commissioner—a Dutchman whose name was, to my surprise, also Glaser, a relatively unusual name in the Netherlands. He had seen my name when I made the appointment and was curious.

"My name's René," he said.

"The same as my brother," I replied, and the ice was broken.

Instead of talking about the purpose of our meeting, he immediately inquired about our common surname. We explored possible family connections, even distant ones, running through a list of nephews, nieces, uncles, and aunts, but none of the names we came up with suggested a link. He refused to give up.

"Are you from Nijmegen?" he asked.

"I'm not, but my father's family used to live there."

"Then we have to be related," he said. "That's where my family is from."

We chatted for an hour, didn't get around to the purpose of my visit, and arranged to meet again a month later. In the meantime, he promised to study the project in more detail.

A month later I returned to Brussels. René welcomed me warmly but didn't beat around the bush. He and his father had run through the entire family in search of a connection. Did I have an Aunt Rosie in Stockholm, he asked. Yes, she was the link! It turned out that his father and Aunt Rosie were first cousins.

"That means my father is also your father's cousin," I said.

My father had never mentioned a cousin. We continued to talk about the family, and after our appointment ended we went to lunch.

I was amused by the discovery. We were family after all, second cousins. Though the relationship was relatively distant, it was still nice to know. But René was even more enthusiastic. For him, it was as if he'd rediscovered a long-lost brother. Almost all of his extended family was massacred during the war: all of his father's aunts and uncles (except one who lived in the Dutch East Indies), and most of their children. René's parents had been lucky. They were in the Dutch East Indies during the war, where Jews weren't subject to persecution. Consequently, I was the first relative named Glaser he'd met. He was delighted to have found a new family member.

The disparity in our reactions embarrassed me. Ria had a great many cousins, perhaps a hundred, but we were only in touch with a few of them and not at all with second cousins. We had grown up in the sixties, when friends took precedence over family. Distant relatives weren't really my thing. But René was a decent guy, and I could understand his warm emotions, even if I didn't share them. Maybe I would feel the same after a while, I thought. After lunch I returned to the Netherlands, the grant for my project approved. We agreed to stay in touch.

My encounter in Brussels continued to preoccupy me, not only because of the new second cousin I had suddenly acquired who considered me close family, but also because of his Jewish background. It slowly began to dawn on me that the family he had lost was also mine. While it may have been an intangible reality to me, it must have been different for my father. After all, we were talking about his cousins, nephews and nieces, uncles and aunts, people who had names and faces and personalities. He must have known many of them, from family get-togethers and from Nijmegen, where many of them had lived. My father had once been chess champion of the Province of Brabant, and I remembered him telling me that a cousin had taught him to play.

When I was alone with my father a few weeks later I told him that I knew the family secret. There was no sign of surprise or sadness in his eyes. I couldn't read his expression, sense his emotion. He simply turned away indifferently and stared into space.

But I was determined not to give up. I mentioned the names of a few of his nieces, names I'd heard for the first time from my second cousin, and I told him that they didn't survive, that almost the entire family had perished.

"That's what it was like then" was all he could say.

The conversation was over. We sat in silence side by side. There was no sign of agitation or unease, as is often the case with silences in a conversation, no signs of anger, vengefulness, or rage, as might have been expected in response to a revelation like mine. Minutes that seemed like hours ticked by in silence, and we sat there, almost relaxed. It was quite clear that he didn't want to talk, that he wanted to leave the past for what it was. But when I made a move to leave, he gave me a piece of advice in a gravely serious voice: "People are sure to be interested in our Jewish background and dreadful history, but do not talk about it. Keep it to yourself. If you don't, sooner or later it will be used against you."

Twice in later years I tried to talk to my father about our family's history, but he remained silent. His lips were permanently sealed.

Often I thought back to that meeting with my distant cousin and to my father's silence. It was difficult to wrap my head around the knowledge that the majority of my family had been murdered. And to absorb the fact that it hadn't happened during the Middle Ages in a distant land, but a generation ago, in these very towns. It was beyond my comprehension. My world was made up of good, law-abiding citizens. A murder in my community would have been headline news. If someone had killed my grandfather or grandmother I could have processed it: Who did it? Why did he do it? Jealousy? Money? Revenge? But an entire family, several families at once? If I dwelled on the atrocity it would drive me crazy. What could I even do? Look for the men who had caused it? Bring them to justice? Who would I look for? They were living amongst us, saying they had served in the Resistance.

A friend drew my attention to a commemorative book about the war published in Nijmegen, the city where a large part of my family has its roots. The book charted the years of the war, he told me, and it mentioned the name Glaser. As soon as I received it I looked inside and discovered a photo of some family members. For the first time in my life I saw their faces and read their names: Sara, Miep, David, Esther, Harry, and many more, all of them murdered. I turned the pages and discovered another photo: three young girls aged fourteen to seventeen, beautiful girls with dark hair smiling at the camera. The text identified them as the Glaser sisters, and I was immediately reminded of my own three dark-haired daughters. The more I looked the more similarities I saw, the glint in their eye, their demeanor, their smile. Maybe it was just my imagination, but it seemed real nonetheless. I was drawn back time and again to the three sisters in the photo. The abstract quality began to dissolve.

Three sisters (left to right): Sara, Frieda, and Miep Glaser

"The story of the Glaser family in hiding is particularly sad," the book read.

> Father David was a cattle dealer who decided to go into hiding in 1942. He asked advice from a farmer with whom he had a good business relationship. The man was unable to take the family himself. His farm wasn't big enough, was too close to the main road, and received too many visitors. But his brother, who had a large farm far from the city, was prepared to take them. On November 17, 1942, the day of the biggest roundup, the family went into hiding. Life was mostly confined to the indoors. It was too dangerous for the children to play outside, so they spent the better part of

the day in the barn. David helped on the farm. Despite the fact that the family was relatively safe, they had to flee from time to time when there was imminent danger of the farm being searched. Then they would wander around for hours, sometimes days, until the danger passed.

Every week a friend came to visit and David asked her at one point whether she would buy the family a chair so they could sit beside the fireplace. She bought a chair in Nijmegen and had it delivered to the farmer, who then made sure it reached its proper destination. It so happened that the woman's brother-in-law, who was aware of her weekly visits and of the purchase of the chair, got into trouble with the police for some trivial reason in June 1943. As a result, he and his wife were forced to watch a parade of German soldiers in the city. The man was unstable and receiving treatment from a psychiatrist. The event disturbed him so much that he decided to tell the police about the chair to get back into their good graces. No time was wasted. Agents of the dreaded Department of Investigation earned an extra hunting premium for the discovery and were dispatched to the address to which the chair had been delivered but they found no one. Then they went to the brother's remote farm and arrested the entire family. They were deported via Westerbork to Sobibor where they were gassed on July 2, 1943.

Some additional details concluded the sad story: the policemen responsible for the arrest received sixty guilders for their part in the arrest; the chair that had played such a crucial role was taken as a trophy and placed on display in the office of the head of the Department of Investigation; the farmer was also arrested but released again in December 1943. I looked again at the picture, and the three sisters gazed back at me. This could have happened to us, I realized, to our three children. It was a question of luck, nothing more. Sheer bad luck. They just happened to have been alive during the war, and that was their misfortune. They had done nothing wrong, but they were still persecuted, hunted down, arrested in a roundup by Dutch policemen—who were paid off for their trouble—and murdered far away and out of sight of the good citizens at home. If the sisters could have looked back at me, they would have seen that I was crying.

ROSIE

Betrayed and Beguiled

THE MORNING OF Wednesday, October 6, 1942, began like any other. It was a beautiful autumn day. While my mother was "home," I cycled to Hilversum, did some shopping, and drank tea on the terrace of the Grand Hotel Gooiland, thinking and worrying about what might have happened to my father and what Kees would find out. I returned to the Coljee residence around five-thirty in the afternoon.

When I arrived a taxi was parked outside. Typical Kees, I thought, never without a taxi. The driver was pacing up and down in front of the door, probably waiting for his fare. Then I spotted a policeman in the kitchen talking to Mr. and Mrs. Coljee. I turned sharply, grabbed my bicycle, and was about to take off. But the policeman was too quick for me. He ran outside, pistol drawn, and shouted, "Stop or I'll shoot."

Escaping was out of the question, so I dismounted my bike and walked toward him. As he returned his pistol to its holster he said, "I arrest you in the name of the law. I know who you are. You're Miss Rosa Glacér, fugitive because you're Jewish and didn't go to Westerbork. You are also in possession of identity papers in the name of Miss Cornelia Donkers." He ordered me inside.

The policeman was well behaved and seemed to be of a decent sort. He let me know he found it unpleasant that he had to do this. I didn't need his consolation, but when I got upstairs and found my mother in tears with a few things packed in a briefcase my emotions got the better of me. I offered the policeman everything I had and beseeched him in the name of everything he held sacred to release me and my mother immediately.

"That would be far too dangerous," he said. "I'm here in response to a telephone call from the Security Police in Amsterdam. They were so well informed, it can only be betrayal." We were each allowed to bring one bag of clothing. Unnoticed, I managed to transfer almost 9,000 guilders and some jewelry to Mr. Coljee. I had to leave behind my entire wardrobe and my mother's clothing.

I was suddenly reminded of the Lohengrin saga. Once his name is revealed, the calamity begins. What sort of apocalypse awaited me now that my identity was known?

The policeman transported us by taxi to the police station in Naarden, where the agents were friendly and offered us tea. They cursed the entire situation, but admitted they were powerless. That evening at seven-thirty Kees reported to the police station, much to our surprise. "Kees," said my mother, "do you know what brought us here?"

"No, Mrs. Glacér. I came as soon as I heard you'd been brought to the station. I hope they let you go soon. I went to Heino yesterday. Your husband was taken away by the SS and brought to Westerbork. I set off for Westerbork, but the train only took me as far as Hooghalen and I had to take a taxi the rest of the way. It cost a lot of money, I'm sure you understand. It took a long time, but when I finally found the camp they refused to let me in. I inquired after your husband but was told that he'd been put on a train that same evening. I realize how terrible this must be for you and Rosie. If only there was something I could do."

Still dazed by our arrest, we were not quite sure how to react to Kees's news. He did not seem to show emotional compassion for my father or for us. Could we trust him? I knew he was an opportunist. He was always talking about money, and he had already lied to me several times. But my misgivings didn't change the situation, so I ended the discussion. I thanked Kees for coming and he left. Shortly afterward Mrs. Coljee arrived. Though she now knew that we had deceived her by concealing our real names, she remained kind, and we arranged to keep in touch.

The detectives interrogated my mother first and then me. During my interrogation I asked the detective how they found us. He knew I'd probably find it hard to believe, but he suspected that there could only be one person who had this on his conscience and that person was Kees. "Without his information the Security Police would never have traced you. I can't say any more."

The next morning they brought us to a prison in Amsterdam, and a week later we were transferred to Westerbork, the camp that my father had supposedly passed through. We were considered "S" (*Strafe*, or punishment) cases because we had refused to obey the initial summons to report to the camp voluntarily. I was told that meant we could expect to be sent to Poland right away. There were rumors that they worked you to death there and might even kill you. I was usually able to manage, but for my mother this was a disaster. Whatever the case, I had to make sure we could stay in Westerbork. I had to attract attention, make myself useful, stand out. The stories we'd heard from Jews who had fled from Germany before the war didn't leave much to the imagination.

When we arrived at Westerbork no one could do anything for us. We were "S" cases and only the Security Police could change that. The situation seemed hopeless, but I managed to draw the attention of the barrack leader, a Russian emigrant. He liked me, and in the midst of all the misery I demonstrated a tap dance. He gave me a job as a nurse. I made sure my mother was admitted to the hospital, making her "unsuitable" for transport. Thus they "forgot" to put us on the train the following day when everyone else was moved to Poland. I was relieved, but for how long, I asked myself. I had to continue plotting.

A few days after our arrival something extraordinary happened. Wading through the mud with a wheelbarrow and a rucksack, I suddenly caught sight of my father standing in the middle of a crowd. We were over the moon and hugged each other for minutes on end. Kees had told us that my father had already been sent to Poland, a contradiction that flashed through my mind for an instant, but it was soon pushed away by the joy of seeing my father again.

I found a job for him in the kitchen. He was not registered as an "S" case and thus didn't have to be on the first transport train to Poland, but a job would perhaps extend his stay. On top of that, there was food to be had in the kitchen.

Now that we were able to stay, if only for the time being, I quickly established contacts outside the camp and wrote a couple of short letters to Mrs. Coljee. I told her how things were going and signed my letters invariably "Lya," since that was how she knew me. She always replied. My first letters were brief:

> I've written several letters to Kees, but haven't heard a word in return. It's not very nice of him. Is he in everyone's bad books again?

We're fainting from hunger here all day long. Our menu consists of six slices of dry bread, a cup of coffee without sugar and milk, and then in the afternoon a bit of some disgusting stew.

I think I'll be staying here for the time being. The place is such a filthy mess. I work 3 days as a nurse and 4 days as a typist. It's hard work, and I earn nothing but my food.

Do you know who betrayed us? I pray a lot, especially for Kees. I hope he sleeps as well as I do.

Mrs. Coljee wasn't my only contact with the outside world. In spite of the censorship and limitations imposed on us, I managed to communicate with friends and students at my school. I also had a subscription to *De Telegraaf*, which came daily in the mail.

Once everything was squared away regarding our stay, I had some time on my hands and decided to write Mrs. Coljee a longer letter. Using the typewriter at work, I explained what I went through during the turbulent period after I was betrayed, and how I had managed to improve my situation and that of my parents not long after arriving at the camp.

Westerbork, October 27th, 1942

Dear Mr. and Mrs. Coljee,

This morning I received your telegram and learned that you sent us another two parcels for which I am most grateful. My mother's parcel is in our possession. She was ill when it arrived and wasn't at home. I haven't received my parcel yet. I normally have to collect it in person, but my father will take care of it this afternoon. Meanwhile, you must be thinking that Lya is a fine one, making a fool of us like that. But nothing could be farther from the truth; it was a question of survival.

I told you we had run away because my father had been taken hostage. The truth is that my father was in Heino labor camp. We kept it from you because we were strangers and saw it as our only way out. Mr. van Meteren knew all of this, but he owed me a favor and promised to keep quiet. How they managed to find us remains a complete and utter mystery.

Please also accept my apologies for the fact that you've heard so precious little from me since we left, only a couple of short messages. But let me make up for it with a long letter, describing what happened after our arrest.

The day they took us away they brought us to the police station in Naarden where we were treated with the utmost kindness. But a police station isn't a hotel and my mother and I had to sleep on the ground that night on a pile of old curtains with our coats and a couple of leather jackets kindly donated by the police as blankets. That same evening Mr. van Meteren appeared out of the blue. Up to that moment we—the police included—had presumed that he was the one who had turned us in, but when we spoke with him we were completely convinced of his innocence. But when I think about it now, I'm not so certain. The question is still open, but whatever it takes I'll get to the bottom of it. I'm determined to find out who played this dirty trick on us.

After you brought us bread the following morning, the police provided tea and bread with chocolate sprinkles from a hotel in Naarden (I forgot the name). Around eleven, an inspector and the same policeman who arrested us that afternoon took us to Amsterdam in a luxury car. We arrived at noon in the pouring rain. We were taken immediately to the headquarters of the Security Police and interrogated. I'll spare you the gruesome details at this juncture!

Then we were taken to the prison and handed over to the German police. Unsurprisingly, we had to hand over all our valuables as well as our suitcases and were only allowed to keep what was absolutely necessary for toilet purposes. To our great surprise we were pushed into a laundry room, the tenth and eleventh in a row, all of them ladies from well-to-do families who had done precisely the same as we had done.

It was disgusting. We slept on straw bags on the floor and had to go to the toilet in a little barrel in a corner of the room, which stank to high heaven all day long. We had to get up at seven in the morning and go to bed at nine. Each day we were allowed, under strict supervision, twenty minutes of fresh air in a so-called "air cell" with bars on top. They kept us there from Thursday October 8th to Monday October 12th. You'll probably have received a request to send me pajamas there. But they turned out to be no longer necessary because they woke us at six in the morning on October 13th! and bundled us onto a train for Westerbork.

First we had to line up with about 200 other victims, all of them sophisticated and sociable, ranging in age from 3 months to 85 years. Then they returned our baggage and our money! When I examined my suitcase I noticed that the following had disappeared: my white winter sweater, a hot water bottle, and two beautiful lanterns. Where they went is a mystery.

We were then taken in police vans to Adama van Scheltema Square, where the Jewish Council for Amsterdam has its office. This was an opportunity to pass on a sign of life through the Jewish Council to you, Elisabeth, and Kees. They gave us bread, coffee, sausage, and even cigarettes. After everything we had been through they were so extraordinarily kind to us that we'll never forget it for as long as we live.

In the afternoon we were told to collect our luggage and were taken in special trams through the streets of Amsterdam, past everything I loved so much and will find so hard to forget, to the central station, where the train for Westerbork awaited us. The train left at 1:24 p.m. I had taken the same train so many times to Naarden. Imagine my feelings when the train passed Naarden and I cherished a secret hope that I might catch a glimpse of you or Mr. van Meteren. I managed to have a good look into Restaurant Ritte but that was all I saw.

In Hilversum station I saw one of Serban's brothers. Serban leads the Hungarian Orchestra at Grand Hotel Gooiland in Hilversum. The boy seemed extremely surprised and I presume he'll have told Kees that he saw me.

We arrived around eight on a splendid moonlit night and were taken by the SS on a one and a half hour walk to Camp Westerbork. I'll spare you the details here too.

After we were registered and enjoyed a cup of warm milk, a military policewoman accompanied us to our barrack as if we were major criminals. I already mentioned barrack 83 in a previous letter. It was pitch dark and there were 200 beds, three high, without mattresses, pillows, or blankets, and that's where we were expected to sleep. Men and women, children and invalids, beautiful and ugly, young and old, all mixed together, and I've never witnessed such filth in all my days.

Although it wasn't allowed, I filled in that night as *Baracken-sanitäterin* [Barrack Medic] (everything here is in German). The next morning no one was allowed outside. We were locked in and had to spend the entire day indoors. Because I had made myself so useful, however, the *Baracken-leiter* [Barrack Leader] gave me a note asking the doctor to put together a first aid kit and that gave me the chance to go outside.

He also appointed me to keep a provisional eye on the sick people in my barrack, to help them and take care of them. I made a great many new friends and acquaintances at that time and also met several friends and acquaintances from Nijmegen, Den Bosch, and Amsterdam. It was delightful. But after a few short weeks, the same people, or most of them at least, had deteriorated very badly.

My first thought was: They won't get me!

Large numbers are transported out of the camp twice a week and it's truly dreadful. We're all terrified of being selected and you never know in advance. It's the most terrible thing you can imagine. The torture people are forced to undergo, especially the mental torture, is beyond description. In the meantime, my mother has fallen ill and is suffering from major stomach cramps. I brought her to Barrack 70, the emergency hospital. She's still there.

It's hard to imagine a filthier place. Men, women, and children together under one roof, all of them sick, and forced to eat and go to the toilet in the same space. I don't have to tell you that my mother is getting worse by the day.

After I'd been here for three days and to my complete amazement, I saw my father. The man almost fainted, as you can imagine. It's only now, of course, that I understand how it was possible for you to have received letters from him asking to let him know where we were. My father was living in Barrack 65 at the time.

I should tell you what happened when we received your parcels. Mother and I collected our own parcels from the post and the parcel with provisions ended up with my father. He in turn presumed that we had received similar parcels.

Our food regime is the following: in the morning a cup of bad coffee without sugar or milk, at noon a plate of thick soup or watery stew, in the evening 6 slices of bread with runny butter and another cup of coffee substitute. You can therefore imagine how urgently we need extra food. I didn't really care at first because they told me I wasn't allowed to stay in this camp as punishment for not volunteering to go to Westerbork. The police had to arrest me instead. I was expecting to be put on the next train heading east. But I just kept on working to get ahead.

It might seem impossible, but I managed to get a fantastic job. I've become private secretary to the *Polizei-angestellte*, the highest-ranking officer of the *Sicherheitsdienst* [Security Service] in Amsterdam. He's a very nice young man and we work together all day long. The other inmates are madly jealous of me, yet they still chase me politely the entire day with a hundred-and-one requests. Imagine, I sit behind a desk with a really nice young gentleman opposite me wearing a large swastika. And he's very kind to me.

As a result of the job I'm allowed to stay here on a permanent basis and can also keep my father and my mother here. It's more than a dream. I've had to pinch myself now and again in the last three days to convince myself that it's real. So I'm staying in Holland, and that allows me to stay in touch with the outside world.

Officially, I'm only allowed to write once a week and I'm limited to one side of a postcard. But this letter won't be passing through the censors so I hope it gets to you. You can write to me as often as you'd like. Your letters won't be checked. Write back soon. I'm so unbelievably anxious to hear from you.

Now that I'm here I've been given the opportunity to take a few days off soon. I plan to make a special trip to Naarden to tell you what we've been through since we last met. You know, there's only one thing I don't understand: Mr. van Meteren has never written. Is he perhaps in prison? Or is he angry at us, or is there another reason? I hope I never have to think such a thing.

For now, dear Mr. and Mrs. Coljee, accept my mother's warm greetings. Send our best regards to all those we got to know and cherish in the short period we were with you. Although you've never made my father's acquaintance, he also sends his best.

Should you want to visit me we can arrange it in due course, now that I no longer have to worry about being sent away from here. So, write back soon.

Much love and a heartfelt kiss to you both.

Your loving Lya
Rosie Glaser, Barrack 63, Lower Westerbork
Post: Hooghalen East, Drenthe
mother has the same address: Mrs. J. Glaser-Philips

Two days after mailing my letter I received a reply from Magda Coljee. The mail still seemed to be functioning as it should. She decided to write back immediately and tell me all about Kees and his extraordinary behavior.

Naarden, October 28th, 1942

Dear Lya,

About half an hour after your arrest, Kees came home. The first thing he said to me was: "Am I too late?" or words to that effect. We told him you had been arrested by the police. He went to the police station immediately. When he came back he said that the police had told him that I had told the police that he had betrayed the Glacér ladies. Furthermore, he said that he wasn't in Amsterdam on Sunday but in Hooghalen near Camp Westerbork. Kees then insisted we give him the strong box with the money you left behind. The next day he wanted to sell the goods you didn't take with you. We refused and kept everything. He told us that he had power of attorney from you to administer your money and property. He also said that he had run up expenses, among other things for the trip to Hooghalen and for a couple of suitcases with underwear he had delivered to the camp. He showed us a piece of paper with your authorization, signed Rosie Glacér. We ignored this too. Then he threatened to go to the *Sicherheitsdienst* if we didn't hand it over. I asked him for time to think about it. And the next day I told him to do whatever he had to do. Can you tell me soon whether we should retain your money and belongings or give them to Kees?

Warm regards,
Magda Coljee

I also received an alarming letter from Henk Coljee, which he appeared to have written without his wife's knowledge.

Naarden, October 29th, 1942

Dear Lya,

My wife is visiting her family for a few days and I'm taking this opportunity to write about something that's been on my mind.

On October 24th we sent two parcels with provisions. One to you and one to your mother. Did you receive them? Did you let your father and mother read my letter? I'm returning your card to Kees (enclosed). He's still with us and sleeps here from time to time.

Let me come to the point. My wife made the trip to Westerbork and handed in three parcels at the gate to the camp. So they're not from Kees as you first thought. You thanked him in your card, but for no reason. She, and not Kees, also sent the telegram. She does everything she can for you and your mother. But I have to tell you that she can only continue to do so on the condition that Kees knows nothing about it, absolutely nothing. It is most urgent that you bear that in mind. He doesn't know that my wife was in Westerbork and that we're still in touch with one another.

The reason for all this urgency is that Kees has been a lot of trouble as of late. One minute he's kind and the next he's threatening. It's the same day in day out. He's determined to have your things. We told him that you had packed everything and had it delivered to a girlfriend, that there was nothing of yours in the house. He searched high and low but found nothing. Now he thinks it was all sent somewhere else before you left. He found out where the speakers from the dance school were, which you had previously brought to a friend. He traced the man and told him you had asked him to look after them for you. Your friend handed them over and Kees sold them for 150 guilders. According to estimates they were worth around 700 guilders.

Dear Miss Lya, please do not be angry at me for writing this letter.

Many warm greetings, especially to your father and mother.

Henk Coljee

I responded immediately to both letters. It was vital. Without money, no food parcels. Without my things, no decent clothing. I hurried to my typewriter and wrote the following letter by return of post:

Westerbork, October 30th, 1942

Dear Mr. and Mrs. Coljee,

I was only able to post a letter to you yesterday thanks to the kind mediation of a very well-informed individual. We have not been allowed to send mail here for a week. I now hasten to respond immediately to the letters I received from you and your wife. While I was grateful to receive them, I was also saddened, because what I had feared has turned out to be true.

In the meantime, my mother has recovered and is no longer in the infirmary. I, on the other hand, developed a huge boil on my forehead a few days ago, half under my hair, which resulted in a sort of infection. My face was terribly swollen and my temperature reached 39.4. I'm feeling a little better now and have been working a couple of hours a day. I can't sit around idle, nor do I want to. The fever is almost gone and my face is less swollen. But I'm still wearing a silly bandage around my head that resembles a turban.

I am very glad that you didn't get into trouble on our account and am virtually certain you will not have to face anything of the sort. In the first instance because you were unaware of the truth, and secondly because as private secretary to the *Sicherheitspolizei* in Westerbork, I was immediately able to arrange for Mr. van Meteren to be arrested in one of the coming days. He will almost certainly be transferred to the concentration camp at Amersfoort.

In spite of the fact that I am a prisoner here, I am still proud of the fact that I remain honest and have behaved honestly, and that people like Mr. van Meteren will receive their just rewards for abusing our weak situation. One thing is certain: while I was unable and even unwilling to believe it, you and my mother were convinced, if I am not mistaken, that something was amiss from the outset.

On the day we learned that my father was in Westerbork, Mr. van Meteren received 375 guilders from my mother, 300 of which was to be handed over to my father and 75 was to cover his travel and accommodation costs. When Mr. van Meteren returned on the Wednesday evening we were already in the hands of the police and we both knew well enough that money would not help us. He told us there, in the midst of all our misery and woe, that Father was already in transit to Poland. Nothing further was said about the money. In my mind I thought he might use the money to send provisions and so forth if I was away, so I decided to let him hold on to it. At the time we had no idea what was going to happen to us. So all that talk about using his own money is nonsense and shamefaced fantasy. I have already handed matters over to the *Sicherheitspolizei*, for whom I work day and night. I am determined to have my way and see this scoundrel punished, and seriously so. He has never spent a cent on my behalf, but my mother and I currently have a claim against him of more than 1,000 guilders, which he most likely squandered on all sorts of young ladies of ill repute. I never at any time granted Mr. van Meteren power of attorney over our property and his claims to this effect are pure deception. Never, never, and again never give him anything that belongs to me or my mother. To do so would be nothing less than a crime. We trust you in this matter and no one else. Your response to his demands was perfect, but please do not think for a minute that anything of mine, no matter how worthless, belongs to him. If you were to concede to his demands I would be forced to warn the police, in spite of the difficulties this would bring.

When it comes to SS headquarters in Amsterdam he should watch his step. It's not a threat, but if he's not careful he'll be getting an inside view of the place before long, if he's not already there of course. He's wanted for intimidation and fraud. It could be worse, but we all seem to agree that this was the only way forward.

Let me repeat: neither me, nor my mother and father, are required to go to Poland and we're staying here. So we can stay in regular contact with each other from Westerbork and that means a great deal.

My confessor in Vught sent me a beautiful prayer book and an extremely kind letter. I have complete faith in what the future will bring, pray a lot, and am absolutely convinced that I'll return from here, get back to my work, and see you all again just as I left you. With the exception of Mr. van Meteren. While I don't expect to see him again, I no longer include him among the people I once knew, let alone loved. It would be better not to send Mr. van Meteren any more messages. Please don't forget: you must hand over nothing to Mr. van Meteren, otherwise police involvement will be unavoidable and immediate. This is not an empty threat, but something I can completely confirm via my activities here. Mr. van Meteren has nothing of mine in his possession except a series of private photos and a few picture frames. I insist on recovering these from him. He kept them in the left-hand cupboard of his desk downstairs. Would you please send them to me by return?

We received the last two parcels, for which we are immensely grateful. Please wrap everything up securely. It's been raining so much of late and everything tends to get mixed together. If it gets damp it can no longer be used I'm afraid.

I didn't see or speak to Mr. van Meteren in Amsterdam. Another of his infamous lies. It goes without saying therefore that I didn't give him power of attorney. Pure fantasy! Please do not believe him. He was never in Amsterdam and he was never in Westerbork. I've written to Miss Elisabeth to warn her, but I haven't received a sign of life from her either.

I warn you, Mrs. Coljee, if you dare hand over anything of my property to him, I'll involve the police and I mean it. I'm so grateful for everything you have done and are still doing to take care of us. But since my mother and myself have already fallen victim to his flagrant scams then I'm sure you will understand my threats and my assurance that I will carry them out in order to prevent you too from falling victim to his wicked character and nature. Once again, please leave my things, including my fur coat etc., where they are. If I need something I will write to you. Mr. van Meteren was never in Westerbork and never delivered a suitcase. I'm here and I'm staying here. Do you need more plausible and more tangible evidence than that?

A visit is more or less out of the question at the moment since you won't be allowed into the camp and I'm not allowed out. In a while, when everything settles down, I can discuss the matter with my boss. The chances that we'll see each other again somewhere are pretty good. My boss is exceptionally kind, and decidedly vexed by the entire situation.

Let me conclude, Mrs. Coljee, by wishing you and your husband much love. My parents also send their best regards and I hope to hear from you soon, if possible, with a parcel. If you send clothing, please pack it separately from any foodstuffs and use sturdy boxes. Everything gets opened here and the wet weather can make a terrible mess.

Your Lya
Rosie

My letter hit the mark. Mrs. Coljee handed over nothing to Kees, nothing at all. In one of the letters I received from her she confirmed that Kees had betrayed us and received a traitor's reward of 500 guilders for each of us. The police in Naarden had already told me about his betrayal.

Mrs. Coljee used the money we left with her to send a parcel of "ordered" provisions every week. If I asked, she also sent other things we left in her care, such as clothing, underwear, socks, and

Westerbork, den 3o Oktober 1942.

Lieve Mevrouw en Mijnheer Coljé-

Eerst gisteren liet ik U door vriendelijke bemiddeling van zeer bevoegde zijde een brief posten, daar hier momenteel deze mogelijk sinds een week niet bestaat.

Ik haast mij dan ook U thans direct een antwoord te geven op de 3 brieven, welke ik van U en Uw vrouw tegelijktertijd ontving, waar ik eenerzijds zeer dankbaar voor was, maar anderszijds, erg bedroefd, omdat ik dat wat ik vreesde nu toch bewaarheid is geworden.

Mijn moeder is intusschen hersteld en weer uit de ziekenbarak uit, en nu heb ik sinds eenige dagen een heele groote steen puist voor mijn voorhoofd, half in mijn haren, waarbij ik een soort infectie heb gekregen, en nu een paar dagen een heel gezwollen gezicht heb gehad met 39, 4 koorts. Momenteel ben ik weer wat beter, en werk thans weer enkele uurtjes per dag, omdat ik niet heelemaal stil kan en wil zitten.

De koorts is practisch voorbij, en m'n gezich minder gezwollen, alleen heb ik een dwaas verband om mijn hoofd, dat aan een tulband doet denken.

Ik ben heel erg blij, dat U geen narigheden hebt gekregen en durf U wel haast/de verzekering te geven, dat U ook geen narigheden krijgt; ten eerste omdat U het werkelijk niet geweten hebt, en ten tweede, omdat ik het momenteel ten allen tijde in mijn macht heb, door mijn werkzaamheden hier als privé-secretaresse van de Sicherheits-Polizei in Westerbork, dat ik na het lezen van Uw brief direct ervoor heb kunnen zorgen, dat de Heer van Meteren, één dezer dagen gearresteerd zal worden en zoo goed als zeker naar het concentratie-kamp te Amersfoort zal worden overgebracht.

Trots mijn gevangen zijn hier, voel ik mij gelukkig, omdat ik weet, dat ik eerlijk ben en eerlijk gehandeld heb, en dat het zeer zeker gewroken zal worden, zooals een persoon als de heer van Meteren van onze zwakke situatie heeft misbruik weten te maken.

Eén ding is zeker, ik heb het niet willen en kunnen gelooven maar U en mijn moeder, waren er geloof ik al vanaf het eerste moment van overtuigd, dat er iets niet in orde was.

Mijnheer van Meteren heeft op den dag, dat het ons bekend was, dat vader in Westerbork was, van mijn moeder fl. 375,-- gekregen, om daarvan fl. 3oo,-- aan mijn vader ter hand te stellen, en om fl. 75,-- te gebruiken voor reis en verblijf kosten.

Toen de heer v.M. terug kwam op Woensdagavond zaten wij reeds op het politie-bureau, en begrepen wij beiden best, dat wij aan geld niets hadden.

Hij vertelde ons daar in al de ellende en narigheid ook nog, dat vader reeds op transport was naar Polen en over het geld werd heelemaal niet meer gesproken; Mijn gedachte was, als ik weg ben kan hij er mij misschien levensmiddellen enz. voor sturen, dus laa het hem maar behouden.

Wij wisten toch immers zelf ook niet wat er van ons zou worden.

Dus dat geld uit eigen zak is onzin en niets als grove fantasie.

Ik heb reeds alles aan de Sicherheits-Polizei, waar ik zelf dag en nacht bij werk in handen gegeven, en zal en wil ik mijn doel bereiken, dat deze groote deugniet gestraft wordt en niet gering ook.

Hij heeft voor mij nog nooit een cent uitgegeven, alleen moeder en ik hebben momenteel een vordering van ruim fl. 1ooo.-- op hem, welke hij er zeer waarschijnlijk met allerlei meisjes

a sweater. She was also able to send money by postal order, which allowed me to take care of all sorts of things in the camp.

After a number of weeks the censorship intensified. Every letter was opened and checked. More rules were imposed. As prisoners we were allowed to write a limited number of lines twice a week, and at certain moments writing was forbidden completely. Since the food in the camp was bad, many of the letters were about provisions, about orders placed and whether they arrived intact or not. Such correspondence was checked by the censor and wasn't a problem, but what annoyed me was the fact that the police told some of my girlfriends to stop sending me letters. They harassed them and told them that if they wanted to stay in touch with me they could arrange a place for them in the camp too. Almost all of them had stopped writing.

After my daily duties I would set out to meet people and discover what I could organize in my new world. Speaking with men had always been easy, and some wasted no time in chatting me up. One day I was introduced to the Austrian/Hungarian pianist Erich Ziegler, who in turn introduced me to the resident entertainers' club that he helped organize. After a week we gave performances in all the barracks with songs and comical sketches galore. I sang, acted, and danced. We were an enormous success.

I also kept busy by talking to the Germans—it was easy for me since I spoke the language fluently. Everyone else was either submissive or kept out of their way, while I actually enjoyed talking with them and listening to their stories from home. I reacted to them just as I did to my classmates in Kleef. They were more or less the same age as me. Most of them simply progressed from the Hitler Youth to the Wehrmacht or the SS without giving it much thought. They talked about their everyday concerns, a brother at the front in Russia, a sick mother in the Ruhr, about being homesick, missing their wives and children.

I quickly found my way, and before long I met a young SS officer, a Dutchman by the name of Jorg de Haan. From the office where I worked—the *Schreibstube*—I was expected to bring him detailed lists of the prisoners who were to be transported by train to Poland. He was good-looking, tall, with a handsome uniform, relaxed demeanor, and clear blue eyes. When he realized I spoke fluent German he invited me for a cup of coffee in his room. The conversation seemed short at the time, but afterward it dawned on me that we had spent an entire hour together. We didn't talk about the lists, rather we talked about each other, about our lives and where we came from. I told him about my dancing and about Kleef. He talked about his two children and his adventures in the *Sicherheitsdienst*. As I left, we looked at each other, smiling.

In the days that followed we had similar meetings. He was charming, kind, and wore a serious yet optimistic expression. Sometimes I caught him staring at me, and when I turned to look at him he laughed. Thinking ahead, I did the same. I had to grasp every opportunity I was given. I had been lucky not to be sent immediately to Poland, but my situation was still risky, too risky to rely on more luck. So, I decided to seduce him to improve my situation. He was an important man, an SS officer in the *Sicherheitsdienst*, responsible in the camp for *jüdische Auswanderung*, or Jewish emigration. It was his job to decide what happened to the prisoners, what kind of work they were given, whether they were transported or exempted.

After a week he asked me inside and told me that starting the following week I was to be his secretary and that he was going to organize a desk for me in his huge office. As a result we saw each other every day, and because there wasn't much to do in the camp at night, we continued the evenings at his house. Thus we became lovers in a strange and exceptional world. He was sweet to me and kind, and I was certain he'd really fallen in love, if only a little. We didn't only go to bed together; we also talked about our feelings, our worries, and our plans for the future. I told him I was married before. He didn't say much about his wife. Behind closed doors we used first names. In public we followed the usual formalities.

During the day we were kept busy with camp administration. He had to assemble a fixed number of prisoners to transport to Poland. It was my job to put together "draft" lists and make sure he got them on time. I also received suggestions from the so-called *Antragstelle*, an internal commission in the camp that suggested exemptions for those whose work was essential. Every time we crossed the camp together countless people approached us with a respectful nod and argued their case for exemption. Sometimes they begged or offered money. I was then expected to collect their written requests, though most of the time he directed them to the *Antragstelle*, which had its own procedures and policies. Its members gave preference to their own friends. Because a large part of the *Antragstelle* consisted of German Jews who had fled to the Netherlands before the war and were there when Westerbork was still a refugee camp, they tended to favor their German compatriots and exempted them first from deportation. Jorg de Haan then had to make a decision on the basis of the various suggestions and draw up a definitive list. The people who'd been selected were given only a day's notice before their departure.

Jorg had regular consultations with camp commandant Gemmeker. Several times he took me along to take notes and draw up the minutes of their meetings. My German skills turned out to be very useful, and the decision was made to have me do secretarial work for the commandant as well as Jorg.

So I worked during the day and spent my evenings with Jorg. I asked Mrs. Coljee to send my red dress, fur coat, and some jewelry, and she did. Besides decent food, I also had a few other privileges, such as the use of a typewriter, freedom to correspond without my letters passing the censor, my own room, and the occasional visitor. I even managed to arrange a visit from a few of my former students. One of them, who now lived close to Groningen, even managed several visits. In short, my circumstances were fairly good. I'd even gained a little weight. And I'd returned to writing songs and poems—about love and men, of course. They were a little cynical, but such was my inspiration. Men had betrayed me, taken me prisoner, and angled for my affection.

Fifteen Minutes

A mere fifteen minutes
Fifteen is all I need
A mere fifteen minutes
I'll catch a man with speed
In fifteen measly minutes
I'm careful, silent, wise
In fifteen measly minutes
He's bound to think I'm nice
In fifteen measly minutes
I make a grown man swoon
In fifteen measly minutes
I show him to the moon

Eve once used an apple
For me it's "sex-appeal"
In fifteen measly minutes
Yes, then he's the schlemiel
A man is a strange element
Imagines he's intelligent
He's "studied" life? He's bluffing

And of women he knows nothing
Yet the art of manipulation
I apply with sophistication
What is a woman in the life of a man?
The greatest thing, some say
No, a kiss is his goal, two if he can
He wants to get his way

Be a woman is my motto
And I know the rule to follow
'Cause men are marvelous creations
Yet they bore me fast, you know
But a woman's life is so
Hence my real bad reputation
What have men shown in the past?
They're potatoes grown cold
Or a novel read too fast?
Oh, the rest they leave me cold
Except . . .

Evenings with Jorg were relaxed and cozy. I was his mistress, of course, but because his wife was so far away and we were stuck in the camp, we lived more or less like a married couple. There were photos of his wife in his quarters. The photos bothered me at first when we made love. It was as if his wife was watching us. But they didn't bother him, and after a while I got used to them. After making love, we relaxed and chatted side by side in the shadows, and Jorg talked mostly about staying happy and optimistic. I could see his eyes glisten in the dark. He spoke as most people do who have all their rights and privileges.

Occasionally I picked up criticism in the camp about our relationship. When I told someone I couldn't have his name erased from the transportation list, he cursed me to my face as a slut. Once an SS officer remarked, "You're still a Jew." I was also not invited when Jorg had dinner with the camp commandant. But otherwise the advantages far outweighed the disadvantages. When there was a party for the camp staff, Jorg and I went together, and I wore the dress Mrs. Coljee had forwarded to me. The parties were wonderful, with music, drinking, and dancing.

At my invitation, Magda Coljee came to visit. I had arranged for an invitation to be sent to her via the so-called *Kommandatur*—the commandant's office—and they simply let her in at the front gate. She stayed the entire day. I really enjoyed her visit, and we had much to discuss. A week after our arrest, Magda had asked Kees if he had already been to the *Sicherheitsdienst*, which is what he had threatened to do if she did not hand over our money. He told her he had changed his mind. A couple of weeks later she received a bill from a hotel in Amsterdam for a dinner. Kees had told her he was in Hooghalen near Westerbork that same day. The truth of the matter was that he had deceived us both.

In the afternoon Magda also got the chance to see my mother. The reunion was warm, and we enjoyed a cup of tea in Jorg's office while he was busy elsewhere. My father was unable to get time off from his work, and without greeting him in person Magda returned at the end of the day to Naarden.

Not long after Magda's visit I discovered that Kees had been up to even more trickery behind my back. A few days after our arrest he had tracked down one of my girlfriends, told her that he had spent a few days in jail because of our arrest, and asked for 2,000 guilders for a lawyer who would arrange for our release, using the argument that my mother was too old to stay in prison and that I was crazy and belonged in a mental hospital. Kees also visited Elisabeth, John's girlfriend, claiming to have some of my possessions that he wanted to hand over to my brother. Of course he was only intent on collecting the 500 guilders traitor's money. He had already been to the false address I had given him. Thankfully, Elisabeth didn't trust him, stayed calm, and told him she was no longer seeing my brother.

I was happy to hear rumors that John was in Switzerland, because I had spread the rumor myself to persuade potential betrayers to give up their attempts to trace him. It seemed that he was still safe.

I worked hard on the diary I had started when I was in Wolvenhoek, the SS prison in Den Bosch. Mrs. Coljee had sent it to me at my request, well wrapped to be sure it wasn't damaged, and by registered mail. I had no shortage of material to write about.

I also continued to write to Mrs. Coljee on a weekly basis to keep her abreast of my situation and to place my orders. Here are some snippets:

> At Christmas I spent 4 days as hostess to a Hungarian SS officer. His *Wehrmacht* and SD roommates had all gone on leave. We had a great time with the others who had stayed behind, and we even danced to music from a suitcase gramophone.
>
> I wish you a prosperous 1943, in the hope that this year will bring back the long-awaited peace.
>
> The mood here is optimistic, but that says nothing.
>
> My brother John sends me good reports from Switzerland where he lives.

After censorship was introduced for incoming letters in January 1943, I wrote her:

This is no fun at all for me because I sometimes got 6 letters per day. But now I have written to my friends, asking them to divide things up. Some address their letters to my father, some to my mother and some to myself. So now I get almost all of my mail.

Someone else is living in our home in the city of Den Bosch. I don't like it, but there is nothing I can do about it.

Don't be afraid that we will lose courage. Mother and I, and especially Father, are bearing up extremely well.

My book is getting bigger and I've found a young man here to illustrate it for me. He's 19 years old and can draw tremendously well.

My father received a package from you, but we don't understand why. I had a hard time getting him to hand it over to me. He meant no harm, but men are egoists. If you send another package just address it to me.

On a winter evening, as we lay staring at the ceiling after making love, Jorg said, "I'm worried about you. The instructions we've been receiving from the German *Sicherheitsdienst* are getting stricter by the day. You should be more careful about what you write in your letters. The censors are much more stringent these days, and they monitor more than they used to. There are also informers in this camp, and I've already picked up remarks about you slipping private mail in among the official letters you dispatch as my secretary." I listened in silence, stroked his face, and thought about my situation.

To avoid jeopardizing our relationship and my privileges,

I stopped hiding my private mail in with the official post that very day and followed a different procedure from then on. An acquaintance who worked at the camp and had to leave every week took my letters with him. Because the rules were more rigidly applied I stopped using the typewriter, wrote everything by hand, and dated my letters a year earlier. That way no one was put at risk. If a letter happened to be intercepted, they would think it was an old one that got lost in the mail and resurfaced a year later. To keep up appearances, I also wrote letters and sent them via

A backdated letter from Rosie to the Coljees

the official Westerbork channels. According to the camp regulations we were allowed only one letter a week and everything had to pass the censor. So the system was satisfied, and I managed to send my other letters unobserved.

On another evening, Jorg was worried again. "More and more people have to be transported, especially people over forty and children. I have to deliver increasing numbers to the camps in Poland. It might be better if you started using your ex-husband's surname Crielaars instead of Glacér. He's Catholic and people in mixed marriages are exempt. Even though you're divorced, it might be of use in the future if things get tougher.

"I'm not sure how long I'll be here. Headquarters are talking about transfers. If I'm no longer here make sure you go to Vught. They're planning a new camp there for young people like you. It's expected to be a model camp, an example for the others. There's work in the place, and you'll be able to stay. Make sure you get out of here. Westerbork is nothing more than a transit camp. Everyone here is destined for Poland sooner or later."

Jorg told me that in Poland the work was much harder, and that many people died. I already knew about the deaths because letters had been found in the empty trains returning from Auschwitz about the execution of prisoners. I said nothing. What should I do with all the new information? Was Jorg announcing the end of our relationship? What would happen to my parents?

I was reminded once again of the Lohengrin saga. When the swan knight revealed his real name, life with his sweetheart Elsa came to an immediate end. Now it was the other way around. Jorg was my swan knight and I had to use another name, conceal my real name to avoid unhappiness.

A short time later Jorg was transferred back to Amsterdam, and someone else took his place, a fool of a man, nowhere near as sensitive as Jorg. He also wanted to take me to bed, but I refused his advances. He was nothing more than a lout. With Jorg gone, my situation changed dramatically, and at night I was forced to return to the barracks where I had officially been living.

Camp Vught was almost ready and was beginning to take concrete shape. I'd always taken responsibility for my mother's care. I felt it was my duty, but now that my father was with her I considered myself free to go to Vught, and I planned to do so. I wrote to Magda about it several times.

> I'm not exactly sure when I'll be going to Vught, but it'll be part of one of the first transports.

In another letter:

> I'll probably be heading for Vught soon. The adventure continues.

ROSIE

The New Camp

ON FEBRUARY 20, 1943, I left for Vught. Saying goodbye to my parents was especially difficult. I had no idea what would become of them in Poland. I controlled myself as best I could, determined not to reveal my concern, not to sadden or upset them. At the same time, my parents maintained their good spirits. They were happy I'd been given the opportunity to go to Vught. After my departure, Magda Coljee received a heartening letter from my mother: "Rosie left last Saturday. She had a smile on her face, strong as always."

When the train pulled into Vught station and I disembarked, I was surprised to find myself sharing a platform with other people, ordinary free men and women waiting for a train. It was as if nothing was wrong. Just a beautiful winter's day like any other. Ladies with hats and fur collars, neatly dressed children with tidy haircuts, a man with a hat and a dog on a leash, a girl with a thick brown scarf.

For them life went on as it always had. They were on the "good" side of the line; they still attended work or school, petted dogs, ate biscuits at tea. And us? We were robbed, censored, condemned to slave labor, guns, uncertainty. Surrounded by armed guards, we looked at them as we passed, and they stared back at us sheepishly. We picked up the pace and marched to nearby Camp Vught. On the way we passed the big lake where I went swimming in the summer and the dance hall I knew quite well. I'd performed there on many occasions, but my situation had since changed beyond description. In those days I enjoyed enormous success introducing new dances. There were people and fun galore! Now I looked like a criminal, surrounded by guns and dogs.

Contact with the outside world was impossible in the early days at Camp Vught. I wrote immediately to my parents in Westerbork, but they didn't reply. My letter to the Coljee family remained unanswered for a full month. I was later told that the letter wasn't sent to the address in Naarden but rather to the *Judenrat* in Amsterdam, where it was finally forwarded to the Coljees.

The rules in Camp Vught were stricter than in Westerbork. There were regular roll calls, although I had no idea why. Probably just to annoy us or to teach us some German discipline. Once we had to stand outside for three and a half hours. Three Dutch NSB members from Den Bosch kept guard over the women's barracks. They were a bunch of sadists, worse than the German SS. They cursed and stomped at the slightest opportunity, and kicked and beat us, often without cause. Censorship was also more rigid. Prisoners had to write in capital letters on preprinted lined paper, no more than thirty short lines, legible, otherwise it wouldn't be mailed. We were forbidden to write about what happened in the camp. Sometimes they insisted our letters be written in German, other times Dutch was acceptable. The rules constantly changed. We were allowed to send only one letter every fortnight, and a *Packetsperre*, a parcel ban, could always be enforced out of the blue.

I quickly assessed the situation and tried to regain some semblance of control over my life. One day, sitting in front of my barrack, I overheard a conversation between a couple of guards. "Do

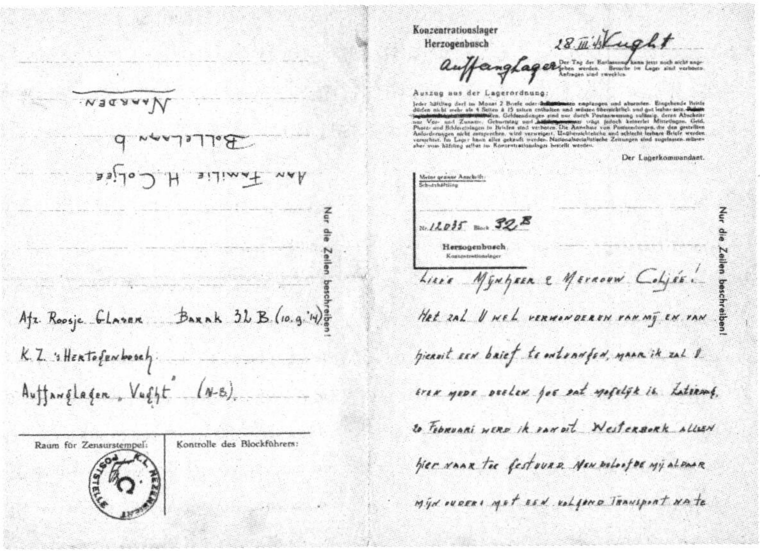

Aan Familie H. Coljée
Bollelaan 6
Naarden.

Afz. Roosje Glaser Barak 32 B. (10.9.'14)
K.Z. 's Hertogenbosch
Auffanglager „Vught" (N-B).

Raum für Zensurstempel:
Kontrolle des Blockführers:

Nur die Zeilen beschreiben!

Konzentrationslager
Herzogenbusch
28.III.'43 Vught
Auffanglager

Der Tag der Entlassung kann jetzt noch nicht angegeben werden. Besuche im Lager sind verboten. Anfragen sind zwecklos.

Auszug aus der Lagerordnung:

Der Lagerkommandant.

Meine genaue Anschrift:
Schutzhäftling
Nr. 12035 Block 32 B
Herzogenbusch
Konzentrationslager

Lieve Mijnheer & Mevrouw Coljée!
Het zal U wel verwonderen van mij en van
hieruit een brief te ontvangen, maar ik zal U
even mede deelen hoe dat mogelijk is. Zaterdag
20 Februari werd ik van uit Westerbork alleen
hier naar toe gestuurd. Men beloofde mij aldaar
mijn ouders met een volgend transport na te

Nur die Zeilen beschreiben!

A letter to the Coljees from Camp Vught

you remember that dance teacher Crielaars?" one of them said to the other. "See her over there? It's her double."

"You're right," the other said. "But that woman arrived here in Vught from Amsterdam via Westerbork, not from Den Bosch. It can't be her."

I couldn't hold my tongue. "Yes, that dance teacher was me," I said, loud enough for them to hear.

They looked at me with delight, and before long we were chatting away, sharing plenty of memories.

After a few days, my fellow prisoners began to notice our exchanges and their consternation was obvious. In their eyes I'd made friends with the NSB. To prevent difficulties, I visited each of the barracks and told them in all honesty how things stood. I said I'd do my best to use my new contacts to the other prisoners' advantage. Slowly, I regained their trust.

Faithful to my word, I managed to arrange for roll call to last no more than fifteen minutes, and the guards agreed not to beat us without reason. I also obtained permission for us to take daily walks through the camp, accompanied by two armed SS men. This gave the women an opportunity to catch a glimpse of their husbands and to quickly pass a note or a small parcel over the barbed wire that separated us. Because of these improvements, my popularity increased, and I was soon appointed leader of my barrack.

The job wasn't very demanding. I was expected to arrange for the sick to be taken care of, mitigate quarrels between prisoners, and maintain contact with the *Aufseherinnen* (female guards who were German or Dutch) and the SS. Beyond that there was nothing else to do. It was different in Westerbork, where I had a full-time job as secretary and spent my evenings with Jorg. Now that I had so much time on my hands, I returned to writing my book. In a new chapter I wrote about my first kiss.

> It happened when I was sixteen, at the Mi-Carême (Mid-Lent) ball at the Vereeniging, where I was dressed as a ballet dancer in a white tulle tutu. As I stood against a pillar in the grand concert hall, which had been transformed into a massive ballroom, I surveyed the colorful crowd. I longed to join the chains of laughing, dancing people careening past, and just as I was feeling very lonely, an elegant, blond-haired young man in a tuxedo approached me.
>
> "May I have the pleasure of this dance?" he asked.
>
> "Yes, of course," I replied, flattered. He took my hand and led me to the dance floor. "With whom do I have the pleasure?"
>
> "Rosie. And you?"
>
> "Hubert." Before I realized it we were gliding to a slow, undulating waltz.

Hubert danced well, but he was not quite sober, and as he danced me around the room his hand eventually slid down my left shoulder blade and under my right arm. I admit, I was turned on. After a sudden drum roll and applause, the dance was over and we let each other go. Then he offered me a familiar arm and led me down the mirrored corridor. "You're beautiful," he said, looking at my reflection in the mirrored corridor. My flushed face turned even redder and I pulled him away with a giggle. I loved this dazzling existence. I was no longer an observer; I was playing the leading role. We made our way to the champagne bar, where Hubert lifted me onto the one remaining barstool, leaned against the bar, and ordered two champagne frappes. It was my first champagne. "To our first encounter," Hubert toasted, raising his glass. After our drink, we glided through the crowd, close together, a splendid warmth flowing through me.

Rosie at sixteen

Before we reached the dance floor I leaned into Hubert's ear. "It's so hot here," I said. He looked at me and we disappeared into the cooler corridors until we reached the emergency stairs. I stopped. "Don't you want to go downstairs?" Hubert asked, pulling me closer. We descended the spiral staircase a few steps, and in the dim emergency light I let him take me in his arms without resistance, felt his warm body next to mine, tasted his lips. We stood on the stairs in

Rosie in the Vereeniging dressed in her white ball gown (seated, foreground left)

a long intimate embrace, forgot time, forgot our surroundings, until our lips separated for a moment and then met again.

The following spring I went to the Vereeniging a couple of times a week. I sometimes met Hubert there and he always asked me to dance, but he never alluded to that wonderful Mi-Carême night. I sometimes asked myself if he still remembered it. But he always came over to say hello, so I imagined he was going to do the same as before.

One day as I was leaving the tennis club on my bicycle, an open-top car turned the corner and stopped. "Rosie, fancy seeing you here!" said Hubert. "I didn't know you played tennis. Come, let me take you home. We can collect your bike tomorrow." He jumped out of the car, took my bike back to the tennis club and locked it up in the bicycle shed.

Hubert steered the car onto the main road and stopped

in front of a restaurant. We found a table outside in the shadow of the beech trees. "Rosie," Hubert said, leaning into me, "am I wrong, or do you have an excellent tan? You look the picture of health."

"And I feel great too," I said in the best of spirits. "When I'm with you there's nothing more to want."

Hubert raised his eyebrows. "That sounds like a declaration of love," he said, laughing. "Since when was it up to the girl to make the first declaration of love?"

Rosie at the tennis club

"I went first?" I asked, surprised. "Have you forgotten the Mi-Carême ball, Hubert?"

"No, why would I?" he answered with a smile. "It was fantastic. I had plenty to drink. I remember it well."

"Is that all you remember?" I asked.

"Yes, more or less," Hubert assured me.

I frowned, looking him in the eye. "Hubert, don't you remember telling me you loved me, taking me in your arms and kissing me? I'd never been kissed by another man. Did you know that?"

Hubert pushed back his chair. The gravel crunched. "Did I really say that, Rosie? Sorry, but I don't recall any of it. Where did I say it?"

"On the emergency stairs," I said, my voice choked.

"Sorry if I hurt you, but when I drink too much I sometimes don't remember what I say and even less what I do."

I cringed. He took my hand. "Sorry, I don't mean to offend you."

"Take me back to the tennis club," I said. "I want to collect my bicycle."

"As you wish," said Hubert and he quickly settled the bill. We drove back to the tennis club in silence and I jumped out of the car. "Have a good life, Hubert, and thanks for the lesson." With my head held high I turned and made my way to the bicycle shed, the sound of his departing car fading into the distance.

The summer passed, the winter arrived, and the next major carnival celebration was just around the corner. The shops and department stores had their windows ready for the big event. "Have you thought about what to wear?" my mother asked.

"Of course," I answered. "I want to be a man this time, a naval officer. I want no one to recognize me at the ball. I'll even ask girls to dance."

My mother raised her eyebrows. "What's the point of that?"

I wasn't sure if I could give her an honest answer. "I just want to see if I can pull it off," I said.

Rosie shopping with her mother

She approved, accustomed to her daughter's whims. "Next week you can have them measure you for an outfit, but don't tell your father I paid for it."

"Of course not, I used my savings," I said with a wink.

On the evening of the carnival ball I took a taxi alone to the Vereeniging. "Have a fine evening, Lieutenant," the chauffeur said as he opened the door. Tossing my cigarette butt nonchalantly in the snow, I took my wallet from my back pocket and paid him.

It worked. The chauffeur had no idea. As usual, the Vereeniging was overcrowded. I was pretty good when it came to dancing like a man, so I began my adventure, bowing left and right to the assembled young ladies, my face aglow from the warmth of my mask. Now it was time to ask someone to dance, I thought to myself, and I impulsively bowed to a girl with black hair. Poor child was probably feeling the same as I did last year until Hubert approached me. As we danced across the floor in four-four time I pressed my black-haired partner close.

"It's hot in here," my partner said.

I nodded.

"Don't you want to chat?"

"No," I said with a shake of my officer's head. When the dance ended I confidently led my partner to the champagne bar, helped her onto the barstool, caught the waitress's attention, and recalled the illusions that had filled me only a year before. I stuck two fingers in the air and pointed brusquely at the champagne. My "girl," who was dressed as a butterfly, spontaneously raised her glass. "Bottoms up," she said. The marine officer bowed, raised his glass, and drank it empty in a single swig.

I danced and cavorted with "my girl" all night but didn't say a word, until I saw that it was almost midnight. That was the *démasqué* moment, when everyone removed their masks. I had to stay one step ahead. Having danced up a sweat we made our way to the building's cooler corridors, and I deliberately led my butterfly to the emergency stairs, to the stairs and their wonderful memories, passionate memories. A voice inside me roared, *Hurt someone . . . hurt someone . . . hurt someone! Let someone else feel what I felt a year ago, here in this same place!* I grabbed her and pulled her close, but this was clearly the wrong move. The girl wriggled free, hurtled down the stairs three at a time, uttered a cry, and raced back to the main hall.

Rosie and her friend Lydia dressed for carnival in 1932

Now I'd had enough. Drenched in sweat, I heaved a sigh and disappeared into the ladies' toilets. "Get out! Get out!" the women screamed. I didn't think the gents' toilets were a good idea either, so I headed for the stage in the main hall, vanished behind the curtains, and made my way to the cloakroom where I'd left a suitcase containing my own dress for safekeeping. In no time at all I was dressed in a green velvet gown with white fur trim and silver shoes, with a carnation in my hair. On my way to the bar I passed the butterfly. It was clear that she was looking around frantically for the naval hero she had sacked, but her naval hero had become a mermaid.

The following morning I awoke to the sound of someone knocking at my bedroom door. "Miss Rosie, your tea," said the maid and she left the tray on the table. Irritated and still

> half asleep I screamed, "Get out, get out, or I'll kick you out," and after a string of curses that would have made a dockworker feel at home I sat upright in bed. Tempted by the tea and biscuits I slowly came to my senses. I looked around the room and saw my marine officer's uniform draped over a chair. That was the end of that, I thought to myself. The thought of my butterfly made me smile. I stretched. Time for a shower.

I couldn't help laughing as I wrote it all down. I was so naive and uncertain in those days, and that business with the butterfly was both crazy and mean. I was making steady progress with my book.

While life was more difficult than it had been in Westerbork, I still tried to maintain contact with the outside world. I continued to receive *De Telegraaf* (*The Daily Telegraph*), but delivery was irregular. Letters were even more problematic. Some didn't arrive at all, others after a long delay.

At the end of April, I received a postcard from my mother in Westerbork written at the end of March. It contained a terribly sad message:

> Tomorrow your father and I begin the great journey into the unknown. We don't know where it will take us. Pray for us often and try to find your dear brother. A tender kiss from your loving mother.

This was a disaster. I had feared this outcome since the beginning of our imprisonment, but at the same time hoped it would not happen. The message made me feel terribly desperate. I knew what it implied, but I could do nothing about it. My hands and feet were tied.

I had to move on. I managed to improve my connections with the outside world through a driver who delivered goods to the camp on a weekly basis. He took my letters outside and smuggled things in. I also had a second contact who lived outside the camp and was willing to smuggle out my messages. But in spite of such conveniences, I still found it a horrid place. The harassment continued unabated. One night the guards made us stand outside naked while they did a roll call. Other times they gave us nothing to eat or set their growling dogs on us. The atmosphere was tense.

Meanwhile, I met some nice women, and because of the tension and boredom we organized a cabaret. We made up sketches and jokes. I wrote songs and lyrics. Our performance was a great success and a welcome distraction.

That May they established a work camp in Vught, and I began working for a clothing manufacturer. I was fine with it. Moreover, I knew from my own experience and from Jorg how important work was. More and more prisoners, especially the unemployed, were being transported to Poland.

Since the censor didn't allow us to write about life in the camp, I included those details in a letter to the Coljees that was smuggled out by the driver:

Vught, June 7th, 1943

Dear Magda and Henk,

Here I sit, three high on my bed (honestly, the beds here are piled three high). After three months, this is finally the first opportunity I have to send a clandestine letter. Thank God I'm here alone in this camp and don't have my parents with me. It can't be any worse in Poland than it is here.

Men and women live separately, and if they're very, very good they're allowed to see each other once a week. Westerbork was paradise by comparison, can you understand that? This place is run by the SS, enough said. The female guards are German and Dutch, the so-called *Aufseherinnen*, the Dutch are NSB members.

When I first arrived here it was truly awful. Things have improved a little of late. The food is bad. We're poorly fed every day, mostly cabbage soup and 4 slices of bread with a thin layer of margarine. Drinking consists of artificial coffee, black.

I was sports leader at first and exercised with people all day, but that made me twice as hungry as you can imagine. I never received food parcels.

I arrived here on February 20th and at the beginning of April I received a farewell card from my mother. A few days later your first large parcel arrived. I was delighted beyond words and was extremely grateful. From then on *De Telegraaf* followed on a fairly regular basis, 3 or 4 times a week; the censor appeared to withhold the rest. A week later I received another parcel from you and that was also wonderful. The cigarettes were particularly criminal. What I need most is bread, butter, sugar, jam, and cigarettes. Everything else is welcome but not essential. If you send tins of milk or porridge the censor confiscates them.

Then there was a 14 day penalty for the whole camp and no one received their parcels. I don't know how many, but there will surely have been some from you. When the parcel ban was over, I suddenly received tiny parcels with your handwriting and Walterlaan (?) as sender. I wasn't sure what was going on. I first thought that Henk had gone to Germany and had stayed at the aforementioned address.

I was also worried about the lockbox. The parcels were getting smaller and smaller and I associated the two. Then I received nothing for three weeks and finally your letter arrived with the old address. I was pleased as Punch, as I'm sure you'll understand. I understood from your letters that you were receiving mine; otherwise you could not have known my laundry and barrack numbers.

I've no further news. I look more or less the same as I did when Magda saw me in Westerbork.

The absence of my parents is terribly stressful, as you can imagine. My hair has turned very gray. Things like that get to you after a while. There is so much indescribable suffering around that you would have to be a monster not to be disturbed by it.

Then I became leader in my barrack. Just when all those provincials arrived. Three of my mother's sisters were among them, one of whom was a year older than my mother and looked just like her. She was suffering from asthma and when they were forced to stand naked in front of the Commander while they were sprayed with delousing powder she died. Sad isn't it?

Then I became leader of the Women for Women cabaret, 40 professional artists participated. We worked in all the barracks with enormous success last week until we received word that this wasn't a so-called *Auffangslager* or reception camp but *Durchganslager*, a transit camp, and then suddenly all the old people disappeared. Yesterday and today they dispatched 3,000 mothers with children and the men were not allowed to go with them. The panic that prevails here I cannot describe. All the children and their mothers have to leave, just like the people over 45. On top of that, 1,000 men have left to work in Moerdijk and

Amersfoort, doing various jobs for the Wehrmacht. All families are torn apart. It is simply terrible. I have enough "content" and continue to work on my book.

I hope this letter will reach you. As for the cabaret . . . In spite of the huge success we enjoyed, it seems pointless after what's happened here in the last few days.

I've signed up for a job with Philips, the real Philips factory in Eindhoven. They've built special barracks in the camp where selected girls work. They're expected to solder wires and radio tubes. They call it *Wehrmachtsarbeit*. It's for airplane communication. I find it interesting. They give me a set of overalls and I have to play the factory girl. It's also useful material for my book.

I write in the middle of transport uncertainties. If I want I could be back in Westerbork tomorrow, but in spite of the terrible conditions here I don't plan to volunteer and I hope I can stay in Vught.

Please send my raincoat. My fur coat was stolen from my bed in a nighttime raid and I had to hand in my black jacket. And please send a couple of summer dresses and those brown suede shoes. Also make sure that I have a food parcel every week; otherwise I would definitely starve to death here. Write to let me know that you've received this letter, and reply quickly with news. Much love and lots of kisses from

Rosie

The address is unchanged.

Despite the awful atmosphere I did my best to stay positive. My fellow prisoners often got into arguments with one another. They usually didn't go beyond cursing and swearing, but occasionally things got physical: hair pulling, scratching, screaming, even biting. One prisoner was left with teeth marks on her arm. Most of the arguments were about minor matters, and as barrack leader I spoke to them after they cooled down. It sometimes helped if I assigned a different bunk to one of the parties, well out of the other's way. Sometimes it took a long time to talk things through. Everyone was irritable and short-tempered. Logical when you thought about it with so many families separated from one another. Children under sixteen had been removed, along with their mothers, since they often got sick and infected one another with whooping cough, measles, dysentery, scarlet fever, and such. The camp leaders feared too much inconvenience. Vught was supposed to be a model for the other camps, and too

Rosie's barrack (photo taken by Rosie in 1953)

much illness might give it a bad name. So they left on June 6 and 7. I saw them go, mothers carrying their babies, toddlers, and older children with sacks on their backs made from old towels. I saw them go, a few thousand of them. Everyone here was devastated, fathers were in tears; you could cut the atmosphere with a knife. What kind of madness was this?

Everyone lost interest in exercising and the cabaret, and with nothing to do boredom returned and some were inclined to passivity. It was a good thing I had a job with the Philips Command to look forward to. I'd heard things were better there. Only a small group of women were involved, and I managed to wangle a place among them. A lot of women were employed making clothes at the moment, various sorts intended for retail trade. You saw them heading for work every morning in their overalls.

One day we were ordered to assemble outside. The camp commandant, the *Obersturmführer*, the führer in charge of labor, and a few other uniforms were waiting to meet us. They walked up and down among us and appeared to be looking for someone. What had we done wrong now? The presence of the commandant and so many officers made me think it must have been pretty serious, but to my surprise they turned out to be looking for someone to model garments from the clothing workshop to the camp leadership and their clientele. To my even greater surprise they selected me from the group. In retrospect it wasn't so curious when you considered that most of the other women were wearing blue overalls and clogs, with headscarves tied around their heads. Apparently I looked a little more fashionable.

From June 15 onward I was expected to make regular visits to the workshop to try on new outfits. They made a sample of each outfit in my size and in a color I was allowed to choose myself. When there were guests and potential buyers I was given my own dressing room with mirrors, face powder, lipstick, the finest underwear, new shoes, and stockings. It was nice to have all the things at my disposal that hadn't been available outside the camp in a long time. After a while all the officers knew who I was. I drank coffee and chatted with them after the show, and had much more freedom of movement in the camp.

A few weeks later I also start working with the Philips Command at a factory making radios for the Wehrmacht. My job was to solder wires to a circuit board, a fastidious task that was reserved for women, but I quite enjoyed it. We sat at rows of tables with hot soldering irons and a powerful light above our heads. We also got extra food, which we called "Philips hash." It was a bit ironic, actually . . . my mother's maiden name was Philips, and she was related to the successful factory family, which had Jewish ancestry. There I was, a Philips, working on the Philips Command and eating "Philips hash." It wasn't the sort of family connection I had in mind. But the work and extra food did me good. I often sang at the factory, sometimes for an hour at a time, not only jazzy songs but also some pieces from opera.

After work, some of the men from the camp tried to chat us up—both prisoners and guards. Some of the women were pretty uninhibited toward just about every man they saw; whatever standards they'd previously held had vanished. On a number of occasions I was approached by one of the SS officers, but I didn't encourage him. You had to be on the lookout for jealous female guards, the *Aufseherinnen*. They had sex with the SS all the time, but they begrudged us the least contact with men.

One day, one of the *Aufseherinnen*—not one of my former dance students—stormed up to me and started cursing and screaming that I should keep my hands off her SS boyfriend. She then got even angrier and started to hit me. I stayed calm and fended off her blows, but when she started to pull my hair and kick me I threw myself at her and she landed on her back with a thud. She scrambled to her feet and ran off screaming. A few moments later a couple of SS guards appeared and arrested me. This was the third time I'd been locked up in a cell. Luckily they let me go after a few days.

Meanwhile, reports in the camp were becoming increasingly worrying. There was a rumor making the rounds that even working prisoners were set to be transported to the east. I had no idea what was going to happen to us. Contradictory reports only confused the situation: we could stay, we had to leave. The camp leadership didn't seem to know what to do with their prisoners or with the Philips Command.

As the uneasiness mounted, I had my driver friend smuggle out my diary and deliver it for safekeeping to Mr. Pijnenburg, my former neighbor in Den Bosch. He could always send it back to me if I needed it. And once my diary was on the outside I figured I should be there too. A week later, the same driver managed to smuggle me out in the trunk of his car. It worked! The feeling I got when the car picked up speed beyond the gate was simply wonderful. But then we ran into problems. My escape had been spotted, and we were stopped at a roadblock outside Utrecht manned by four motorized SS officers. The driver and I were brought back to the camp, but they soon let him go when I said I had hidden in the car without his knowledge.

A week later, on September 10, 1943—my birthday—I was transported by train to Westerbork together with a group of roughly three hundred young people. Our final destination was Poland. That evening the train passed through Den Bosch, where I used to live, and Nijmegen, the city of my birth. Seeing my cherished cities on my birthday made me sad and reminded me of the many birthdays I had celebrated in both places with friends and family. Now I was all alone, peering out of a dark train, and things were very different. I had managed to pass on a message to Mrs. Coljee via a certain P. Derks, letting her know not to send any more parcels to Vught. I knew from Jorg what Poland meant and decided to do my best to stay in Westerbork when I arrived.

Jorg may not have been there anymore, but I still knew plenty of people in the camp.

But I didn't get much of an opportunity to try my luck. In Westerbork I was locked up in an enclosed space for two days and then we continued our journey eastward, to an old village at the foot of the Beskid Mountains, a village called Auschwitz.

PAUL

Letters

IN 1994, FOURTEEN years after my initial conversation with my grandmother and ten years after my meeting with my second cousin, I received a call from a stranger in Naarden. It was 7:00 p.m. on a Wednesday, and I'd just arrived home from work. The man sounded excited, and I couldn't figure out what he was talking about. Perhaps he'd dialed the wrong number, I thought. But after a brief exchange it became clear that I was the person he was looking for. He had found some old letters written by a woman who shared my surname. He asked if I was related to a woman named Rosie. I jumped to my feet. Now I was the one who was excited. This was important—maybe even the key to learning more about my family.

We arranged to meet that same evening, and I jumped into the car and headed for Naarden. The whole ride there I wondered about the letters. What would they have to say? Would they provide new information?

Two hours later I rang the bell at the address provided, and a man of about fifty-five opened the door and ushered me inside. In the living room he introduced me to his wife, who offered coffee, and as she was pouring it they came immediately to the point, telling me it wasn't easy to find me. They had called other people asking if they were Rosie's family, but I was the first to say yes.

As members of their local church, they volunteered to visit elderly people in a nearby nursing home. That's how they got to know Mrs. Coljee. She had no family or friends, and the other people in the home found her grouchy and didn't get to know her. They visited her for several years. After her death the manager of the nursing home asked them to clear out her room, and to their surprise they found some letters in a desk drawer. They handed me the letters.

As we poured a second cup of coffee, I told them about my quest for information about my family's past. I asked what the letters contained.

"We've read them and they left quite an impression. It was moving to read Rosie's letters and to experience a little of her daily life. It was quite extraordinary for us."

We continued to talk as I thumbed through the letters. They were written during the war on an almost weekly basis from Camp Westerbork and later from Camp Vught. How could that be? I had always been led to believe that Aunt Rosie lived in Sweden during the war. Wasn't she married to a Swede?

Besides letters, the bundle contained other documents such as money orders, proofs of delivery, and a few messages dictated at Rosie's request. I found short letters from my grandparents, from a certain Kees van Meteren, mailed in Dessau, Germany, where he apparently worked for the Germans in the aircraft factories.

There was also a photo album, which we went through together. One of the pages had a photo of Mrs. Coljee's brother, proud in his SS uniform, killed at Stalingrad, and another brother in a Wehrmacht uniform, who disappeared on the eastern front. The same page had a photo of Rosie with her parents and brother, my father. For me this single page symbolized the tragedy of the war.

A'dam 25-8-43

Fam. Colfie

Zoo als u misschien al gehoord
heb mogen zy in Vucht geen pakjes
meer ontvangen dat schryf ik
maar dat u geen pakjes meer weg
stuurd anders word het maar
verdeeld onder de S.S.
U zal wel opkyken hoe of ik
aan uw adres kom. dat zal
ik vertellen hoe dat zit
Ik ben de Chaffeur die op
Vucht ryd en het Rosje Glaser
gesproken. en die het my ge-
vraagd of ik het even schryven
won en als u haar toch
een pakje wil sturen

A letter to the Coljees, written on Rosie's behalf:

As you may already have heard, parcels are no longer being accepted in Vught. I'm just letting you know, so that you won't send any, otherwise their contents will be distributed among the SS.

You may be surprised at how I managed to get your address. Let me tell you how this works.

I am a driver and I deliver to Vught where I spoke with Rosie Glaser. She asked me to write to you to ask to send a parcel to her. Please give it to me before Tuesday evening and I will bring it with me to Vught on Wednesday. My address is Hemonystraat 28, third floor, Amsterdam (South)

A. G. de Bruyn
And Rosie Glaser sends her warm regards

Rosie at eighteen, 1932

Mrs. Coljee's brothers died and so did Rosie's parents, my grandparents. There were no winners, only losers.

It was past midnight when I left.

In the days that followed I read every item, sometimes several times over. Most of the letters were uncensored. I also did some supplementary reading on the camps during the war: Presser's *De Ondergang* and books by camp detainees such as Gerard Durlacher, Etty Hillesum, and Rob Cohen. The books and the letters combined gave me a clear impression of what it must have been like for Rosie in the camps. It was like walking into a different world, and it continued to amaze me that only one generation stood between me and these events.

I was also struck by the buoyant tone of Rosie's letters. She had every reason to complain, indeed many people did, but there was

Rosie at carnival with Wim and Franz, 1933

Rosie in Maastricht, 1934

no trace of self-pity in her missives. Instead, she tried time and again to gain control over her own life, to improve her situation, and to enjoy what she could.

Other sources confirmed some of the things revealed in Rosie's letter. In her book *Schroeiplekken* (*Scorch Marks*), Carla van Lier offered a portrait of life in Camp Vught that referenced Rosie.

Rosie with musicians, November 1940

Writing about the many suspicions and rumors that circulated in the camp she speculated: "How was Rosie able to talk about so many established facts that were later confirmed?"

The couple who discovered Mrs. Coljee's letters later wrote me a letter offering a further glimpse of Rosie: "During the summer holidays we met a woman who told us she also worked on the Philips Command. She knew Rosie well, and informed us that she sang and danced and was very beautiful."

After seven months in Vught, Rosie left on September 10, 1943. She was working for the Philips Command at the time. The reason behind her sudden departure wasn't clear. Had she been given too much authority? Had she overplayed her hand? Was she being punished for something? Or was she simply deported with other Jewish women? The letters said nothing about it.

I made copies of the material for my brothers and sister, and when we got together for a birthday we talked about Rosie as a family for the first time. But we didn't dwell on the subject, and the atmosphere was absent the kind of curious enthusiasm one might expect. My sister and one of my brothers were clearly troubled by all the new information. They found it difficult to digest.

I also made copies of some of my grandparents' shorter letters for my father. I didn't copy Rosie's letters, aware that they'd lost touch and afraid to open old wounds. My mother had told me that my father had severed ties with Rosie because he felt she had been reckless when she was supposed to be in hiding, wandering around all over the place with false identity papers. He thought she had not paid enough attention to the risks involved and that her behavior had ultimately led to their arrest. In his eyes, Rosie's recklessness was to blame for their mother's death. Based on the letters, I formed a different opinion, but I decided not to bother him with it. He'd closed the door on the past, and I intended to respect that. Nonetheless, I told him that it saddened me that he and his sister were no longer in touch, especially since they both had the good fortune to survive the war. It didn't make the slightest difference, and I hadn't expected it to, but I needed to get it off my chest.

Then it was Christmas Eve. I figured our three daughters, who were in their twenties, were old enough to hear my story. That evening I told them for the first time about our Jewish roots, about the fate of the Glaser family, and about their great-aunt Rosie.

ROSIE

Dancing in Auschwitz

On September 16, 1943, I arrived at Auschwitz-Birkenau at five in the morning in a train full of men, women, and children. After a three-day journey in a tightly packed freight car without food, drink, or sanitation, the fresh air was a great relief. Everyone was happy that we had arrived.

There was a big crowd when we got off the train, and a young Polish prisoner passed me and said in German: "*Nicht krank werden und kein Angst*" (Don't get sick and don't be afraid). We had to leave our luggage where it was and weren't even allowed to bring a handbag or a parcel of bread. Men and women were told to stand apart, children in between. Then they started to select people one by one. I stepped out of line to get a better view of what was going on. Most people were being loaded onto trucks, and I thought them lucky to not have to walk; some were old and not steady on their legs. I learned shortly afterward that they were all immediately gassed.

When I had a question I walked up to a tall, handsome *Hauptsturmführer* standing at the head of the row and asked him where I should be standing. He looked me up and down and asked in a courteous tone, "Miss or Mrs.?" I smiled and shrugged my shoulders. "So, out with it, hurry up." When I told him I was divorced, he started to laugh. "That makes you a Mrs." And he sent me to a group of around a hundred other good-looking women standing apart from the rest. An officer commanded us to follow him. In the distance I could see barracks, too many to count. After a walk of almost four miles we arrived in Auschwitz. We passed a couple of wooden barracks, but beyond them the buildings were made of stone, street after street. We stopped at a kind of bathhouse, took off our clothes, had our heads shaved, and were given camp uniforms. It was awful. Some of the women wept in silence as they sat in the barber's chair. They cannot get to me, I thought to myself as I looked up at the sky, my tresses slipping to the ground over my naked shoulders. In the next room a number was tattooed on my forearm. You didn't need a name in Auschwitz, but when they asked me, I said Crielaars, as Jorg had advised. I was given number 62472. If I added all the numbers together I got three times seven. Maybe it was a lucky number, I thought.

After a short walk, we arrived at one of the stone buildings, Block 10, a building specially equipped for women in the men's section. I figured it was some kind of brothel at first, but I was wrong. Block 10 was what they called an experiment block, where the German doctors Josef Mengele and Carl Clauberg conducted medical experiments on the prisoners. Most of my companions considered themselves fortunate to be there. They didn't gas you, and you didn't have to work yourself to death. We were "in luck."

The atmosphere among the occupants of the block was good. The experiments lasted only briefly. An injection here, an incision there, a blood sample. On the surface it wasn't so bad. After the experiments we were allowed to rest, and when we were feeling better we could go outside and search for herbs such as sorrel and caraway in the fields surrounding the complex. They called it "herb detail." It was quite pleasant. Can you imagine? In Auschwitz, wandering in the sun in search of herbs? One of the guards was extremely young and quite nice as soon as we were a reasonable distance from the buildings. He chatted with us now and then, and you could see the kindness in his bright blue eyes. He was different when the other officers were around, more severe, or at least he looked more severe. Sometimes he doled out orders at the top of his voice, making sure that his comrades had heard him. And because we liked him, we immediately did as he said. That way the other soldiers could see him putting the fear of God into us and think he had our group completely under control.

We were on herb detail almost every day, especially when the German doctors were conducting their experiments in other camps. Nearby, the river Sola flowed down from the mountains at great speed. It was wonderful to be able to sit on the banks and go for a swim. It was like being on holiday. It all sounds very pleasant, of course, but *pleasant* is a relative word. It's true, compared to many others our lives were reasonable. We were a small group of women in a world full of men. Almost everyone had a "boyfriend" who arranged extra rations and the occasional distraction. But ultimately we were in a concentration camp and fearful of experimentation and being gassed.

We talked a lot to pass the time. We also made music. I played the harmonica, which I managed to lay my hands on somewhere. In the evenings we sang songs sometimes, and more than once a few of us enjoyed a dance. All the other women would then watch from their bunks. I also began to write songs and poems again. I dreamed of love. They couldn't take love away from me, and my desire kept me warm in that loveless place. It was at this juncture that I wrote my kapo song. Kapos were prisoner functionaries who were assigned by the guards to supervise other prisoners.

Kapo Song

Text and Music by Rosita Glacér, Experiment Block, Auschwitz 1943

I smiled at a Kapo in Auschwitz
He brings me parcels and joy
He's my personal mister fix-it
My Kapoman, he's my boy.
All night I dream of my Kapo,
Until the new day smiles
I pretty myself for a walk with my beau
Then my Kapoman's by my side.
I like him so much. He's my star.
And he knows he is, he knows he is
I smile, but I'm restless thus far
And my smiles are exclusively his.
Sometimes I'm a little uneasy
Afraid the *Aufseherin* will start to groan
At my Kapo friend, who wants to please me
Wants the sun to shine for me alone
May the *Schwarzbetrieb* soon be ended
This dreadful dark affair has had its season
When I go home, it will be splendid
Then I'll pretty myself, I have my reasons.
I'll kiss my Kapoman until my lips are sore
He'll beam with joy, there's nothing I want more
And that is the end of this story
Yes, yes, that is the end of this story

There was a courtyard next to our block with a wall at one end where prisoners were executed on a daily basis. We had a euphemism for it. We called it "filming," being filmed. You couldn't see what was going on because the shutters on that side of the building were closed. But the command to fire, the shots, and the cries of the victims cut to the quick. When they brought prisoners to the wall you heard all the footfalls and commands. A few of the victims begged, but most of the time they were silent, which was worse. They knew what was about to happen and so did we. My room in this "hotel" happened to be a couple of windows away from the wall, and I heard everything, clear as a bell. It was a harsh reality and unreal all at once. I saw nothing. I just heard. I heard everything as I sat in my room. Sometimes reality got closer to home. A Jewish doctor who helped us after the experiments was forced to pay for her efforts. I couldn't work out why. She was tortured but managed to survive. We comforted her and tried to cheer her up.

As time went by, the experiments became more invasive. A few of the women died in terrible pain as a result of experiments that appeared to go wrong. Once when I was sent to Dr. Clauberg's room I was told to undress immediately and lie down on a stretcher with knee supports that held my legs apart. There were three nurses in the room. They said nothing. The lights were bright, and as I tilted my head backward Clauberg appeared and injected a syrupy fluid into my uterus. The lights went out, a metal plate was held over my belly, and pictures were taken. Violent stomach cramps followed and persisted. Then it was over, and I was told to step down from the stretcher. I heard from one of the nurses that Clauberg had sterilized me. I hobbled out of the room and hurried to the bathroom to excrete the fluid. The pain diminished, but it took days before it disappeared completely and I was able to walk normally again. During my next visit, Clauberg injected me with typhoid, took blood samples a few days later, and then gave me injections to fight the disease. He was trying to find the best serum treatment for typhoid. I was fortunate, to a certain degree. The injections worked, but I knew that I'd never be able to have children. It made me want to cry when I thought of it. But at that moment in time it wasn't important. I could worry about the future later. Life there was lived one day at a time. After the experiments I decided to cut myself off from all the misery. I steeled myself in isolation in the midst of thousands. I would survive, come what may.

Eventually Dr. Clauberg left to conduct experiments at another camp, and it was quiet in the block for a while. But after a few weeks he returned, and the experiments started anew. Because the experiments were now even more invasive and there was a need for cooperation, we were given a choice: volunteer or be relocated to Birkenau. Everyone was determined to never volunteer. But the regime in Birkenau was harsh and unforgiving, and people were literally worked to death. Birkenau also housed the gas chambers, and that spelled death too. We were then told officially that those who did not volunteer for the experiments by the following evening were to go to Birkenau.

We talked a lot. Why risk your life in Birkenau? The experiments didn't last long. Besides, the food there was still reasonable and herb detail got you outside and could even be relaxing. Birkenau probably meant death. The women signed up one after the other, and the remaining few objectors were made to see sense by friends or *Blockältesten*, block leaders. Dr. Clauberg had won. I had already decided not to sign up as a "volunteer." It was bad enough that I was unable to have children. I didn't know what the consequences of my decision would be. Everyone feared the worst, but the experiments were getting increasingly invasive and I refused to undergo any more. I would take my chances in Birkenau. Because I refrained from voicing my decision at the outset, the other residents of the block left me in peace.

The following day, three other objectors and I were forced to walk the nearly four miles to Birkenau. An ordinary soldier with a rifle was our only guard.

We were not allowed to speak, and when I said something in German to the guard he gave me a dirty look. I smiled, but decided to hold my tongue. He was just a bumpkin, as far as I was concerned, a country boy who thought a lot of himself. That kind wouldn't listen to reason. The SS man on herb detail was an entirely different sort. He chatted with us like a normal person, and when his mother came to visit she greeted us, asked how we were getting on, and even if her son was looking after us properly. The soldier accompanying us to Birkenau came from a decidedly different upbringing. He was an unpredictable, dangerous type, so I said nothing and tried not to stand out.

Thinking about this guard, and based on my now fairly extensive camp experience, I was beginning to see a pattern. The lower the rank, the dumber, more malicious, and more bigoted the guards tended to be. It was as if they were taking revenge for their inferior intelligence. Some of the guards were little more than scum, especially in Auschwitz. Officers in the SS or Wehrmacht were often better, but not always. Those who were genuinely convinced that the Jews represented a threat to the German people, a threat that had to be dealt with, could also be hard and merciless. But the worst were the dumb, gullible subordinates. Brutal fanatics to the last. It would take more than a string of horrors to make an idiot like that see any sense. But what could I do about it? I had to stay calm and docile, otherwise there would be hell to pay. Perhaps it was time to be more laconic than I sometimes was, and no less careful.

I followed our peasant guard, deep in thought. Walking was a bit of a struggle because of the experiments. I thought of my parents. They couldn't have survived this. Almost all the adults over forty were brought directly to the gas chambers. Jorg told me more or less the same thing in Westerbork, and after working for him and the *Zentralstelle*—the central administration of prisoners—I knew well enough what kind of criteria the Germans maintained. If you were over forty your chances of survival were slim. They might even be more rigorous now.

I thought back with regret to the day I left my parents' home in Nijmegen, and how catty and quarrelsome I was. I was lucky they weren't angry when I moved back in with them in Den Bosch after my divorce from Leo. They welcomed me right away, and not a word was said about my ugly departure. My mother did mention once that my father had been extremely angry at the time and saddened. Fortunately it didn't last long. My father wasn't spiteful or vindictive. Besides, business setbacks and the general economic crisis meant he had other things on his mind. My parents were selfless in taking me back, and when we lived together in Den Bosch life was good. They even fully supported my running a dance school in their attic. *Ja, so war es einmal*—that was how life once was. Intense sorrow engulfed me as I thought of my parents, but I pushed the feeling away. I thought instead of the happier times, to help me keep my chin up and keep walking.

When we arrived in Birkenau we were brought to the area where the gas chambers were located and were immediately put to work. Our job was to accompany and reassure the prisoners before they went for a so-called shower. I handed out towels in the dressing room, but their fear remained. It was a conveyor belt of murder. You could read the terror in people's faces. There were children too. I remember one boy with dark brown eyes, not much older than ten as far as I could tell, standing alone, a threadbare scarf around his neck. When he caught my eye I smiled at him. He hesitated, and for a moment the distance in his eyes disappeared and he smiled back. After thirty minutes we were ordered to drag the still warm corpses outside. The little boy was among them.

I was determined to cut myself off mentally, and I was surprised at how quickly I succeeded. I steeled myself, shut down my thoughts, or better yet, tried to think of nothing at all. But it was only partly true that I could think of nothing, because I had to focus on survival, survival, survival. I was surprised at how indifferent I could be to the pain and death of others, to the endless stream of warm corpses with contorted faces, some covered in drool and shit, eyes open, a mother clasping her child. We took them outside and laid them on a plank or a ladder. I conserved my energy by dragging without lifting. Emaciated adults and children weren't so heavy. The men of the *Sonderkommando*—Special Detail—carried the bodies away on the same planks and ladders, checked for gold teeth, removed them, then brought the bodies to the crematorium. I saw and felt dead people all around me, but at the same time I didn't see them anymore. A fellow prisoner couldn't cope with what she saw and went crazy after four days. She did not care when she herself was sent to the gas chamber.

The difference between day and night was enormous. At night I slept deeply and I was somewhere else, far from the barbed wire, the screams, the corpses all around me. In the morning it all returned, like a wild animal gripping my neck that I couldn't shake off.

After six weeks of working at the gas chambers, I discovered a cousin of mine among the warm corpses, and at that moment my armor failed me. It wasn't as impenetrable as I'd thought. I realized that I couldn't keep this up for much longer. Overcome with anger and desperation, I marched up to the group leader and spoke to him in German. I told him I couldn't do this anymore and that I wanted to go to the "Union" factory (a nearby facility where shells and grenades were made). He was dumbfounded and—to my great surprise—acquiesced.

In hindsight, I was lucky. It was the custom to send anyone making critical remarks or not working hard enough to the gas chambers, and it was up to the group leader to decide. I was taking an enormous risk talking to him directly. I had seen a fellow prisoner in my group, whose spirit was broken and who could do no more than move mechanically and stare listlessly, sent to the gas chambers.

At the Union factory I was given better clothing and, more important, better food. On the first day they took me to the huge workshop. As I entered the building I saw a high ceiling supported by concrete pillars, bright lights suspended over the machines and their operators, massive containers full of raw materials, stacks of crates, and trolleys. Steam wafted upward in one corner. Wheels turned, instructions were yelled, and the smell of metal and oil permeated the air. It was bustling.

A female guard brought me to a machine where another woman was working. As soon as the guard spoke to her she stopped and glanced at us nervously. She looked tense and thin, her eyes sunken. She said something I didn't understand. When I asked the guard, I was told she was Greek. The guard explained to me how to operate the machine and signaled to the Greek prisoner to demonstrate. She looked at me with questioning eyes, and I smiled back warmly, signaling that I wanted to learn. She then relaxed and showed me precisely what to do and how to do it. I copied her, and she corrected me if I made a mistake. After practicing a couple of times, I had completed my occupational training, and I was put to work next to the Greek. Standing at the machine I saw her look at me with a smile once in a while, and I nodded my head to say hello.

I spent the first three months working on a large press and

various heavy lathes, making parts for hand grenades. The boss of the factory went by the name Schröder. The female guards who milled around the workshop abused us verbally on a regular basis and sometimes beat us as well, especially if they thought we weren't working fast enough or if a stupid peasant was among them. Some of the guards from the German part of Ukraine were particularly coarse, short-tempered, and brutal. The rest weren't so bad, and even Schröder, who appeared on the factory floor now and again, seemed to be a gentleman dressed in an SS officer's uniform.

I worked part night shift, part day shift, but despite the long hours, the work was much easier and less heavy than at the gas chambers. It was pleasantly monotonous, gave you the chance to think about other things. And that was a source of new energy.

We were occasionally startled by the sirens announcing an air raid on the factory. Then everyone ran outside, where the guards scuttled into their shelters behind the building. We prisoners remained outside. I always looked for the same place, a dry ditch behind a wall about three hundred feet from the factory. If there was a direct hit I was protected from the blast and from shrapnel. All of us hoped that the Allies were on target, but sometimes they missed the mark. Dozens died outside a workshop not far from ours. But air raids were an exception, and it was otherwise relatively quiet.

On the day shift I met two young Belgian women, Rachel and Martha. We shared the same barracks, and I'd seen them before. We were not allowed to talk when we were working, and if we disobeyed, the guards barked at us, but at night in the barracks we were free. Rachel, Martha, and I became friends, and exchanged places with other prisoners so that we could sleep in adjacent wooden bunks, three high. We often lay on our backs and talked for ages about family, love, and the guards, until the others asked us to be quiet. Almost everyone wanted to get to sleep right away to regain their strength or forget where they were.

Sometimes in the silence I saw the little boy I had smiled at just before he died. He had smiled back for a moment, but otherwise his expression was adult and cheerless. Had I betrayed him? We were there to reassure people for as long as we could, but we knew they were going to be gassed. Was my smile a cowardly deception? Or was it kind benevolence? When I thought about it, that smile must have been his last. I only wanted to be kind, and my kindness was rewarded by the smile he returned and the momentary sparkle in his dull eyes, a brief moment of joy in a too-short life.

In the morning we would pick up where we left off. I was the only one who'd been married. Rachel had been engaged, and Martha had had a couple of boyfriends but nothing very serious. We also talked about home and our youth, Martha about Antwerp, and Rachel about Tielt, a small town in the countryside of West Flanders not far from Bruges. It cheered Rachel and Martha to know that I was familiar with both places. I'd been to Blankenberg and Oostende on numerous occasions and even visited the world exhibition in Brussels. When we were together we were cheerful and relaxed. We talked constantly, laughed a lot, and even sang sometimes.

One day Rachel returned from the factory with a limp. A female guard had beaten and kicked her, and dragged her by the hair. Her left arm was black and blue from fending off the blows and there were scratches on her face. But it was nothing compared to her lower right leg, which she had injured by falling on a sharp-edged concrete slab. It didn't look broken, but there was a gash close to the bone and obvious muscle damage. It was also extremely swollen. The bruises on her arm and the scratches on her face healed quickly enough, but her leg refused to get better. The wound festered, and it troubled her for a long time to come.

At that time my job was to take crates of finished shells to a nearby storage depot where they were numbered and accounted for. One day the woman who usually did the paperwork wasn't around, so I looked for the SS officer in charge of the department to tell him the numbers. When I spoke to him in German he was surprised. He muttered something about the shoddy administration, and when I told him I could do administrative work and that I had grown up in Germany, he asked me to follow him to the *Schreibstube*—the "office"—and take a seat. From then on I was responsible for the paperwork.

My job was simple. I assisted production planning by tabulating shell part quantities and coordinating production schedules. Thus, I was free to visit various departments whenever necessary.

Because I spoke German and told them that I was from Kleef people treated me normally. The guards knew I had freedom of movement in and around the shell factory, and if I asked them something, they responded in a normal, professional manner. But I was still well aware of the reality of the situation.

Still, there was no one looking over my shoulder. All I had to do was make sure that the production schedules and the paperwork tallied. Now that I had a little more time to myself and a typewriter at my disposal, I began to write poems and songs again. It helped me escape, albeit fleetingly, from the camp. I sang these songs myself, but after a while everyone sang them, even the soldiers.

Meanwhile, my new boss and I discussed production growth improvements. After a while we talked about other matters. His name was Fischer, Kurt Fischer from Magdeburg, and he worried about his family now that the Allied bombings were getting closer to the center of the country. Even Magdeburg had been affected. As we talked, his initial reticence toward me began to evaporate.

The office where I worked during the day was small but quiet, secluded from the noise and uproar in the factory, a tranquil island in a stormy ocean. My conversations with Kurt about administration and scheduling were getting longer and longer. It was not necessary, of course, but it was a pleasant and welcome distraction for both of us.

He told me about his sister and her triplets, the dog his parents gave him, his adventures in the Hitler Youth, and about his brother in Stalingrad. He seemed to be quite sensitive and much more timid than his SS uniform would have everyone believe. In contrast to Jorg, he was not out to seduce me and he made no advances. He was just nice to me, nothing more, nothing less. But I saw potential advantage in our relationship and decided to win him over. I told him about my passion for dancing, my professional success, and the failure of my marriage to Leo. He told me he had been engaged for almost two years ago but had to break it off for one reason or another—he wouldn't tell me why precisely.

There was something endearing about his shyness that I found attractive. He hadn't touched me, not even once, and after a while he confided that he was not impressed with his posting to Auschwitz. A year ago he was still in France. A beautiful country, nice people, and good wine. But a fellow officer had framed him for an unfortunate incident, and because of that he was transferred to Auschwitz. He'd been here for almost a year now. He was not a Nazi "believer," but he thought Hitler had done a lot for the German people, especially after the humiliating peace treaties that followed the First World War. The misery they caused was immense: unemployment, hyperinflation, internal divisions, poverty. After years without work, his father had found a job, and the poverty they had experienced at home became a thing of the past. Not that they were rich, but they now earned enough to live like normal citizens. But when it came to Russia and England, he thought the Nazis had overstepped themselves. They should have stopped the war when they had occupied enough territory. They should have demonstrated greater self-control—then they would have a Great German Reich with secure borders: former ally Stalin to the east; the Arctic Ocean, non-hostile Finland, and neutral Sweden to the north; the Atlantic Ocean and the North Sea to the west; and allies Spain and Italy to the south. But now it was all a mess, and they were being beaten back on all sides. And as far as Kurt was concerned it was all due to the Nazis' unlimited lust for power. I listened to him talking about geopolitical prospects, about the Great German Reich, but I said nothing in response. I could see only my present situation. And I wanted to hold on to the atmosphere in my little office for as long as I could.

During one of our "planning discussions" I learned that the SS officers met regularly in the evenings to pass the time. After all, they too were stuck in a camp far from home. The nights involved drinking and singing, but after a while even that became a bit routine. One day I took the plunge and offered to play piano and dance during their evening get-togethers. I knew a lot of German songs. Kurt responded evasively, but after a few days I was told that I should come along to one of the evenings. He had apparently been talking about it. They wanted me to come and dance for them. Prison uniforms weren't exactly appropriate, so he arranged for me to have different clothes and more elegant shoes.

A soldier accompanied me to the warehouse where they kept the clothing. There were mountains of clothing, all of them from people who had died in the gas chambers, separate piles of jackets, shoes, dresses. The entire warehouse was full. I tried on a few outfits and took more than I needed. I stuffed two dresses, underwear, stockings, three blouses, and two sweaters into a burlap sack. I also grabbed a pair of boys' shoes to replace my worn-out pair, and three pairs of ladies' shoes for dancing. It being winter, I slipped into my "new" stockings right away and put on a sweater under my camp clothing. I also grabbed a couple of combs and a few hair clips from an adjacent room. I hid the dresses and other clothing at the back of my desk in the *Schreibstube* and took some inconspicuous underwear and stockings back to the barrack for Martha and Rachel.

As evening fell I went back to my office and changed out of my camp clothes. I combed my hair, which had grown back since they shaved it off when I arrived. It even had some shape to it. Kurt had arranged things so I no longer had to be shaved like most of the other prisoners. I practiced a few dance steps in my new dress, rubbed my legs to warm and loosen them, and waited for Kurt, who was coming to get me.

So there I was, spending an evening with the SS. There was a piano in the corner of a cozily furnished room, a record player, lots of noise, drink, and cigarette smoke. Heads turned when we arrived. To my surprise there were women among them, above all the dreaded *Aufseherinnen*. Schröder, the factory manager, wasn't there. He was sure to think such activities beneath him and probably restricted himself to parties organized by colleagues and the camp's senior officials. Some of the attendees were clearly already a little tipsy. They sang German songs like "*Süsse Heimat*" (Home Sweet Home) and "*Warum ist es am Rhein so schön?*" (Why Is It So Beautiful on the Rhine?).

And then it began. I was expected to dance to the music from the gramophone. I took a moment to decide what record to put on, then Kurt raised his hand. Silence fell as I introduced myself and the dance I was about to perform. It was a mazurka. First slow, then faster. I demonstrated three different dances, and after half an hour it was over. No one clapped, but I was given a whole loaf of bread as a reward and was sent back to my barrack.

In bed that night I told Martha and Rachel all about my adventures, and shared the bread I had kept hidden under my clothes. All three of us fell asleep in the lingering excitement.

The next day I put on my ordinary camp clothes and went to work at the *Schreibstube*. But instead of my dowdy striped jacket, I changed into a blouse with a sweater over it. Not too eye-catching, but still. Kurt smiled when he saw me, saying nothing and disappearing into the factory. Late in the afternoon he told me I was expected for a second performance that evening. I was given extra food during the day in the *Schreibstube*, and I felt a lot better and stronger. After that, these occurrences became frequent. Almost every night I danced, sang German cabaret songs, and played piano. Afterward I was always given extra food as a reward, usually a loaf of bread, just like the first time.

Meanwhile, Kurt talked more and more about home, the threat of losing the war, and the evenings in the camp. He didn't find it so easy to talk to his colleagues about such things, especially the war and how badly it was going. It was not allowed. You had to keep believing in the *Endsieg*, or final victory, but with me he was less inhibited. Even though they weren't cheerful subjects, our conversations helped Kurt to relax.

One evening after my performance was over I suggested that I teach the officers the latest dances from Germany. In reality they were from Paris and London, but no one needed to know. I chose new dance steps based on old tunes, and avoided jazz and swing since they were considered *entartet*—degenerate. The dance I demonstrated didn't appeal to them—most of those present came from simple backgrounds and were more interested in learning the polka or the waltz—but the decision was made to start earlier in the evening next time. And so I began teaching a new group of dance students. They were a little timid, of course. Most of them weren't used to that kind of thing; they were boors and peasants with big mouths who didn't dare expose themselves for what they were. Not everyone participated. Some stayed on the sidelines drinking beer and schnapps, but after a couple of evenings the atmosphere warmed up, and even the wallflowers came out of their shells. I also taught etiquette. How did a man invite a lady onto the floor? What sort of behavior was inappropriate? No hands on your dance partner's bottom, I instructed. A "shallow bow" is required when asking a lady to dance, and a curtsy is expected from a lady when it's over. It was bizarre when I stepped back and looked at it. There I was teaching etiquette to SS men in Auschwitz.

Around 11 p.m., Kurt would escort me to the office, where I changed back into my camp clothes, then we parted company, me to the barrack, Kurt back to the group to chat, sing, and drink. Kurt told me that various men and women often ended up in bed together.

Up to now they had let me be. One or two had tried to grab me, but in the group, in full view of their colleagues, it didn't go beyond that. I was apparently still attractive enough, in spite of everything, I thought to myself with a degree of pride. But at the same time I was a little worried that it was all going to turn sour, sooner or later. How did you steer clear of louts like that?

One evening, Kurt walked me back to the office as usual, but this time he watched me as I changed. We looked at each other and said nothing. Then he moved toward me. I could feel his breath—his eyes so close, serious, painfully serious. We threw our arms around each other, fell to the floor on top of my discarded clothing, and made love. Afterward he was shy, quiet, a little confused. I saw a reticent, serious man who was concerned about his family at home. I comforted him, ran my fingers through his hair, and whispered, "We didn't ask for this nastiness. Live for the moment." We lay in silence for a minute or two, side by side, touching. Then Kurt got to his feet, put on his trousers and jacket, gave me a quick kiss, and returned to the group. I dressed slowly, combed my hair, and thought about timid, slightly apprehensive Kurt. He had finally taken the plunge, and I decided to give him my love in spite of the bizarre circumstances and to seek comfort in being with him. With Kurt at my side I also felt protected from the other guards, some of whom couldn't keep their hands to themselves, especially when they'd had a drink. I no longer needed to worry about contraception. When I thought about not being able to have children a feeling of emptiness and sadness came over me. But with Kurt it was a small advantage.

Kurt and I got together after dance class more frequently after that, a little love in the midst of despair, in that factory of death, that demonic enterprise. It was a love dictated by circumstances, but it offered some moments of freedom and it had a healing effect on me.

During the day, when I was at my desk working on production schedules, I often thought of Kurt—his smell, his hands, how we had made love the evening before on the floor behind this very desk. His shyness had disappeared, and he was much less reserved when we talked. He felt more self-assured.

Then suddenly the dance classes stopped. No more agreeable SS evenings, no more singing. Something was going on. One evening, as Kurt and I lay side by side on our blankets behind the desk, he shared his concerns with me. "It's a rotten business. We're losing the war. Everybody knows it. We talk about it but keep it to a whisper, since the *Eindsieg* is still the official stance. The Russians are coming from the east and the Americans are advancing from the west. What's going to happen to us? I've had no mail from my family for a week, not my parents, not my sister."

I comforted him, tried to cheer him up, make him smile, but it didn't work. He was despondent and frightened. There was little left of the energetic and kind SS officer I once knew.

I wanted him to pull himself together, be strong. But I didn't tell him. To lift his spirits I said, "You've always treated the prisoners correctly. Keep it up, then they won't have anything to accuse you of after the war. If anyone asks me, I'll say you were good to me." He said nothing, ran his fingers gently through my hair, got to his feet, and returned to his quarters. I went back to my barrack.

Kurt and I enjoyed one more encounter behind my desk after that. But he seemed troubled and told me we'd be leaving soon. The Russians were nearing the camp.

PAUL

Getting Acquainted

WHEN MY SECOND cousin René, whom I met at the European Commission in Brussels and with whom I promised to keep in touch, telephoned out of the blue, he didn't beat around the bush: "I've moved to The Hague," he said. "We didn't get much of a chance to talk the last time. Why don't you join us for dinner?" The memory of our first meeting was still fresh in my mind, and I was eager to learn more about my family. "Excellent," I said. "Is the end of the week okay, after work?"

"No problem, but I'll be at the synagogue after work, so why don't you meet me there? Sabbath begins on Friday evening. And then we can go to my house for dinner."

That Friday afternoon I drove into the center of The Hague. I'd never been inside a synagogue, and I was curious to see what it looked like and how the service would go. I parked the car, grabbed my briefcase, and made my way along a quiet, narrow backstreet. There wasn't a soul in sight. The entrance to the street was blocked with wooden barricades reading "No Entry" and "Work in Progress." I walked until I reached a gated door bearing the address I had received from René. It didn't look like a place of worship. I surveyed the empty street, and in a window diagonally opposite I glimpsed a man with a rifle. He quickly pulled out of view. The mood was ominous. I was on my guard. I looked back at the gate, checked the number, and rang the bell.

Immediately someone opened the gate and let me in, peering at me with a serious, inquisitive gaze. A second man hurried into the vestibule and closed the door behind him, before edging past us and locking the gate. Before I knew it I was standing in a small enclosure with two nervous men. This was strange, I thought to myself, putting down my heavy briefcase. What's going on? I instinctively stood with my back to the wall and adopted the defensive position I learned in the boxing ring, ready to fend off punches with the right and jab with the left.

"Is this the synagogue?" I asked the men. They nodded and asked what I had in my bag. "Papers from work," I said. Did I mind if they took a look? After checking its contents they calmed down a little and asked if I'd arranged to meet someone. I gave them my second cousin's name. One of the men disappeared behind the door he had hurriedly closed moments before. Now that the atmosphere was a little more relaxed, I asked if this was the usual procedure. "Yes, security measures," the other man answered tersely. He was clearly not interested in chatting.

"Has the service already started?"

"It's halfway finished." His colleague returned and told me that my cousin was expecting me and I could go inside. The other man visibly relaxed.

After a friendly good-bye, the door gave way to a beautiful and spacious courtyard with a huge tree in the middle, an oasis of tranquillity in the heart of the busy city center. Then René appeared, welcoming me warmly and thrusting a *kippah* into my hand before ushering me inside.

It was a handsome building, with wide, arched windows that allowed an abundance of light to flood in from all sides. Galleries to the left and right were decorated with elegant latticework, and a large brass chandelier hung from the ceiling with about twenty-five electric candles in it. An ornate wooden platform surrounded by a decorative railing occupied the front of the room, almost as tall as it was wide. This was quite different from the elongated Catholic churches I was used to, with their small, stained-glass windows and somber, almost melancholy, air.

Among the wooden pews, roughly seventy-five people stood and sat. The genial atmosphere was a stark contrast to the suspicion I encountered when I first arrived. There was plenty of chatter among the adults—in addition to Dutch, I heard snippets of English, French, and Russian—and children were not on their best behavior, just as I recalled from Catholic churches. At the lectern, the rabbi alternated between spoken word and song. I could follow most of the time, except for the Hebrew segments, and if I lost my place I asked René.

After the service we made our way back to the main courtyard. The sun was shining, and a number of the congregants hung around to chat. René explained that it was a special service, a bat mitzvah, hence the size of the congregation. We offered Ruth, the bat mitzvah girl, our congratulations as we walked to a stately building on the opposite side of the courtyard where coffee and snacks were being served. Everyone was chatting, and René introduced me to a number of people.

We stayed for an hour, and when it was time to leave, four of us made our way to the exit. But a man with an earpiece held us back. No more than two at a time were allowed through the door, and only on his signal. René went first with someone else, and after a couple minutes I followed, stepping out onto a broad and busy thoroughfare. What a contrast to the narrow side street where I entered! When I turned right I saw René waiting down the block next to another man with an earpiece. He told me there were even more security guards dotted along the street, communicating with their colleague inside.

That evening René introduced me to his wife, and we talked about the family over dinner, especially his parents' family. He didn't know much about Aunt Rosie. Apparently his father had told him little more than how they were related and had said nothing about what she had been through or her present circumstances. Perhaps that was all he knew.

Driving home around eleven that evening, I thought back to the synagogue and its strict security measures. They surprised me. I'd heard about terrorist threats, of course, but I had no idea what that actually meant for the Jewish community. René and the other congregants took the situation in stride, as if it were perfectly normal. But wasn't it remarkable, I thought, that so many years after the Holocaust, these people still had to fear for their safety? I realized I'd missed my exit. Too much on my mind.

ROSIE

The Road to Liberation

On January 17 I took my first steps toward liberation. The day was bitter cold and everyone was restless in the barrack. We'd been released from work earlier than usual. Our guards, whose arrogance and aggression had abated in recent weeks, looked nervous as they tugged chests and supplies back and forth. Everyone could sense that something was about to happen. The gas chambers hadn't been used for weeks. News had already reached us of the Allied victory at the Battle of the Bulge. In the last couple of days we'd heard the rumble of artillery fire in the distance. But now the Russians were getting close to the camp. You could hear the thundering of the cannons. In the barrack, everyone was talking at the same time. Then the woman in charge of us appeared with news: "We're leaving tomorrow. The camp is being evacuated. Those who can walk are to follow. The sick are to stay behind."

That night I thought about our imminent departure. Martha, Rachel, and I had been at the camp for a long time. The duration of our stay was almost enviable, considering that most of those we had arrived with were dead. We were a genuine team, a team of strong-willed, hardened optimists. Our bizarre circumstances had only reinforced our bond. Even when the bombs had started to fall, we operated as a group, huddling together for protection in a ditch. We huddled together at night now, too, ever since the barrack windows had been smashed.

The next morning we had to get ready for the journey. Because Rachel still had problems with the wound in her lower leg we weren't sure she would be able to join us. She could manage a short distance, but we still didn't know how far we would have to walk. Not even the barrack leader knew. On the other hand, Rachel wasn't really sick enough to be left behind in the infirmary. And even if she was, most people were convinced that the SS would shoot anyone who stayed. They'd done the same to sick people often enough in the past, to make sure they didn't fall into enemy hands and testify to SS crimes. Weighing all this, Rachel decided to join us.

As everyone packed their belongings, I hurried to the *Schreibstube* to collect the extra clothing I kept there for the dance evenings. When I returned, I gave Martha and Rachel spare skirts and a sweater to help them dress against the cold. I myself put on a pair of long trousers and two skirts, then rolled a pair of long socks over my trouser legs, making sure they were closed tight. I wrapped a rag around the bottom of each leg, covering my trouser legs and the tops of my boys' shoes. Then I used part of an old blanket, laces, and a hairpin to create a pouch around my waist, which I stuffed with a towel, some rags, extra gloves, and, of course, my songs and poems. In addition to being useful for carrying things, the pouch also protected me from the icy wind. We used the rest of the blanket to wrap Rachel's lower leg, keeping it extra warm and sturdy. As always there was a shortage of food, but if we were careful we would probably have enough bread to keep us alive for a few days. We also tied our drinking bowls to our belts. We could fill them with snow and drink it when it melted. Our preparations were in order, but we were still worried about Rachel. She dragged her leg when she walked and couldn't rely on it for support.

As dusk began to fall, the SS arrived. "*Schnell, schnell, raus.*" Searchlights glared down on us from the watchtowers. The evacuation had started.

We entered a different world as we left the camp. It was cloudy and dark with no stars, swirling snow, crackling footsteps. In spite of the presence of thousands barely a word could be heard. I liked being outside in the snow and started to hum. Eighteen months in Auschwitz had been long enough. We were going home, heading west, although I wasn't sure about our exact destination. On either side of us, armed SS men were lined up in warm winter clothing, Alsatian guard dogs at the ready. We passed bare trees silhouetted with snow. Drab lines in ashen gray with dirty white edges. It looked like a picture from Grimm's fairy tales. Stark and eerie and strangely serene.

The reality of the situation was much more savage. Trigger-happy Russians marched behind us, American Flying Fortresses roamed above us, and hordes of armed SS men confined us on either side. Looking around I thought to myself: stupid Germans. Who in their right mind would deploy so many well-trained soldiers, armed to the teeth, to accompany a bunch of ragged beggars, instead of deploying them in defense of *der Heimat* against the advancing Russians?

A nearby gunshot brought me back to the present moment. Stragglers and dropouts were being shot dead. A woman in front of me was pulled to the side of the road and killed with a flash and a loud bang. Almost no one looked up or back. The SS hurried us along. The Russians were close. Many of the prisoners fell behind. The pace slowed down. Too many of us were malnourished, suffered from leg cramps, weren't dressed properly against the cold, and were frozen stiff; some had shoes that pinched. As prisoners were unable or unwilling to continue, more and more executions took place at the side of the road. There were corpses everywhere.

After hours of walking Martha was doing well, but Rachel was having a hard time with her leg. We talked about what to do. Rachel knew she couldn't keep it up much longer. How much farther did we have to walk? It seemed the Germans would be tired too and in need of a break. Then the report reached us that the Russians had penetrated German lines. We had to keep going, pick up the pace. By that point, Rachel had to drag her leg so much she could barely walk. Without our help she would be finished. As the three of us marched arm in arm, Rachel talked about leaving us. Martha and I didn't argue with her. She was a realist. Rachel asked us to go to her home, find perhaps a brother or sister. Her parents had been sent to the camps a long time back. "Tell them that I enjoyed being with you and that we laughed a lot. The café at the end of the street is where Pierre lives. I don't know if he's with someone else now, but kiss him for me and tell him I still think about him often." This was her last will and testament. "It's time to let me go. You won't make it if you have to drag me along. Soon the pain and the fear will be gone. I've made my peace. I love you dearly. Kiss me and adieu."

I stared into her eyes for what seemed an age and saw a warm tranquillity. She said nothing, and I kissed her on the lips. Martha's face was awash with tears, and she too kissed Rachel. We kissed her again and again. We said nothing. I stepped out of the line and asked a nearby SS man in German if we could take a moment to say good-bye to our dying friend. He was a little baffled; prisoners weren't supposed to talk to SS, but he nodded almost imperceptibly and motioned to a spot at the side of the road with the remains of a wall. Rachel hobbled toward it together with Martha and me. We laid her down, ran our fingers through her hair and over her face, promised to carry out her wishes, and kissed her for the last time.

The SS man waited for a moment but quickly rejoined the advancing column of prisoners. When another appeared, ranting and raving, pointing his rifle, Martha and I hurried back to the line. I looked back, saw a flash, and heard a bang. Rachel sat up and fell over, her hair still fluttering in the wind, a final gesture of farewell. After that all I could see was the snow. Nothing else.

Martha and I continued on in silence. What was there to say? Our tears turned to ice on our cheeks. After forty minutes or so, orders were given. We didn't hear them, but everyone stopped. I bumped into someone in front of me, who treated me to a string of abuse. Then it registered. A rest period! We'd been waiting for hours. For Rachel it was too late. People sat in the snow or sought shelter against a wall adjacent to a couple of bombed-out houses. We were close to the remains of a small village.

The Germans tossed us a few lumps of bread, and scuffles followed. Martha and I watched from the sidelines. We still had bread from the camp, and Rachel had given us her portion shortly before we said good-bye. It all seemed so unreal, like a dream you wanted to wake up from but couldn't. Then a group of Germans passed us on the road, some pushing a handcart. Refugees from the east. "The Russians have broken through," they shouted. Everyone was too tired to react.

That night we slept outside in the biting cold with only a couple of walls to protect us from the wind. Martha and I stayed warm by snuggling up together and rubbing each other's face and hands. We kept our shoes and clothes on. After a year and a half in Auschwitz, our first day outside the camp had come to an end.

The journey continued the following morning. When we woke there were corpses everywhere. Many had succumbed to the bitter cold. It was tempting to let yourself slip away in sleep. Some even died while they were sitting.

That kind of death wasn't for me, but I could imagine how tempting the soft white snow must be. When we stopped for a break around noon on the second day it started to snow again. I sat at the side of the road and stared at the thick snowflakes, swirling down. Some blew past me, caught by the wind, or turned in another direction. The snow muffled loud noises, making everything seem at peace. I wasn't bothered about being snowed under, slowly but surely. I was mesmerized by the perpetually tumbling flakes, by their soft, ethereal beauty. I thought of Rachel, who must be completely covered with snow by now.

After a while, a clamor of commands disrupted the tranquillity. I looked up. It was time to move. I brushed off the snow, found Martha, and marched on. All my joints were stiff.

An hour later we suddenly had to stop because of the thunder of artillery fire up ahead. We sat at the side of the road in small groups. The artillery fire intensified. Shells exploded in several places around us. You could hear them coming: first a high-pitched whistle, then a flash of light and an explosion. It was just like thunder and lightning. The higher the pitch of the whistle, the closer the shell. At one point, a shell exploded nearby, and one of the SS guards was hit. He fell to the ground with his face in the mud, his helmet still in place. When we looked over we saw that both his legs had disappeared. There was no sign of them, just a shoe with a foot in it a few yards from his body. It was amazing what a single shell could do! I was stunned. This was the first time I'd seen them in action. It was hard to imagine that I had made such effective things when I was in Birkenau. In those days it was about production and planning. Then it was still theory, but now I saw them practically. It was a shame the Russians didn't have better aim. The soldier's family would receive a handsome certificate with old-fashioned ornamental letters, telling them their son died a hero's death, for his people and the fatherland. They were just being fooled. There was nothing heroic about bad luck, about being blown to pieces by sheer accident. That was not how heroes died.

At night we lay on the open road. Martha and I huddled together like spoons to keep warm. I'd built a wall of snow around us to protect us from the wind. It was like an animal's den. A shallow pit, my rucksack as a cushion under my head and rags as scarves around our heads to keep in the warmth and keep out the snow. Lying there warm and at rest in the snow I was reminded of past holidays in Sauerland near Winterberg or skating on the lakes in Oisterwijk, not far from Den Bosch. Once again I imagined how tempting it would be to submit to the snow and not get up.

Early the next morning the guards woke us with their usual clamor. We were half covered in snow and stiff when we got to our feet. But some didn't move. Tired or dead? It was hard to tell. Most were dead. The rest would follow soon enough, with or without the help of the SS.

On January 23, after six days on the road during which we had walked more than fifty miles, we arrived in the village of Loslau, where we were packed into an open-top coal train. We continued our journey by train, traveling both day and night. It was amazing how well the railways still functioned amid the disorder. There was plenty of water and coal. If a station was bombed, the train was diverted along other routes via other stations. The Allies tended to bomb the big stations and ignore the smaller ones, forcing the train to make the occasional detour while continuing on its way.

The conditions on the train were abominable. In my car alone there were 160 hysterical prisoners, packed together without food or drink in temperatures of twenty below. Some died of exhaustion. Others we strangled to get a bit of space for ourselves. Every morning when the train stopped, the naked corpses were thrown out of the car, after we removed their shoes and clothing and searched them for food. You could hear a thud as each corpse hit the ground. Now and then you would hear something crack. But the sound no longer affected us. The most was fourteen in one night. We urgently needed more space in the car and more clothing to protect us against the cold and the wind.

Of course, no one alive was allowed to leave the wagons. If you tried, as some did, the SS shot you dead on the spot. It still amazed me that so many SS guards continued to bother themselves with a bunch of decrepit, undernourished prisoners instead of fighting at the front or returning home. I still thought it was a stupid strategy. The train sometimes went into reverse after a stop, instead of moving forward. It was clear that the front couldn't be far off and that the Russians were advancing apace. Our journey was taking us farther and farther west.

We crossed over the Oder-Neisse line, between the advancing Russians and the withdrawing Germans, until one night we stopped at a railway yard near Berlin, where we were treated to a spectacular show: an intense air raid on the city. We finally arrived at Camp Ravensbrück, completely exhausted from cold, hunger, and thirst. Of the 160 people who had been packed into our car, almost half had died on the way. We were lucky that our train wasn't targeted by airplanes. Such attacks happened often enough, but we had been spared. When we arrived everyone was indifferent, listless. My feet were frozen, and all my toes were black. Martha was at the end of her tether, but she too had survived the brutal journey. Only just, but that was what counted for now.

In the camp it turned out that I'd picked up typhoid at some point, in addition to my frozen toes. Typhoid could be fatal and I was brought to the infirmary, but my illness wasn't considered serious enough, or at least not advanced enough, and I was told to go. They no longer had vaccines against typhoid anyway. When I told the female doctor in charge that I was a nurse, I was allowed to stay and help in spite of my illness. I also had something to eat, although it wasn't very much.

In the chaos I lost track of Martha. She had probably been crammed into one barrack or another. The camp was bursting at the seams. Tents had been put up to house the influx of new arrivals. Tents in January! But it was still better than the street.

Fortunately my feet returned to normal after a few days. They still tingled a little, but the blackness disappeared. Work in the infirmary began to organize itself, and I got on well with the doctor. We talked a lot. She was also a prisoner. Her father was once a communist, and that made her a subversive. I told her that my parents were Jewish, and that that made me extremely dangerous as far as the Nazi regime was concerned. We both laughed. She was from Düsseldorf, which wasn't far from Kleef. We both longed for the days of our youth, for humanity, and we chatted a lot in the midst of all the commotion.

Then one day the typhoid flared up. My temperature went through the roof, and because of my poor physical condition I was on the brink of death. Now that I was seriously ill, I was allowed to stay in the infirmary as a patient. The "subversive" doctor insisted on it.

Quite unexpectedly, the Swedish Red Cross appeared at the

camp completely unannounced and was permitted to hand out packages at the gate to Scandinavian prisoners. Ravensbrück's once systematic German administration was now creaking at every joint. The influx of new arrivals and the lack of organization in the camp gave me the opportunity to convince the German in charge of the distribution that I was Danish. The doctor helped by going along with my story, and I managed to get my hands on one of the packages.

Back inside the hospital, after sneaking a sausage and some crackers from the well-filled package, I handed it over to the doctor in exchange for an injection to fight typhoid. She had apparently kept some antiserum aside for herself as a precautionary measure, but now she was willing to trade it for the package, in order to satisfy her permanent hunger. She too had to stay strong if she wanted to help the multitudes of needy patients. The antiserum and the extra food helped me back to my feet.

The package from Sweden saved my life. My health returned after about five days, and during a walk outside the infirmary I bumped into Martha again in the mud and chaos. From that moment onward we stayed together.

After only three weeks in Ravensbrück we had to move on, this time to the Spreewald, a wooded region near Berlin, where we helped dig trenches. Martha, myself, and a number of other prisoners were brought there by truck. As we drove through Berlin we saw the consequences of the endless bombings. Much of the once-magnificent city was in ruins, and the atmosphere was oppressive. Entire rows of houses had been reduced to rubble. Women on the street wore anxious gray faces, some pushing carriages or wooden carts filled with furniture and firewood. A man with stubble on his chin stood with one arm of his jacket hanging empty. Women waited in line at a functioning pump or tap. There seemed to be a shortage of everything.

It was apparent that Berlin was getting ready to defend itself against the advancing flood of Russians. The cars that were still running belonged to the army. Groups of soldiers were dotted here and there. Paving stones had been piled up to form a dam. Sandbags lined the entrance to the metro. A tram was lying across the line, blocking the road.

We arrived at a crossroads with a huge cannon in the middle guarded by an older soldier and group of boys in black uniforms, fourteen- or fifteen-year-olds. They were wearing black caps instead of helmets, and armbands with swastikas. The soldier put us to work immediately, not clearing rubble, but filling burlap sacks with sand from a nearby bomb crater. We were ordered to bring them to the crossroads and piled them up as protection for the soldiers and the cannon.

The people on the street and the young soldiers looked on with curiosity as the handful of prisoners went to work. And vice versa. At one point a man with crutches and one leg who seemed to know one of the boys with the black caps tried to convince him and the others that it was time to quit and go home. He pointed to his missing leg. The two exchanged words, voices were raised, they swore at each other, yelled about betrayal. The man slunk off.

In the afternoon, after we'd been lugging sandbags for half a day and our work was showing signs of progress, I got the chance to talk to one of the boys who was standing near the group. I asked him why the cannon had such an incredibly long barrel, and he was surprised that I spoke German. He told me in a slightly uneasy voice that the cannon was a Flak, a *Fliegerabwehrkanone*, used for shooting at planes high in the sky. Now it was being deployed to keep the Russians away from the streets surrounding the crossroads. While I pretended to rearrange the sandbags for better protection, I took a good look at him. He was still a child. I smiled, and for a moment he smiled back. When he was summoned back to his group—talking to prisoners wasn't allowed—I noticed he'd left a couple of cigarettes on the ground. For me? I quickly shoved a sandbag in front of them and grabbed them.

We worked until it was almost evening, then returned to the truck, where we were given something to eat and loaded into the back. As we rode, the headlights turned off, we could hear planes droning and the thunder of exploding bombs in the distance. It was a familiar sound. There was nowhere to take cover, just as in Auschwitz. A truck was no protection. And just as I did in Auschwitz, I didn't let it worry me and tried to stay calm. The thunder was still quite far away. I chatted with the others, but it didn't evolve into a real conversation. Everyone was too tired and cold.

As I snuggled up against Martha, I let my mind wander. Hitler had to be here somewhere, perhaps in the Reichstag or in a luxury underground bunker where he was having a party with champagne and music or drinking coffee with his girlfriend Eva. Perhaps they were dancing. A Chopin waltz? Certainly not that degenerate jazz and swing. Could he dance? I didn't think so. In the newsreels I'd seen he looked as stiff as a rake, his movements spastic. Eva was a different story. She was beautiful and nimble, that was what Kurt had told me.

Or was he doling out orders from his residence, still intent on the *Endsieg*? But orders to whom? There was not much left of what was once the most powerful army in Europe. A couple of boys trained to use a Flak and the remains of a military unit here and there. They couldn't stop the bombings. No one mentioned the Luftwaffe anymore. Why die for nothing? The man with the crutches was right, but nobody listened, at least not yet. And here I was, having helped to construct Berlin's defenses.

The truck stopped suddenly, and we could see the dark silhouettes of abandoned houses from behind the tarpaulin. Debris on the street prevented us from moving forward any farther. We had to sleep in the back of the truck. It was a reasonably quiet night, the bombings still far off on the other side of the city. Two armed soldiers kept guard, but I thought how easy it would be to escape. Whole neighborhoods were in ruins, I spoke the language fluently, and I was wearing ordinary clothing underneath my camp uniform, clothing I brought from Auschwitz. I wouldn't stand out among the city's defeated inhabitants. But why take the risk? The Russians would arrive before long, and I didn't have any papers. They might think I was German. It was better to meet the Russians as a German prisoner. With these thoughts careening through my mind, I fell asleep.

I used to visit Berlin regularly. It was a handsome, vibrant city with elegant people and many cultural venues. The songs from that era were well known and were even sung in the Netherlands. Berliners had a sense of humor, were quick to laugh, lighthearted. The Berlin that I remembered was different from the rest of Germany. Other Germans were more disciplined, more serious, always ready with a polite bow. Although Berlin was the capital and housed the Reichstag, it wasn't typical. It was cheerful, both edgy and relaxed. There was music everywhere, not only in the concert halls, but also in parks, on the street, in basements.

Shortly before the war I saw a film about Berlin directed by Curt and Robert Siodmak based on a screenplay by Billy Wilder. It was called *Menschen am Sonntag*. It was a silent film with music that focused on couples in love and how they spent their Sundays in Berlin, flirting in pedal boats on Wannsee Lake, picnicking in the park. I knew that Berlin well. The beautiful houses, broad streets, well-dressed people, packed trams, cigarette smoke, parks. I'd walked its streets, sat at its café terraces, visited its basement cabarets, talked and laughed with its inhabitants. But that world was gone, gone for good. The only appropriate music now was funeral music. It was criminal how the Nazis had brought this beautiful city to hell.

The sight of the ruined city, streets, and neighborhoods, the purposeless soldiers, the people wandering with their troubled faces, didn't fill me with satisfaction as it did most of my fellow prisoners. Even Martha was elated, but all I felt was sadness, sadness at a world that had been lost, a world left in ruins.

We spent the next two days clearing rubble from the road, filling wheelbarrows with our bare hands, and sleeping in the truck. And then at last we reached the Spreewald, just south of the city. It was a beautiful area, filled with nature trails and waterways. Berliners often came to hike or fish. But now the Germans were apparently trying to transform the forest into a line of defense against the advancing Russians. The truck delivered us to the banks of a tributary, where we were given shovels and ordered to dig trenches.

The work was easier than expected. The soil by the river was soft, and there weren't many stones or roots, and our guards weren't so stern and loud anymore. Everyone was nervous about what lay ahead. The first trench had to be thirty feet long, parallel to the river and near its edge. We were told to pile up sand on the river side, and a machine-gun post was installed on the mound. Then we started the next trench. Everyone knew it was a lost cause. But deserters were still being shot without mercy by the SS.

After a few days we stopped working, even though the trenches were unfinished. We were loaded back into the truck and departed for Hamburg, at least that's what we thought. To our surprise we ended up in the salt mines next to Bergen-Belsen. Telefunken had a factory there, and we were put to work assembling lamps. We spent a week there, then left, as unexpectedly as we had arrived. This time we were really heading for Hamburg. After traveling for days on poor roads full of potholes and on detours through the countryside, we arrived in Wandsbeck, a labor camp and a branch of the Neuengamme concentration camp near Hamburg. In Wandsbeck I was ordered to work in a rubber factory, but the regular bombings caused power failures so frequently that they eventually moved us to another workplace nearby, a furniture factory where I was expected to cut out rifle butts using a band saw. The same power shortages there led to yet another change of work, this time in the *Strassenkommando*, or street detail, clearing rubble in Hamburg, rubble from buildings bombed by the English.

At six in the evening on April 30, 1945, a selection was made, and a group of prisoners was brought to Hamburg's central station. The majority of people were Scandinavian. Only Martha and I were not. I then remembered that I had passed myself off as Danish in Ravensbrück; I must have continued to pass. I hadn't had a passport in ages, and it was possible that I was still listed as Danish on one or another list of prisoners. I'd been using the name Crielaars, which might sound a little Danish to a German ear. If a German had heard me and Martha speaking Dutch in Ravensbrück, in the midst of all those other languages and in the general chaos, he could easily have mistaken us for Danish. Whatever the case, from the moment rumors began to circulate that we were being picked up by the Swedish Red Cross, I understood the situation. Martha and I quickly buttonholed an English-speaking Dane and asked him to teach us a couple words of Danish in a hurry. Formalities were the most important, such as "My name is . . ." or "I was born on September 20 in Copenhagen" and "I'm tired." I decided not to say anything else. If I ran out of words, I would pretend to faint.

At last, two trucks arrived with Swedish plates and whitewashed tarpaulins with red crosses. There were no further checks as I had feared. The head of the Swedish Red Cross simply walked up to the German guards and handed over some papers. Communication was difficult, but the young man who taught us a few words of Danish was deployed as an interpreter, and that sped things up. The entire group had to get into the back of the two Red Cross trucks. It was organized in five minutes.

Then the engines started and we drove off. The young Danish "interpreter" smiled at me. When I asked him why there were only Scandinavians in the group, he told me that the Swedish Red Cross had made arrangements with the Nazis to collect Scandinavian prisoners from the camps. Many of them were policemen who had refused to arrest Jewish citizens on German command. These policemen were now being freed. I stared at him in amazement. What luck! Martha and I buried ourselves in the blankets we found in the back of the truck as we left Hamburg central station.

PAUL

Family Remains

ON THE OCCASION of my father's seventy-fifth birthday, one of my father's cousins, whom I'd never met, paid a visit from Amsterdam. She was a vivacious, enthusiastic woman named Suzy Rottenberg-Glaser, my father's youngest cousin, and the only one in the family—the surviving family—to have kept in touch with him. I'm not sure why she was the exception, but it probably had to do with the fact that she simply showed up when she felt like it, on special occasions such as this. After the party she invited me to visit when I got the chance, and a few weeks later, spurred by my curiosity, I went to see her in Amsterdam.

Suzy was happy I'd come, welcomed me warmly, and after conversing over tea for a half hour, she told me her story. She was the sole survivor from her family and had managed two narrow escapes. On the first occasion she climbed over a high wall surrounding the Jewish orphanage where she worked, before the Germans stormed through the front. She was the only one who managed to escape. The second time, one of the women with whom she was in hiding pretended to have scarlet fever during a house search. The Germans turned on their heels and left. "They were always afraid of catching one or another infectious disease," she said with a smile. "I wasn't able to say what I'm telling you for a long time. It took many years and professional help before I was finally able to talk about it," she said as her smile faded. "It's easier with you than with my own children. I can't get them to talk about it."

As the afternoon wore on, she told me other stories: about her mother and her brother, both betrayed and murdered in Auschwitz; about her husband, who managed to escape on foot and finally reached England after a year on the road; and of course about Aunt Rosie.

Rosie was her older cousin by eleven years. They had no contact with one another before the war because of their age difference, though she admired Rosie from afar. Her mother was less smitten. "If we saw Rosie during one of our walks, my mother made me look the other way. My mother was terribly straight-laced, and she didn't think that Rosie's head-turning good looks were appropriate for a young girl to see.

"After the war we established a good relationship. Not immediately after the war, but a couple of years later." Rosie visited her in Amsterdam, and Suzy visited Stockholm. "The things Rosie went through, it's enough to make your hair stand on end," she said. When I questioned her further she wouldn't say any more.

Later in the evening she relented. "Rosie was betrayed by her own husband, imprisoned in several concentration camps, and experienced the unspeakable. A friend who survived Auschwitz told me shortly after the war that she had met Rosie in the camp and that Rosie was sleeping with an SS officer at the time." She paused. "But who am I to judge. Rosie survived in that hell and that's all that matters."

"Two people I met shortly after the war who had returned from Auschwitz asked if I was Rosie's relative, since we shared the same surname. 'Rosie,' they said, 'the one who slept with the German officer.' I said we weren't family, despite the surname." Suzy continued, "Shortly after the war everything was still black and white, and if you had cooperated with the Germans it was wrong. Going to bed with a German was certainly wrong. But you had to know what it was really like in a concentration camp. If you wanted to survive you needed more than a little luck. You had to lie, steal, and cheat, most of the time at the cost of the other prisoners. If you stole someone's bread, you survived, the other died. If you pretended to be a professional, you got the chance to work for the war industry, and those who didn't were gassed. Anne Frank might have survived were it not for the fact that a fellow prisoner stole her bread a few days before the liberation of the camp. That was the raw truth."

I was familiar with Holocaust stories from history books, commemoration days, and documentaries, of course, but they tended to be distant and abstract. Now, as I heard about my family's first- and secondhand experiences, about impossible dilemmas, about cowardice, injustice, tragedy, courage, betrayal, and murder, my perception changed. These stories touched me, confused me, and I was ashamed of my earlier indifference.

Two things in particular stood out to me in Suzy's recollections. "Not a single government was willing to help; no one was interested. Not only the Dutch, but the British, the Americans, and the French, the so-called Allies, failed to intervene. We were completely alone. The Allies knew about the gas chambers in Auschwitz. They flew low over them, bombed half of Germany, but not the gas chambers, despite repeated requests. The Americans and the English were both guilty of turning back ships full of Jewish refugees. Only a few individuals provided concrete help." When I asked why so few survivors retaliated against those who had betrayed them, people who often lived only a block away, she explained, "After the war we were so exhausted we didn't have the energy to do anything. Liberation was double-edged. We were happy, of course, that the Germans were gone, but then we were faced with uncertainty about which family members would return, and the sadness for those who did not return. There was no room in the Netherlands for that grief." She continued, "Max Tailleur, a Jewish comedian popular in the Netherlands, said shortly after the war, 'I laugh to keep from crying.'"

After almost two hours of conversation we said good-bye. As I left she invited me to celebrate her next birthday with her, this time a special anniversary. She was organizing a party in the Apollo Hotel, and her family would all be there. "It's your chance to meet them," she added. I promised to think about it.

On the way home, stuck in a traffic jam, I thought over our conversation. I had always thought there had been much resistance during the war, that the Dutch government had done as much as possible for its oppressed citizens, and that the sense of solidarity had been strong and palpable. The Germans had arrested many Jewish citizens, but their fellow countrymen had been unable to do anything about it. At least that was what I had always been told, what I had learned at school. But the story of my father's cousin, the story of Aunt Rosie and my other relatives, was entirely different. Ruthless manhunts were organized, and Jewish game was hunted down without mercy, driven from its hollows and smoked out by Dutch policemen, Dutch civil servants, Dutch mayors, Dutch SS officers, Dutch bounty hunters and traitors. They were so effective that the Germans only had to round it up and dispose of it. Many of my fellow citizens participated and profited. There was more betrayal than resistance.

I was tired when I arrived home.

Still intrigued by Suzy's stories a few days later, I decided to go to her birthday party after all. I wanted to know what my family, albeit distant, looked like and to see them interact. Perhaps I'd learn more about Aunt Rosie and my father.

When I arrived at the party Suzy introduced me to some friends and family members, among them her children and her younger nieces and nephews. It was clear that they all knew one another. They talked incessantly. A few older people were gathered at a table. One of them, a first cousin of both Suzy and my father, was an elderly gentleman named Richard, who asked after my father. Without talking about the war I could see that it had left its traces. He mentioned the names of family members who didn't survive in a calm, measured tone. He knew Rosie and described her as beautiful and unconventional. "Rosie was extremely enterprising, independent, had a way with words. She did whatever she wanted, and she was our prettiest cousin."

Another elderly man told me he couldn't talk about the events of the war with his children because they didn't want to know about it. Absolutely nothing. "It confuses and saddens me, because it's something they ought to know, and I don't have a lot of time left," he said. "I understand how they feel to a certain extent. They're busy and have other concerns, but at the same time I refuse to accept that you can't share important facts and feelings within your own family. It's important. I know what happens if you don't talk about it. Before you know it, it leaves a cavity. I couldn't talk about it myself for years, but things changed after therapy and I want to tell my children about it, come what may." I was struck by the contrast: his children didn't want to know, and my father refused to tell.

The guests of my own generation were different. They showed none of the enthusiasm that René exhibited upon meeting me in Brussels, almost the opposite in fact. I'm usually pretty good at striking up conversations with strangers, but that night I made little headway. I realized that the Holocaust was still a heavy burden on both the survivors and their children, despite the fact that the past was receding. Standing alone with one of my relatives, I asked if he ever talked with his parents about the war. He said he didn't. A couple of his friends did, but one became suicidal and the other was left with a nervous tic, in spite of psychiatric help. "I will not take that risk. I want a normal life, and the past has to remain outside it," he whispered resolutely. The exception was a young woman who talked enthusiastically about her work on an ambitious film project by Steven Spielberg. I only learned later in the conversation that she was filming the testimonies of the last survivors of the Holocaust. I'd never heard of such a project before and was surprised by it.

Whatever their views on the past, the people at the party were my family, or what was left of it. A great-aunt, a couple of great-uncles, a few second cousins, and a lack of communication between generations. These were the remains of my family, distant and close at the same time.

ROSIE

Dance of Liberation

IT HAD BEEN raining for close to a week. The truck was moving at a snail's pace. Gray skies and hardly a light in sight. The road leading to the border with Denmark at Flensburg was full of holes, and the holes were full of water. The rest of it was a dirt track.

Once we left Hamburg, I had a sense that I could give in to my fatigue. I had ignored it until now. Tired or not, I'd had to keep moving. Hungry or thirsty, I'd had to be on my guard. Now that I finally surrendered to the fatigue I felt even more exhausted. Martha and I lay in the back of the truck with a number of other prisoners, huddled under blankets. We said little. I dozed constantly. I was so tired and undernourished that I was no longer interested in what was going on around me. I heard voices but paid little attention. The only voice I recognized was our Swedish driver, whose language I didn't understand but whose cursing was unmistakable. For me it was a reassuring sound, almost like music to my ears after spending so much time in the camps.

Sometimes planes thundered overhead and emptied their machine guns. They were Allied fighter planes, mostly English Spitfires, and they shot despite the fact that the trucks were painted white and had a giant red cross on top as a sign of neutrality. Apparently there were still misunderstandings, as German military vehicles regularly positioned themselves between the Swedish trucks. If a plane dove toward the trucks, we all jumped out and threw ourselves into a ditch. But on one occasion the shelling came so quickly, silently, and unexpectedly over the edge of an adjacent forest that there was no time to jump out of the truck and seek cover. Five prisoners were hit, two fatally and three wounded, and the driver was wounded as well. After a lengthy delay to tend to the wounded, we continued on our way. Our Swedish "interpreter" took over driving, and the wounded driver sat next to him with a bandage over his left arm and shoulder. He seemed to have run out of curses.

Beside the Spitfire attacks the journey was uneventful. We slept and napped in the truck, stopping now and then to eat and take care of our needs. One night I saw a village in the distance, on fire. It had probably just been bombed, since the flames were still raging and there were sparks hurtling into the air. From a distance you would think they were fireworks. It looked almost celebratory.

After three days we reached the border and joined the line of Swedish Red Cross trucks waiting to cross. We were not free yet, I realized, not really free. We first had to be exchanged for other prisoners—prisoners from the camps for German soldiers taken as prisoners of war when Norway and Denmark were liberated. A great deal of hustle and bustle ensued. Lists of prisoners were exchanged on both sides of the border. Armed soldiers surrounded the truck. The cargo area remained silent. Then the waiting began. I prayed that real freedom would come.

After two hours I heard commotion and loud voices; there was clearly some kind of disagreement. The German officer in charge of the prisoner exchange was quarreling with the convoy commander. The latter refused to exchange deceased prisoners for living German soldiers, and the former was insisting. A Swedish diplomat joined them. He looked like a gentleman, but he was clearly furious. I could see his face turn red through a gap in the tarpaulin covering the back of the truck. In addition to the two prisoners killed in the air attack, two others died on the way from their wounds and the rigors of the journey. The German officer refused to budge. The diplomat was equally determined not to concede, and he repeated his position in a loud and unforgiving tone, barking the kind of German the German soldiers understood so well. He even insisted that the German officer would have to face personal consequences, with their defeat so close at hand. In spite of being without a weapon, the diplomat courageously stood his ground. As a result, telephone calls were exchanged with headquarters in Berlin, the government in Stockholm, and the headquarters of the Swedish Red Cross. That night, the trucks remained at the border surrounded by soldiers.

The exchange finally took place the following morning. We were told to get out of the truck one by one and were permitted to cross no-man's-land to the other side of the border. At the same time, three German prisoners of war walked past in the opposite direction.

When the name Crielaars was called out from the list I was free to leave the truck. The Swedish driver helped me and accompanied me to the place designated by the German officer. The German looked pale and his expression was impassive. His uniform was impeccable. Even when they were losing, *Ordnung muss sein*—order must prevail. He asked my name. I didn't have any papers to show him. I also told him my prisoner number. A soldier matched the name on the list to the number tattooed on my arm. He then nodded and pointed to the right. The driver told me in English where I had to go and pointed to a group of people about three hundred feet ahead. They would bring me to

A newspaper clipping from Rosie's archive shows the Swedish Red Cross waiting in the mud at the Danish border

Sweden, he said. He wished me good luck and went back for the next prisoner.

At the same time, three men set out from the other side dressed in German uniforms. We passed each other halfway. We looked at each other out of the corners of our eyes, and I was hesitant to look straight at them. As I got closer I could see their faces. They were not undernourished, but their faces were dull and serious, and a little downcast. So I was worth three of them, I thought to myself. I took in every detail. One of them had a mustache, another was limping and old. The third was still young, quite handsome in fact, and he looked back. Like me he was visibly relieved at being set free; we smiled at each other if only for a second. Who were they? What had they been through? What had life been like for them up to now? I wanted to know, to talk to them. We passed each other and said nothing. After three hundred feet I was finally free.

Across the border, former prisoners were welcomed with hot tea, coffee, and a bite to eat. We were told not to eat too much. For the severely malnourished it could be deadly, they insisted.

Martha and I complied, but we enjoyed every morsel that passed our lips. We were given new blankets and were brought to a small public square with all the other former prisoners. A Danish soldier saw me, walked toward me, shook my hand, and asked, "May I have the number on your uniform as a souvenir?"

Me? Without a number on my uniform? I didn't dare give it to him. That kind of thing was punishable by death. I remembered the four Polish prisoners who, over a year ago, when the snow lay three feet high and the big pine tree was decorated with electric candles for Christmas, were hung in front of our eyes for not wearing a number. They were considered potential escapees.

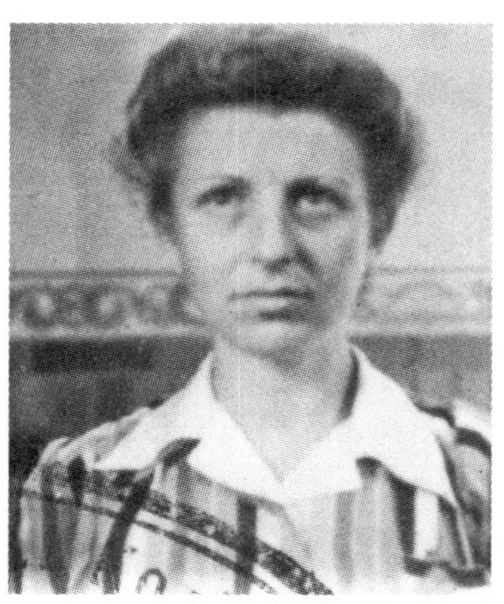

Rosie one hour after her liberation at the Danish border

We were then brought to a building where the Danish authorities provided us with new papers, a sort of provisional identity card. In Germany I had always used the name Crielaars on Jorg's advice. Now that I was truly free I decided to go back to my old name: Glacér. I'd had enough of the Lohengrin saga and all that "hide and seek." With my card and passport photo I was a brand-new person, on paper at least.

After everything was settled we were reloaded onto trucks and driven to Copenhagen. There were a few minor hitches on the way, but the journey went relatively well. Everyone was in good spirits. Gone were the oppressive fear, cold, hunger, and screams. Only the stench of our own bodies remained, but no one was bothered by it. We were free and without fear. That was the most important thing. The tarpaulins covering the truck had been thrown open.

Martha and I sat side by side. We didn't say much. When we arrived in Copenhagen on May 3 the first thing we noticed were the flags hanging from the buildings. A few people brought something to eat or drink for the emaciated prisoners. Everyone was kind. The people there looked good and seemed to be interested in us. Some waved awkwardly. Some were shocked at what they saw. Then I realized I was still wearing my camp uniform over my ordinary clothes. On top of that we were grimy and extremely thin, and some had soiled bandages on their wounds. These good people hadn't experienced the war at close quarters and knew about it only from the newspapers, abstract and at a distance. A mother with a baby in her arms stared in bewilderment at the recently liberated prisoners. I could see her shoulders convulse as she sobbed.

Her tears were infectious. Martha couldn't hold it in anymore and started to cry. She continued to sob and mutter incomprehensible words long after we passed the woman with the baby. It sounded like a Flemish dialect. Her weeping got louder. She shed the tears of sadness she'd been unable to shed till now, that she hadn't been allowed to shed. I threw my arm around her and ran my fingers through her short hair. She didn't seem to notice. She sobbed without respite, her shoulders shaking. It sounded more like the cry of a jackal in the night than a human being. It brought a lump to my throat, and I began to cry gently with her. And so we sat, pressed tightly together in the truck, for what seemed like hours. Why did you first have to be rejected before you could be chosen? I thought to myself. I pictured my parents. They couldn't have survived. I pictured my brother John, our dead friend Rachel, the countless numbers who died in the gas chambers, the boy with the brown eyes and the fleeting smile, my niece. I thought about the crimes committed by Clauberg, the fact that I couldn't have children. I thought of all the years of discrimination. Why? All because I was who I was.

The other prisoners said nothing and waved enthusiastically at the people on the street. They left Martha and me to our grief.

On May 4 we were boarded onto a ship that took us across the strait to Malmö in Sweden. On the ship we were offered a real "dinner." How difficult it was, all of a sudden, to be a "lady" in my striped, dirty, and shabby prison clothes. I was sitting there and being served . . . eating with a fork and knife. When we docked at Malmö we were greeted by a crowd. I waved and said to Martha, who was sitting next to me, "Life is about to start again." The chairman of the Swedish Red Cross, Count Folke Bernadotte, gave a speech I will never forget, but when the Dutch national anthem was played no one could or wanted to sing it.

After our reception, the medical staff of the Red Cross took us to a large hall where we would be given medical help and allowed to recover. Many were sick, infested with lice, and badly undernourished. I weighed eighty-four pounds. Compared to the camps, the building was like a luxury hotel. We had running water, central heating, and a spacious dormitory where everyone had their own bed. It was safe there, and there was no need to be on our guard. We had plenty of food, and everything was clean and neat. Even the toilets were clean. But the most important thing was the friendliness of the people who welcomed us. I didn't understand Swedish, but their tone of voice was clearly amicable. Some of the caregivers even spoke English.

In the three weeks of quarantine that followed, everyone began to regain their strength. The Swedish Red Cross provided me with new clothes, and from the Dutch embassy in Stockholm I received a new winter coat, despite the fact that it was May. I still hadn't seen or spoken to anyone from the embassy, a shame because I had so many questions about the Netherlands—my family, my friends.

While we waited, people searched for fellow citizens who spoke their language, everyone eager to talk about the future. The group of Dutch women I met had mostly come from Ravensbrück, but I didn't know them. They were a cultivated bunch, and I could tell they came from wealthy families. But hours of discussing the reconstruction of the Netherlands began to irritate me. Dutch society needed to be more just. Women should be given more power. It should be more socially minded and more honest. Idea after idea was proposed for the new social order in the postwar Netherlands. The Dutch women here were full of new ideas.

I participated less and less in these discussions. The group was infectiously enthusiastic, but at the same time naive and idealistic. Society wasn't what they thought it was. It didn't work that way. Anyway, what did their so-called renewed Netherlands have to offer to me? Were my parents and brother still alive? Were the rest of my family and friends? My experience in the camps didn't make me optimistic. On top of that, I had to consider the past. The Dutch had made it impossible for me to operate my thriving dance school. I had twice been betrayed by the Dutch and put in prison. The queen had escaped to England when her people needed her most. Magda Coljee had helped me, but she was German. A Dutchman shot at my brother while he was defending The Hague.

Looking back on all that had happened, I could only conclude that when push came to shove, the Dutch were not my confederates. Of course there were plenty of kind and good Dutch people, but the memory of everything that had happened continued to haunt me. The people in Sweden were kind to me. They, not the Dutch, were the ones who liberated me. The Dutch Red Cross did nothing for me. The Swedish Red Cross took care of me. They saved my life. My choice was clear.

I spent my time in quarantine thinking about my decision. Was it the right thing to do, or was I being impulsive? But each time I thought about it I came to the same conclusion. My mind was made up: I was going to stay in Sweden. With that assurance I began to inwardly unwind.

Eighteen days after Rosie's departure from Hamburg, standing with former German prisoner Ilse Schmidt and nurse Huvud Lottoo

Because I spoke German, Dutch, French, and English, I ended up working as a liaison officer between the various nationalities. I also played the piano, and people regularly gathered to listen or sing along. When boredom set in after a couple of weeks, I organized a group that met every day for an hour of exercise. It was a small group at first, but before long almost half of the women joined. Some were still too weak and sick to participate. After each session, when my muscles were sufficiently warmed up, I did ballet exercises in the main hall of the school building.

Now that people were physically better, I thought it was a good idea to organize something fun. I imagined a cabaret with some dancing would help and started to work out some ideas on paper. A week later, when my initial plans had taken shape, I set off in search of people willing to participate. Before long I'd collected a group of eight women.

We devised a number of sketches together and learned them by heart. I wrote a few songs in different languages—German, Dutch, French, and English—set them to familiar melodies, and tried them out on the piano. One of the women was an opera singer. She had a beautiful, powerful voice and sang most of the songs while the rest of us joined in at the chorus. I played piano. After a week of rehearsing, it was time to hit the boards in the main hall. It was a cabaret by women for women. The decor wasn't much: some improvised curtains, flags, and some vases. But the lighting was good and the room was large enough. Everyone came.

Rosie at the piano, rehearsing songs for the cabaret in Sweden

The audience responded enthusiastically to our first song. It was a familiar tune, a real showstopper. They laughed loud and hard at the sketches too. Our often awkward and clumsy presentation only enhanced the hilarity. Sometimes the audience listened to a song in silence, since they didn't all understand the language, but as soon as there was a familiar chorus they all joined in, robustly. Germans, Dutch, French, and Belgians, all from different backgrounds. Some stood on their chairs; others danced in the aisles, alone or with a female partner. A few embraced and kissed each other just a little too long. We seemed to be discharging all the tensions that had been pent up during years of captivity. After we finished there was thunderous applause. After shouts of "Encore, encore!" the opera singer sang a tearjerker and everyone sang along. The applause seemed to be endless. There were flowers for the entertainers. Two of them had tears in their eyes. They hadn't received flowers in years.

During the intermission the enthusiasm and commotion seemed unstoppable. People mixed and mingled, gabbled in a jumble of languages, talked about the cabaret, and laughed to their hearts' content. It was exactly as I had wanted it.

After thirty minutes or so one of the women rang a bell to signal that the intermission was over, but the gesture was ineffectual. Everyone kept on chatting noisily; almost no one moved. After several more signals, we started to speak to everyone individually, shepherding them in the direction of the hall. It took fifteen more minutes until everyone was finally reseated. It was time for the dance performance.

As the gentle tones of a Chopin waltz filled the room I started to move. Although I'd been dancing since my childhood, I taught it professionally, and my performances had been shown on newsreels, dancing was never a matter of routine. It was always new to me. The rhythm in my body was in harmony with the music. There was something divine about it. When the Chopin ended, the audience went wild.

My next dance was set to Ravel's *Bolero*, beautiful music that began with a slow, distant melody and gradually gathered speed, swelling to a powerful rhythm and concluding with a tremendous explosion of sound. I had prepared a ballet-style performance, and as I danced a bead of sweat ran over my lips. I tasted salt. The dance was spontaneous. I was almost in a trance. Only when the music reached its abrupt conclusion did I return to the present, dazed, breathless, and sweating. I could see the audience looking at me in silence. As my arms fell to my sides, they burst into rapturous applause. Commotion and elated shouts filled the room. I was back, and I began to wave and smile at everyone. I wanted to hold on to that fantastic moment for as long as possible. I wiped the sweat from my brow.

Rosie's dance of liberation

The bolero wasn't an ordinary dance for me. It was my dance of liberation. I had already been free for a couple of weeks, but it only became real to me that night. I think many of the women felt the same way.

I was anxious to hear news about my brother, John, the rest of my family, and friends. I'd written several letters but received no reply. When I asked for information, representatives of the Dutch embassy said they couldn't help me.

Then, finally, I received a letter from the Netherlands. Bad news. Disastrous news. After days of grief I wrote about it in a poem.

LETTER FROM THE NETHERLANDS
Malmö, 26.5.1945

A letter from the Netherlands, a joy to see it come
It helps me to forget my pain, I wonder who it's from
At night I lie in bed and think, perhaps there will be mail
To free me from my loneliness, and lift this murky veil
A letter from the Netherlands, my own dear mother's hand
A sunbeam in the darkness, so wonderful and grand

That is what I need, a greeting from my homeland,
Ties no one can sever, that close-knit loyal band.

Do you know what it's like to be locked up
In a cell, or a camp or behind barbed wire
What's the point you might wonder
What is meant by these atrocities.
Toil and slavery, endless work, to captivity consigned
Hunger, darkness, exhaustion, fatigue, worn out every day
Then deep from within a longing grows for the one you left behind
So let there be a letter from her, that is what you pray

Days fly by like hours and the world is burning still
What has become of my dearest friends, the friends I miss so much
Some lost to typhoid, others murdered, slaughtered, killed at will
I can only guess when my day will come, when I will feel death's touch
The rules are stern, the guards so mean, the mail cruelly withheld
A blatant insult to international law, for none of us upheld
Despite all this, my thoughts retain but one ambitious goal
A message, yes, a message, no message is too small

After three long years in this dire hell my joy returns anew
On a sultry night in spring, unexpected by one and all
The struggle is abandoned out of the blue
Far, far away from the Netherlands this time of bliss drew near
Thin, emaciated, grimy, dirty, my eyes were filled with fear,

A silent prayer stole heavenward on this golden hour in
spring
For my mother and my cherished land, the land to which I
cling

A letter from the Netherlands
The letter came, it finally came, but in a stranger's hand
As I sat on my bed at night, yes then the mail arrived
With news that left me without doubt, no single doubt
survived
That letter from the Netherlands was not in my mother's
hand
A shiver ran through my every limb
I read and read until the writing was a haze
Greetings from the Netherlands, but not in my mother's
hand
Why I still miss her so much, I still can't understand.

The letter wasn't entirely unexpected. When I was in Auschwitz I was already convinced that my parents wouldn't survive, but there was always a sliver of hope, against my better judgment. Extraordinary things happened in the chaos of war. But now, that hope was extinguished for good. Knowing that my parents were dead was yet another reason not to return to the Netherlands. Lack of cooperation and concern on the part of the Dutch authorities intensified my decision. I had recently received a bill for the warm winter coat that the embassy had sent in May, immediately after our liberation. They wanted me to pay for it. The Swedish authorities had provided clothing, housing, food, and medical care for free, and the Dutch wanted me to pay for a coat.

Complicating matters was the fact that I was told I couldn't stay in Sweden. The Dutch government and the Red Cross had agreed that former prisoners should return home as soon as they were able. Nevertheless, I had made up my mind. The Netherlands was not my home. I was staying in Sweden. I didn't care what the state authorities said. I didn't trust them. I didn't trust them at all.

Martha had managed to establish contact with her family in Belgium. Some had been lost, but most of them were still alive, including her mother, two brothers, her grandfather, and several cousins. She wanted to go home, and the Belgian Red Cross took care of it. As we said our good-byes like a couple of old friends, we promised to stay in touch.

If I was to carry out my plan I had to learn Swedish as quickly as possible. Although the reception camp was only temporary, they nonetheless offered language classes outside in the schoolyard when the weather permitted. I joined in and picked up the

A Swedish lesson on the school playground

language quite quickly and I practiced every day with the Swedish caregivers.

A private Swedish lesson

Once the quarantine was lifted, sixteen of us Dutch women were brought to a smaller refugee camp in Gothenburg, the nearest city, where I lived in a small wooden house. During my time there, I managed to compose three songs that were recorded and broadcast on the radio. At one point I was photographed playing piano by a photographer from *Life* magazine. I also managed to find a job as a nanny for a wealthy family. Having come from a wealthy family myself, I related to them quite well. In the early days I spoke an awkward mixture of German and Dutch, but before long my Swedish improved and I began to speak the language fluently.

HEY! HEY! HEY!
Text and music by Rosita Glacér, July 1945, Gothenburg

It happened on a pretty lake
In the Swedish mountain country
It was glorious summer weather
And many a heart was free
Young folk aplenty having fun
As young folk like to do
Cute faces taking in the sun
But then things went askew

Refrain:
Hey! Hey! Hey! Why are you walking past me?
Hey! Hey! Hey! Pretty girl, is your heart still free?
Far sa gott, he said, I always know the next line
Jag älskar dí, he said, does that make everything fine?

The girl could only stand and stare
At that strange young Swedish lad
He seemed quite cute, but did she dare
She didn't see anything bad
He offered her chocolate, a cigarette
A walk in the nearby brush
And then the fun began, you bet
Their faces began to flush:

Hey girl, I'm in love with you
I'm wild and it's bliss
Please tell me I can marry you
Come on, give me a kiss
Your nice blond hair and sweet blue eyes
I simply can't resist
So don't say no, just improvise
Come on now, I insist.

Boy, I need to think this through
I didn't expect your advance
I'm not so quick to lend my heart
But I'm willing to give you a chance
I'd like to stay in Sweden,
A nice place to remain
I find the country dandy
Now listen to this refrain:

Hey! Hey! Hey! I know that you love me.
Hey! Hey! Hey! Young love, my heart is free.
Far sa gott, I also know the next line
Jag älskar di, and everything was fine.

Meanwhile, the Dutch embassy continued to insist that I return to the Netherlands. I was one of the few Dutch people who hadn't returned, and there was another ship leaving soon. When I told them that my parents were dead, that I didn't know if my brother had survived and didn't know where to go, they told me not to worry about it, the Dutch authorities would take care of temporary housing and put me in a camp.

Why should I let them put me in a camp in the Netherlands? Hadn't I been liberated? After three years of living in one, I refused to go back. Was that all the Netherlands could offer? I had already made up my mind to stay in Sweden, and this only strengthened my resolve. I asked the ambassador to check more carefully to see if my brother was still alive. I had asked them before, but they said they didn't know. Now they knew it was important for me to have somewhere to go in the Netherlands, and they promised to do all they could to trace him. But their efforts were unsuccessful, and they started in again about a shelter camp in the Netherlands. As the embassy continued to badger me, I had to consider the possibility that they might have me arrested and taken into custody. They'd done it before, twice in fact.

Then I had an idea. There was another Dutch woman in this reception center who planned to return to the Netherlands but had to wait three months before the damage to her house was repaired. The embassy appeared to approve. With this in mind, I quickly wrote a letter to Mrs. Coljee to ask if I could stay with her for a couple of weeks in three months' time. I wasn't planning to go back to the Netherlands, but this way I could keep the embassy at bay and it also gave me a provisional address if things went awry. I could then work out how to get back to Sweden.

Gothenburg, July 29, 1945

Dearest Magda and Henk,

Here I am again. I hope you are well. I'm alive and in good health. So many things happened in Germany, of course, as I'm sure you can imagine.

Sadly my father and mother did not survive and I've not heard anything from my brother John.

I've been through a great deal since I last wrote, but that's not the purpose of my letter. I hope I can tell you all about it in person when we meet. Here in Sweden I'm doing quite well. The people are exceptionally kind and hospitable, the food is excellent, and they've given us quite nice clothes to wear.

The people here—I've made so many good friends—all want me to stay, but the Dutch diplomatic mission signed an agreement to repatriate all the Dutch people and I have to leave.

That's all well and good, of course, but what makes it so unpleasant is that I haven't heard anything from my brother, have no address to go to in the Netherlands when I arrive, and they want to put me in another camp. I'm sure you can imagine how dreadful the very thought of it is to me.

In the meantime I've been in touch with my fellow Dutch dance teachers and have decided to open a new school at the first opportunity. I need about two weeks to make all the necessary arrangements and meet with my contacts in the Netherlands. But I can't do anything if I'm stuck in a camp, because all the formalities would simply get in the way. That's why I have a huge request for you.

Would I be able to lodge with you for 14 days while I settle my affairs? It would be such an enormous service to me, invaluable in fact. I hope you can help me rebuild the work I was innocently forced to abandon three and a half years ago. All I need is a telegram from you stating that I can stay with you for two weeks. I still have a lot to do here so it will be three months before I can travel. Will you let me know if I can stay with you for a couple of weeks in November? I can then give your telegram to the Dutch diplomatic mission and then I would have an address to go to on my arrival.

I truly hope you will be willing to help me, but even if that's not possible please send me a note. Warm greetings and a heartfelt kiss,

(Lya Donkers)
Rosie Glacér

After a telegram from the Coljees, the Dutch authorities left me in peace.

Then I received good news from the Swedish Red Cross. Really good news. My brother was alive and well. When the south of the Netherlands was liberated in 1944 he got engaged to his girlfriend Elisabeth. They had just married. I was over the moon, but I didn't understand why the embassy knew nothing about it. He was registered shortly after the liberation in 1944, and from what I heard he had also been paying his taxes. Were the staff at the Dutch embassy too busy with receptions and lunches?

I quickly got bored with my job as a nanny. The father of the family had eyes for me, and his wife had started to notice. The

Götenborg, den 29 Juli 1945

Lieve Magda en Henk,

Hier ben ik dan weer en hoop, dat jullie
het goed maken. Ik leef en ben gezond. Heb van
zelfsprekend heel erg veel meegemaakt in Duitsch
land, zooals je je zeker wel begrijpen kunt.
Mijn vader en moeder leven helaas niet meer, en
van mijn broer John heb ik nog niets gehoord.

Ik heb heel erg veel meegemaakt, maar daaro
ver wil ik hier niets schrijven, dat hoop ik jul
lie allemaal zelf te kunnen vertellen.

Ik heb het hier in Zweden heel erg goed.
De menschen zijn erg lief en gastvrij, het eten
is heel erg goed, en we hebben behoorlijke mooie
kleeding gekregen. De menschen hier, ik heb hier
heel erg veel vrienden gekregen, willen me alle
maal hier houden, maar dat is niet mogelijk want
de Nederlandsche Legatie heeft indertijd ervoor
moeten teekenen, dat alle Nederlanders repatrie-
eren.

Rosie's first letter to the Coljees after the war

atmosphere was getting tenser by the minute, and I wanted out of the situation. As soon as my Swedish was good enough I found a job as a secretary and handed in my notice.

Meanwhile, I visited the city on a regular basis, and colleagues from my new job invited me out. They were kind to me, and I enjoyed their company. There was a place to go dancing in the center of the city, and on Sundays it was packed. The dance floor was perfect, the music upbeat, and there were two bars. It reminded me a lot of the Vereeniging. I went there to dance and meet new friends every Sunday, and that was where I met my new husband. He was a nice man, a naval engineer who lived in Gothenburg. His name was Elon Nordström. We got engaged that same year, 1945, and we married on February 15, 1946. So began my new life in Sweden.

A wedding portrait of Rosie and Elon

PAUL

Encounter

AFTER MEETING MY distant relatives, I wanted to know more about my family's past. My father still refused to talk and despite my curiosity, I didn't insist. I was inclined to think that allowing his children to grow up without the burden of the war may have been the right thing to do, although in hindsight I may have been rationalizing his decision. Though he spoke about his youth in Kleef and Nijmegen, I still had no idea what he or his family looked like back then or what kind of house they lived in. There were no photographs. He claimed they were lost.

The only way forward was to contact Rosie. The idea of just calling her out of the blue was out of the question. I was too afraid she'd refuse to talk about the past after so many years of silence. On top of that, Rosie and my father were not on good terms, which only increased the probability that she would refuse to speak to me. No, if I wanted my chance I would have to present myself in person. During a business trip to Helsinki I decided to change my return flight and take the night ferry to Stockholm, where she lived.

I approached the magnificent Swedish coastline early in the morning. At five o'clock I stood on the deck without a soul in sight. As the boat deftly moved between the numerous uninhabited islands that flanked the mainland, I took in the light, bright and soft. A red sun burned low in a cloudless sky. The sea was calm, and the engines were humming gently at my back. I made my way to the bow and looked down into the water as the boat cleaved it in two. I stood there for what seemed like an age, alone in the world.

The ferry docked at six a.m., still too early to call my aunt, so I waited awhile, drank a coffee, and called her at 8:00. After introducing myself, I told her I was in Stockholm harbor and that I would like to pay her a visit to talk about the past. She told me quite directly that I was not welcome. I made it clear that I was not there on my father's behalf, that he didn't know I was in Stockholm, but she continued to refuse. So there I was with all my good intentions, alone in Stockholm harbor. Finally, I told her that I knew about my Jewish background, and only then did she begin to talk about the past.

She packed everything into ten minutes. It was like an explosion. She rattled on at such a pace that I didn't catch everything. But I couldn't forget the tone of her voice and her final words: she had said all there was to say, I had what I had come for, and I still wasn't welcome. In a final attempt, I told her that I'd be in Stockholm until late Sunday evening, that I planned to look for a hotel, visit the city, and see the famous Vasa warship. "I'll call you again in the morning. My father refuses to speak, and you're the only one who can tell me about the past, what it was like, how you lived. I'll ask you tomorrow a second time if we can meet, and if you say no I'll respect your decision and wish you a long and happy life." Without waiting for an answer I hung up.

The next morning, also at eight—I was very impatient—I called her again. Half an hour later I was at her door.

I rang the bell, and a woman with gray hair and bright eyes

emerged. In spite of her age she seemed healthy and strong, no fragile old lady. She smiled, looked at me inquisitively, and shook my hand. This was my aunt Rosie. Before I could go any further, Rosie instructed me to take off my shoes and offered a selection of slippers from the hallway. I chose a green pair and made my way inside.

It turned out to be an extraordinary day. There was so much to talk about. Rosie, who was divorced from Elon, showed me photos from before the war. She had hidden them underground somewhere in Den Bosch in 1942 and later dug them up. For the first time in my life I saw my grandparents and other members of my family. They looked elegant and beautiful in their handsome clothes. I saw them walking, at dinner, on the banks of the Rhine, on vacation, and at their houses in Kleef and Nijmegen. I saw my father as a young man and in his soldier's uniform in front of the station in Den Bosch. I had hundreds of questions, and Rosie responded in a clear voice, opening a window on a life I believed was lost. An image of my grandparents and family slowly emerged from obscurity. Rosie paused for a moment, took a photo of my grandparents from her album, and gave it to me. "A memento," she said. My father was in the same photo, a child. She pointed to him and said, "You can cut that part off."

When she got up to retrieve a pot of tea from the kitchen, my attention was drawn to a segment of barbed wire with an electrical insulator hanging on the wall between the paintings and photos. "A souvenir from Auschwitz." As she spoke, it struck me that she had no problem talking about the past and that she remembered many details. Despite the serious topic, she sometimes made a joke or told an anecdote that left us both laughing.

It was clear that she had managed to preserve her joie de vivre, her passion for dancing and music, her active interest in people, and her optimism, despite the terrible things she endured. "From the beginning of my new life here in Sweden I always signed my letters Rosie, as I did before. But there's a difference. In the *R* of Rosie and my official name Rosita, I draw a smiley, a grinning face, laughing at life. A snub to those who wanted to intimidate me, to break me. They didn't succeed."

When we talked about the family she lost in the Netherlands she observed, "When I was young and living in Nijmegen I didn't attach much importance to family, but things have changed. When I married Elon I acquired a new family. The Swedish are very close and family-oriented." She told me with pride that Elon's brother had named one of his daughters after her: Rosa Nordström.

Every now and then we stopped talking, went for a walk, had a drink, and looked out across the beautiful Mälaren Bay. Gazing out over the water Rosie said, "When I'm dead, that's where I want my ashes to be scattered."

As night fell we made our way to the subway station. The weather had turned gray and misty. We'd talked all day, but when we reached the platform we said nothing. I stepped into the train, and the doors closed automatically. We continued to look at each other, our faces serious, no smiles. The train began to move. I saw her wave, alone on the platform. She got smaller and smaller as the train accelerated, and finally disappeared into the mist. That was the last time I saw her.

ROSIE

A Future with Memories

IN SWEDEN, I built a new life for myself and finally settled down. I had a job, a husband, a new family. For the first time I felt calm. My husband played a large role in this. Like many Swedish people, he had a tranquil temperament. He was completely devoted to his work, to me, and to the family. He didn't seek adventure and rarely got excited. But despite our diametrically opposite personalities, I was happy with him. Not only because our marriage allowed me to stay in Sweden, but also for the simple reason that he was a kind man who doted on me. He was reliable to a fault, almost boringly so! He was exactly the kind of husband I needed as a thirty-one-year-old woman.

We had a nice house on the outskirts of Gothenburg, on a quiet street where the only activity was the postman's arrival and the sound of children playing. I decorated the house on my own, using furniture from Elon's old flat. It was a shame I didn't have anything from home. Over the years we accumulated a few things, including, of course, a piano. I practiced and sang every day, just as I used to do.

I also still liked to joke. Elon wasn't sure what to make of my humor at first and would sometimes give me a funny look, but eventually he came to appreciate my wit. He called my jokes Dutch humor.

I stood out a little from Elon's family. I wasn't the passive housewife type, I was enterprising, talkative, I sang, I danced, and I was always up for a bit of fun. When they didn't understand my jokes, Elon and I looked at each other with a smile and thought: Dutch humor. I was often the center of attention. Elon was proud of me, fond of me, and that felt good.

But for me the tranquillity of our life in Sweden had its dark underside, and from time to time I suffered from unexpected spells that could last for days, and when they did the memories came flooding back, memories I was usually able to keep at bay. Normally I was able to keep out the misery, even in the worst of situations. It helped me keep my chin up and even write songs and enjoy a laugh now and then, a genuine laugh. But at these times, besides the memories, my mind was awash with questions. We were all born loyal, and loyalty is seen as a virtue, but at the same time it can destroy you. We pledge allegiance to king and country, to leaders, the church, the boss. My brother served his country when it could have killed him. He came close enough when his glasses were shot from his face in The Hague, by a fellow Dutchman no less. He almost died a hero, and for nothing. Shortly after the war, the same grateful homeland demanded he pay taxes for my father, a man the authorities had imprisoned and murdered, and they even included interest.

Government ministers delivered patriotic and heroic speeches, and their vassals supported them blindly. Many Germans must have regretted their loyalty to the fatherland. They believed in certainty and fairy tales, the certainty and fairy tales provided by the Nazis. Fairy tales are for children; at least that was what most people thought. But the opposite was true. Adults needed them too. But for the Germans, the fairy tale was over.

And God? Where was God when we needed him? Was there a virtuous God for the Germans? And a treacherous God for the prisoners? The idea of God was now absurd. God was an expression of human weakness. The dying called on God. I saw it for myself, I heard their cries. God was a fancy word that blinded us from reality. In Auschwitz there was no God. Where was he when those young women, those girls, were hanged and we were forced to watch? Where was he when that young boy smiled back at me? Where was he when thousands perished? I always came to the same conclusion: I didn't believe in God or the state. What was left? Only people.

After the war everyone talked about the good citizens and the bad citizens. But who were they? Of course there were criminals, common criminals and war criminals. But if the Germans had won the war, who would be righteous and who benighted? A Dutchman had shot at my brother. Leo's betrayal put me in prison. Kees betrayed me too. Dutch policemen arrested me with a smile and put me in prison once again. On the other hand, Jorg and Kurt were kind to me, as was the German doctor in Ravensbrück. Magda Coljee, who had been so kind to me and my mother, was also German. There was no black and white. There were only people. Some were kind; others were not. The vast majority were honest, naive, obedient, and opportunistic.

Time and again I reached the same conclusion, and after a couple of days lost in my thoughts I returned to my daily routine. I couldn't talk to Elon about it. He wouldn't have understood. I sometimes tried, but then I saw the vague, questioning look in his eyes. So I told the world I had a migraine. Everyone understood a migraine. The explanation bridged the enormous gap between the surface and what was going on under the surface.

The proportion of Jews murdered in the Netherlands was higher than in any of its neighboring countries, including Germany. No, I was happy I had stayed in Sweden. The Dutch mentality continued to amaze me. I didn't understand their attitude. The way they treated me after the war, you would think I had committed a crime. It was as if being treated as a criminal during the war made me a criminal after it. The world was standing on its head. I was unlucky not because I had been born Jewish, but because I had been born

Dutch. In Sweden they saw me as a respectable fellow citizen, perhaps a little more interesting because I was from abroad.

Those opportunists who betrayed me in the Netherlands would probably side with the Allies now and boast about their courageous resistance against the Germans. They probably thought I was dead or so crippled by my experiences that I'd never bother them with my suffering. Many of my fellow prisoners had become passive and apathetic to some extent. But my betrayers were wrong. I might live far away in Sweden, but I would ensure that their bad deeds were not swept under the rug. In 1945 I wrote a detailed letter to the Dutch authorities reporting Leo Crielaars and Kees van Meteren for treason and Marinus Crielaars for collaboration. I described the facts and events in as much detail as possible. I received a reply and read to my relief that all three had been arrested and imprisoned.

Then I received another letter from the Dutch authorities, this time about my parents' tax assessment. My brother had already informed them that our mother and father were dead, but it now appeared that they wanted us to pay up, and with interest, because there was no civil registration of their death.

Our house, our stolen property, and the jewelry we handed over at the beginning of the war were not returned. The money that the government forced my parents to deposit with Lippmann, Rosenthal & Co. was also not returned, at least what was left after my father withdrew some of it and gave it to Venmans for safekeeping. It was all rather complicated, the Dutch authorities informed me. When I responded that it was in fact quite simple, and that our stolen property should be returned without further delay, the Dutch authorities protested that it was indeed a complicated matter and that they'd look into it further.

I couldn't afford a lawyer, and I wasn't even sure if I could trust one. I remembered how most lawyers, the vast majority in fact, simply dropped their respected Jewish colleagues like a ton of bricks during the first years of the occupation. All their lofty legal principles and legal etiquette simply vanished into thin air. Mr. J. B. Hengst, my ex-husband Leo's lawyer, even had the audacity to send me a threatening letter, despite his client being declared guilty of betrayal:

MR. J. B. HENGST
ADVOCAAT EN PROCUREUR
'S-HERTOGENBOSCH
TELEFOON XXXX 8837
POSTCHÈQUE EN GIRO 23448.
Dondardags Gesloten

H/F 'S-HERTOGENBOSCH, 14 November 1946
STATIONSWEG 7.

Fröken Rosita Glacer,
c/o herre Manden
Egmontsgatan 10,

Göteborg
Sverige

IN ZAKE: L.J.Crielaars

Geachte Mevrouw,

Wellicht zal het U intereseeren te weten, dat de Heer Crielaars tenslotte zonder eenige oplegging van straf in vrijheid werd gesteld en zeer terecht, want de aanklachten zijn zoo goed als alleb ongegrond gebleken, integendeel is kome n vast te staan, dat Uw relaties met de moffen veel en veel ernstiger waren dan die U van hem vertelde.

Er is dan ook geen twijfel aan, dat, wanneer U in het land mocht komen, U niettegenstaande Uw oogenblikkelijke Zweedsche nationaliteit het risico loopt, dat er maatregelen tegen U worden getroffen en ik meen goed te doen U dit mede te deelen, teneinde niet het verwijt te zullen hooren, dat ik U niet vooraf gewaarschuwd heb.

Hoogachtend,

A letter from J. B. Hengst, Leo's lawyer

Dear Madam,

It has become clear that your relations with the Jerries were much more serious than those of which you accuse your ex-husband. There can be no doubt whatsoever, therefore, that should you endeavor to enter this country you run the risk of having measures taken against you, in

> spite of your Swedish nationality. I mention this for your benefit, and to avoid any potential accusation that I did not warn you in advance.

Shortly after the liberation, the Dutch government had actually crafted legislation that intentionally prevented the return of stolen money and property. Parliament had approved the law. All very democratic. It was the kind of legislation the Nazis would have been proud of. It took years of legal action to get even a percentage of it back. Very few were able to start proceedings. If you had no money, because all of it had been stolen, you could prove nothing, and as the family was dead, you had no papers—in short, if you had absolutely nothing left, then you were out of luck. It was as simple as that. None of my possessions were ever returned to me, not even those confiscated by the Germans and later handed over—at least what was left of them—to the Dutch authorities. The only money I got back was what remained of the fund I had given to Mrs. Coljee for safekeeping.

The same Dutch state had carried on about the honor of the nation and called on the population to fight for king and country. What kind of homeland was that?

The procedure established by the Dutch government for the disbursement of German reparation money to the victims of the war was simply endless. Ten years after I was exchanged for three POWs, Germany announced it was going to pay compensation to the victims. They called it *Wiedergutmachung*—literally, "to make good again." I had applied to the Dutch authorities charged with distributing the *Wiedergutmachung* citing imprisonment, slave labor, the murder of my parents, the medical experiments, and the loss of my dance school and possessions to justify my claim. When I received no response I finally decided to write again nearly twenty years after the war. I asked for an update on my claim and an advance, bearing in mind the duration of the process. I received an answer from the head of the office responsible for investigating claims:

> Amsterdam, July 31st, 1964
> Frau R. Nordström-Glaser
>
> Re.: your claim
>
> I received your letter dated July 28th, 1964 in which you request that a short-term advance be granted on the basis of the aforesaid claim.
>
> While I can certainly sympathize with the reasons you put forward, I regret to inform you that it's impossible for me to satisfy your request.
>
> My office is overwhelmed with written and telephone requests similar to yours.
>
> The supplementary treatment of such requests would involve an incredible amount of extra work, which would of course lead to a serious delay in the settlement of regular claims.
>
> I must therefore ask you to be patient, even if you were born before August 1st, 1902 and your claim has—for whatever reason—not yet been settled.
>
> In order to avoid additional work, I would also appreciate it if you would refrain from further correspondence, or telephone calls.
>
> Head of the Central Settlements Office—
> German Reparations
> Mr. J.G.A. ten Siethoff

In other countries, the *Wiedergutmachung* settlements had already been disbursed. After a while I received a letter telling me that the Netherlands was refusing to pay my compensation because I was Swedish and not Dutch. The fact that I could prove I was Dutch when it all happened made no difference. To make matters worse, I received a letter from the Dutch embassy expressing serious doubts about my identity and the misery I had experienced. I sent them the identity papers I was given at the Danish border and provided them yet again with the number that was tattooed on my arm at Auschwitz. No response. I then turned to the German president, who informed me that Germany had deposited money designated for me with the Dutch government. I was back to square one. I was caught up in a heartless, frustrating bureaucracy and there was no way out.

In contrast, the French authorities insisted on fairness when it came to situations such as mine, but this was no help to me. The Hague continued to refuse. I then turned to Queen Juliana and tried to arrange a meeting with her during her royal visit to Stockholm. I succeeded, and she was extremely nice to me. I followed up our meeting with a letter explaining my situation in more detail and received a reply. She was willing to intervene, and thanks to her efforts I was finally granted compensation of 2,000 guilders for the medical experiments that led to sterilization in Auschwitz. I was also to be compensated for being forced to wear a Star of David, a sum based on the number of days I had to wear it. It was a little unusual for someone who had never really worn the star, except for the one day when I had to go to the police station in Den Bosch. But in the end, forty-two days were deducted because of the forty-two days I spent in the SS prison in Den Bosch, during which time I was unable to wear the star in public. They refused to budge on the matter. Petty Netherlands at its best. As a result of the deduction, I fell under an officially established minimum and no longer qualified for supplementary compensation.

Despite the annoyances generated by my hostile native country, I remained optimistic and enjoyed life to its fullest. I hadn't survived for nothing, and I wanted to celebrate it to my last breath. With Elon I had a nice, domestic life, the kind I hadn't experienced since my youth. His family was very close, and we had regular parties, picnics, and other outings. I got along especially well with Elon's brother and his wife. I was crazy about their children, and they were crazy about me. I took them to the zoo, the park, the harbor, and when they were older to the theater. I taught them to dance and play music, especially during Sweden's long dark winters when they celebrated St. Lucia's Day. Together with the children, we put on our Sunday best and wore crowns with burning candles. Elon knew that I couldn't have children. I hadn't told him when we got married, but he didn't react as badly as I had feared.

My ambition was to start a dance school in Sweden. Now that I was Swedish it was legally possible, but the young people didn't dance as much there as they did in the Netherlands, Belgium, and Germany. Moreover, Elon didn't like the idea of spending long evenings home alone while I worked. I consequently applied for a secretarial job, adjusting my résumé to show that I worked as a secretary in London during the years I had spent in the camps. Nobody was looking for an employee with a difficult past, one so few could understand. I managed to find a job as an executive secretary at a major electronics firm, where I was responsible for commercial correspondence with a number of German companies. Experience working in my father's business came in handy, and I didn't have an aversion to the Germans because of the war. German was still my mother tongue, Dutch my second, and Swedish now my third.

Although I had made my home in Sweden, I still kept in touch with friends in the Netherlands, with my brother, and with a couple of nieces and nephews who had survived the war. I wanted to pay them a visit, but I worried I might risk being arrested, as Leo's lawyer had insinuated in his letter. I'd been arrested twice before and didn't care to have it happen again. Fortunately, I checked with the Dutch police, and the lawyer's claims were complete nonsense. A month later I traveled to the Netherlands. Elon stayed in Sweden. He was busy building ships, and the commissions were piling up. Moreover, he wasn't really interested in the idea, though he understood perfectly well that I wanted to catch up with old friends and see my brother John and his new family.

Our reunion in the Netherlands was warm and emotional. At John's insistence, we agreed that nothing should be said to his children about our Jewish background and also nothing about the camps. It was all just excess baggage, he argued, and didn't concern the children. We shouldn't burden them with the past. The future was theirs, and they should be free to develop unhindered. Since John's wife, Elisabeth, was Catholic, the children had been baptized. John made no effort to keep in touch with the few cousins who had survived the Holocaust. He thought it was better that way, for him and his children. They didn't quarrel, far from it, but he didn't attend the annual meetings held by the few survivors in the family, despite the invitations he continued to receive. I had always liked maintaining contact with people. But John was my introverted little brother, and that was the way he'd stay forever.

Rosie in the Netherlands

The first time I returned to the Netherlands I also decided to see my ex-husband, Leo. He had told me through his lawyer to stay away from the Netherlands, suggesting I might be arrested. So I wanted to show him that I was not to be intimidated, that I was doing well, and that I was happy he had been arrested for his base and cowardly betrayal during the war.

He was the first person I visited when I arrived in Den Bosch. I put on my prettiest dress and my red coat and went to see him. As I walked through the streets and the neighborhood where he lived I began to slow down unintentionally. I recognized the houses. There was a little park on the corner of one of the streets, so I found a bench, smoked a cigarette, and watched two children play. The neighborhood was just as it had been. What would I say to him? What if he wasn't at home? I began to question whether this was a good idea after all. As it started to drizzle, I pinched myself for being such a coward and reminded myself that I'd been in worse situations. I got to my feet, found his house, and rang the bell.

Leo himself opened the door, muttering something unintelligible. He looked old and run-down. I was pleased to see it. "Hello, Leo," I said. He muttered something in response. The rain got heavier, and he asked if I wanted to come inside. I told him I preferred to stand in the rain. He stood and stared, his mouth half open. I told him he looked terrible, that I found his betrayal appalling, and that his incarceration in Camp Vught was justified. I wished him a miserable life, turned on my heels, and walked off into the rain. As soon as I turned the corner, out of his sight, I stopped and caught my breath. It had gone just as I wanted.

I then made my way to my parents' house near the station, which had been heavily bombed by the British. The rubble had been largely cleared, but you could still see damaged walls and roofs. I had heard that our house and a few neighboring houses were completely destroyed, so the sight didn't shock me. There appeared to be nothing left of the place, just the walls separating our house from the house next door—which was also a ruin—and part of the scullery wall. The rest was a massive pile of rubble.

Rosie's home with the attic dancing school in Den Bosch

When I climbed over the wall I saw the remains of the barn in our backyard, which had been used as a safe house. It was also where I had buried my family albums and films of the dance school. I looked for the spot, waited until dusk so as not to attract attention, and started to dig with a small shovel I had brought in my huge handbag.

I quickly found what I was looking for. The albums were in pretty bad condition, but the photos were still in fairly good shape. The negatives and the films had also survived. I removed the photos from the damp and damaged albums and put everything into my handbag. It was completely dark by that time, and I checked to see if the coast was clear before climbing back over the rubble. Back in Sweden I stuck the photos in new albums and added captions. I was happy to have saved at least some memories of my youth, my family, and my dance school.

The next day I continued to explore the city, viewed and photographed ruined buildings, and paid a visit to my old neighbor, Mr. Pijnenburg. He had always been kind to me and my parents—he had taken us to the station when we fled—and I had not forgotten it. He now lived with his family in emergency housing, since his own house had been bombed, just like ours. Bad news for both of us, really, because I had sent my book to him for safekeeping when I was in Camp Vught, and it was lost in the bombing. Apart from that he was doing fine and looked exactly the same. His children were also doing well. We talked about the past, although it was only a few years ago, about the dance school, about my parents and people we knew in Den Bosch.

Rosie visiting a former neighbor and her children in Den Bosch

The following day I took the train to Naarden to visit Magda Coljee. I bought her flowers on the way. When I turned onto her street I recognized everything, down to the last detail. The trees on one side, the bend to the left, and the house itself. Memories flashed through my mind. The last time I was there I was with my mother and a policeman with his pistol drawn. Before I knew it I was at her front door. The welcome was warm and affectionate and sealed with ten kisses.

My brother had already paid a visit to collect our possessions and the remaining money, which she handed over with a careful breakdown of the expenses and packages she had sent. It was a shame that the money was worthless now. In an effort to combat undeclared "black" money, the government had introduced new currency after the war, and the old money was no longer legal tender. My brother contacted the ministry involved, but an official told him it would have been better if my father had deposited the money with the bank designated by the Germans. Then it would have been registered. There was nothing he could do. Some of the jewelry was also missing, probably appropriated by Kees. A shame, since besides its material value it was also the last remaining tangible memory of my mother.

Despite our joy at seeing each other again, Magda appeared concerned. She was thin and had bags under her eyes. She told me her husband, Henk, had been arrested. The ministry had reasoned that since he was married to a German, was a member of the NSB, and had boarded Jews who were handed over to the Germans, he must have betrayed us. She had been forced to engage a lawyer to defend her husband, but she barely had enough to pay him. Magda also told me that people were disrespectful to her on the street because of her German background, even people who had been extremely nice to her in the past. One of the shopkeepers had even refused to accept her food vouchers. I did my best to cheer her up and told her that I'd write a letter to the ministry exonerating Henk as soon as I got back to Sweden. The help she gave me when I was in dire straits was incredible, and I planned to let them know. We talked about Kees, who I told her had been imprisoned in Vught. I asked if she knew where he was now, but she didn't. In spite of my flowers, my thousand thanks, and my efforts to cheer her up, Magda remained downcast and dispirited.

The next day I traveled to Belgium, where I met up with Martha, and we made our way to Tielt, where Rachel used to live. It was a sleepy little town not far from Bruges and Ghent. A medieval tower stood in the middle of an old market square, which was surrounded by old houses, a few cafés, and a terrace.

The address that Rachel had given us was occupied by another family who knew nothing about her. The house had been allocated to them by the authorities after their own house in Antwerp was bombed, and they had no knowledge of the family who lived there before them, at least that was what they said. When the door closed we were stunned, not knowing what to do next. No trace of Rachel? Impossible!

We tried the house next door. The neighbors, an elderly couple, seemed friendly, and they told us that none of Rachel's family had returned. Poor souls, she called them. The greetings, kisses, and good wishes we had promised to give to her family evaporated into thin air. The elderly woman invited us in. She ushered us into the living room and quickly removed the slipcover from the sofa. We drank coffee, and the couple talked about their former neighbors and about Rachel. They remembered her as a young girl, cheeky, cheerful, and full of mischief. She often popped in. She also loved to go fishing, and Uncle Lambiek, as she called him, used to take her to the nearby canal, just opposite the timber factory. The water was cloudy there and full of sewage, but for some reason the fish seemed to like it and there were always plenty to be had. They would sit there half the day, and he would talk about giant carp, eels, and bream, and Rachel would talk about school. She attended a girls' school run by nuns. She was smart, the best in the class. Overcome with emotion, our host hesitated and stopped. His wife took over. She told us about Rachel's first boyfriends and Pierre, the love of her life, to whom she was engaged. They never understood why the two had broken up. Rachel hadn't been fishing with Uncle Lambiek for a long time by then. Their canal conversations had dried up, as she didn't find it as easy to talk about crushes as it had been to talk about school.

Pierre's surname was De Jaeghere, and he lived in the café at the corner of the street. It was clear that these people loved Rachel. When they asked what had happened to her we told them she died a gentle death after a period of illness. We hadn't agreed to do so in advance, but her elderly neighbors were such nice people we decided to spare them the truth. They loved Rachel. Why hurt them more by telling them what really happened? After a second cup of coffee we said our good-byes and kissed them both on the cheek, even though we had just met. Perhaps we did it on Rachel's behalf? Whatever the case, it felt like the right thing to do.

The café on the corner turned out to be closed that day, and when we rang the bell a woman with blond hair opened the door. "Is Pierre here?" we asked. The woman gave us a suspicious look and told us that Pierre was not at home. We were happy to have found the right place, but the woman claimed she didn't know when he would be back. We arranged to return later in the day and sauntered to the market square for a coffee on the terrace of one of the cafés. We talked about our adventures with Rachel, the fun we had together in the barrack, the jokes we told, and the almost hilarious situations we sometimes found ourselves in. We talked about the wound on Rachel's leg, the wound that ultimately killed her, and all because of a beating from some stupid guard. A meaningless beating, for no reason. We later heard that the sick prisoners who stayed behind at the camp weren't killed as we had predicted, but were the first to be liberated by the Russians.

After a couple of hours we returned to Pierre's café. The blond woman opened the door again and called to her husband. Pierre appeared in the doorway. He was a strapping lad with broad shoulders and a large tattoo on his upper left arm. He listened to our story, nodded now and then, but didn't seem to be interested. When we asked him about his time with Rachel he shrugged his shoulders. He turned and walked inside. The blond woman closed the door with a slight grin on her face. And that was that. We had found the love of Rachel's life but hadn't managed to get beyond the front door. Life can be incredibly stupid.

To come to terms with my wartime experience and for my own mental health, I spent part of my trip visiting well-known sites such as the beach at Normandy where the Allied invasion started; Bastogne, where the Ardennes offensive took place; and Berlin, where I helped to build the defenses. I also visited all the prisons and camps in which I had been held. I took pictures of everything, and when I was back in Sweden I arranged them in albums during the long winter evenings. Everything had its place.

Near Camp Vught

Next to a picture of the ruined city of Kleef I wrote a free-form poem. It seemed sadly ironic that the city that had inspired Wagner's *Lohengrin* was destroyed by Hitler, who was so obsessed with the composer:

Lohengrin Saga
Opera Lohengrin
Lohengrin—Wagner
Wagner—Hitler
Hitler—Bomber
Bomber—Kleef
Hail to you my dearest Swan [the symbol of the city of Kleef]

In memory of my lost years, I decided to write a book about my life. I had already written a similar book, but it was lost in the war. Now that I had the time, I started again. I needed my past to help build my future. A future with memories.

I picked up my pen and wrote the foreword:

> I started to write this book in prison in Den Bosch in 1942. I continued to write when I was in hiding. I started again when I was in Camp Westerbork and continued in Camp Vught. I sent the manuscript by courier to my neighbors in Den Bosch where it was destroyed by bombs in 1944.
>
> I started writing again after my liberation in Sweden. I dedicate this work to my deceased parents and to all those who share my point of view: Difficulties and risks are the acid test of our character.
>
> Rosie

Cell block 10 in Auschwitz (photo taken on a later trip)

PAUL

Roses

IN MARCH 2000 I received a call from my sister Marjon. She told me Aunt Rosie had passed away. An official from the city of Stockholm had contacted her after finding her address among Rosie's papers. He told her that Rosie had died at home a couple of months earlier and that he had been looking for family members for quite some time. The fact that Rosie had no children hadn't made it any easier. He had also spoken to her husband Elon's family. Elon had died in 1967. After some happy years of marriage, Elon started to suffer from depression, which led to heavy drinking. One morning he was found dead in the snow. When he lost his job, Rosie supported both of them. Though their relationship had deteriorated, she considered it her duty to look after him. After Elon, Rosie appeared to have had other serious relationships, one with a bank manager from Stockholm, another with a hospital director from Nuremberg, but she never remarried. In the absence of children, it appeared that we were her closest family.

Marjon, my brother René, and I decided to go to Stockholm to pay our respects and to make whatever arrangements were needed. My oldest daughter, Myra, who was curious about her great-aunt and had been planning to visit her with me in the spring of 2000, joined us.

A week later we flew to Sweden and went directly from the airport to Rostock Crematorium in the east of the city. A clergyman directed us in broken English to a small chapel. Between two burning candles we found an urn containing Aunt Rosie's ashes. He left us alone. Silence engulfed us. While we knew in advance that we would be collecting her ashes from the crematorium, we were still caught off guard, making the silence even more intense.

It was time to go. The official who had been in touch with us was waiting. I took the urn and put it in my backpack. Quickly, we walked to the city hall. We had to hurry because it closed in an hour, and then the weekend began. It was strange to walk with Aunt Rosie on my back. The blood rushed to my head, and I broke into a cold sweat. We arrived at the city hall just in time, and the formalities were quickly taken care of. I arranged to take the ashes with me to the Netherlands, signed the relevant papers, and received the key to Rosie's apartment. We planned to take a look over the next few days and decide what to take with us. It wouldn't be much since we had weight restrictions on the plane. The official promised to have the rest of Rosie's property cleared from the apartment and the proceeds donated to charity. Before we finished he asked me what the number tattooed on Rosie's arm meant. I wasn't in the mood to talk about it, so I told him I didn't know.

Rosie's apartment was just as I remembered it. We placed the urn on the table, opened the doors to the balcony, and looked out over Mälaren Bay. The weather was tranquil, frosty, and hushed. We were no longer in a hurry. The sun began to set, and we looked for candles, then lit them on either side of Rosie. She was home again.

The following morning I started to search for papers and photos. The postcard with Marjon's address was still on Rosie's desk.

Among her things we found cameras and no fewer than fifty photo albums. The majority offered a picture of her new life in Sweden. She appeared to have prospered, done a lot, and laughed a lot. There was Rosie on the deck of a handsome cruise ship, behind a sledge being pulled by six huskies in Antarctica, in a submarine next to the captain (of course!), with the queen of the Netherlands in Stockholm, on countless picnics with friends or family. Rosie was often in the foreground, smiling, wearing a stylish summer dress or an elegant fur coat in the snow. There were also several photos of mountains, factories, rivers, ships, ice floes, bridges, buildings. These subjects must have excited her.

We then found an old album from Rosie's youth: her father and mother, her friends, Wim, the dance school, Leo, Kees, and John. The photos extended from her youth to the middle of 1942, and they bore handwritten captions in Swedish. My brother and sister saw our grandparents for the first time. I had already seen some of the pictures when I first visited Rosie in Stockholm, but that was just a small portion of what we found. For the first time we saw what life was like after she moved out of her parents' house. There were newspaper clippings about dancing, many of them featuring photos of a radiant Rosie, and her old passport, which referred to her as a dance teacher by profession. We also came across two films, which I watched later when I got home. They had no sound, but they showed Rosie dancing, teaching, chatting with students in her attic dance school in Den Bosch. In one scene she was talking to her mother, our grandmother. Another captured my father and mother dancing together, young lovers gliding over the dance floor. I had never seen them like that before. There was nothing from the images to suggest that the war was already two years old and that the situation was grim.

We found a folder full of poems and songs, all of them written by Rosie in Westerbork, Vught, Auschwitz, Birkenau, Gothenburg, and Stockholm. We also came across a small diary with a lock. It was like an autograph book: Rosie invited friends she met after the war to write something in it. The first was the man who liberated her, Folke Bernadotte. He wished her *lucka till*, much success.

Then we discovered the diary she had spoken of in one of her letters from Westerbork, in which she had begun to write again in 1945 after the first one was destroyed by British bombs. It was in a folder with a green cover. I glanced inside and saw a foreword, written by hand in neat, elegant letters. The rest was typed, page after page, chapter after chapter, each with Roman numerals. The last pages were written in pencil with many erasures and corrections. Apparently she would write by hand first, then type up her draft. It looked well cared for.

We found reports of witness interrogations made in 1946 by the Dutch State Police of the people who had betrayed her. The reports not only exposed the betrayal of her ex-husband Leo, they also detailed the activities of her lover Kees, and of the people both men mixed with.

A separate folder was dedicated to correspondence with the Dutch government and other official authorities. Most of the documents were requests for the return of money and property or for compensation. Year after year, letter after letter, frosty treatment, poor results. A kind letter from Queen Juliana's secretary stood out amid the official letters of rejection. At the back I discovered a chart of notary invoices that listed all our murdered relatives and what was left of their estates. It wasn't much. The family was gone, and so was their money and property.

Little by little the pieces of Aunt Rosie's hidden existence came together. All this new information widened and sharpened the picture. It told the story of a passionate, intense, and adventurous woman who, despite adversity, remained positive and optimistic.

The last thing we found was behind a painting on the wall: Rosie's last will and testament. In Swedish, it conveyed her wish to have her ashes scattered in the bay she had looked out over for so many years. I hadn't forgotten her request, but I decided not to mention it to the official for fear that he would refuse to release the urn. Scattering ashes in the bay is prohibited. But Rosie's life was full of rules and regulations, and much of the time she simply ignored them. We decided to do the same and respect her last wishes.

Paul and his daughter Myra after scattering Rosie's ashes, 2000

That Sunday morning the four of us walked along the edge of Mälaren Bay. It was early March, and the sea was still frozen. A bird on the horizon flew low above the water. The sky was blue and cloudless. It was silent as a grave. Suddenly, in the distance, a tiny boat plowed its way through the thin ice. We waited until the silence returned, then I clambered onto a rock that jutted into the water and broke a hole in the ice. After a short ceremony, I poured Aunt Rosie's ashes into the bay. Marjon had brought Dutch roses and she threw them onto the water. Roses for Rosie. Silence.

AFTER THE WAR

WHILE ENJOYING HER new life in Sweden, Rosie continued to keep track of the people who had played an important role in her earlier life. She wasn't able to trace everyone, but some basic information is provided below.

ROSIE

Of the twelve hundred people who were on the train that transported Rosie from the Netherlands to Auschwitz, seven hundred were gassed upon arrival and five hundred were put to work. According to reports, only eight of the original twelve hundred survived.

On December 8, 1945, Rosie sent a long letter from Gothenburg, Sweden, to the Dutch department in charge of investigating wartime abuse, providing information about her betrayal by her ex-husband Leo and her lover Kees. "I can't help laughing as I commit this to paper," she wrote. "I'm 31 years old and my eyes have opened. I've changed so much you wouldn't recognize me anymore; perhaps three and a half years of concentration camp did me good. Who knows, but let me come back to the point."

Rosie wrote a year later in one of her photo albums about her relationships with Leo and Kees: "I met my second misfortune in March 1937, namely Kees. Leo and I rented our dance halls from him in Den Bosch. This man is responsible for the entire unfortunate situation that has followed me like a shadow for ten long years. I fell in love with him and he with me. A dangerous game developed, involving money, ethics, and honor. Everyone lost. We all three lost love, money, and our good reputations. Hate, in the most profound sense, left deep wounds. It was an unforgettable three-sided affair. We are now all three married. I think I'm the better off. I want to forget them as one forgets a nightmare. Maturity has helped me succeed."

Rosie survived both Leo and Kees.

Shortly after her liberation Rosie wrote a letter about the bombings she experienced: "The most horrendous air raids on Auschwitz, Breslau, Berlin, and Hamburg left me completely indifferent. After a while I didn't even bother getting up, whether I was in a wooden barrack, the back of a truck, or in the open air. While the shrapnel whizzed past our ears, we told each other jokes. Why worry about the future. You had to enjoy life in the present. No, life in Germany made me hard and cruel."

When I visited her she explained, "Each command assigned to the gas chambers was relieved after three months. The old command was then sent into the gas chambers itself. I wasn't aware of that then. I never saw anyone from my group again. I'm so lucky that I was allowed to go to the Union factory. Without realizing it at the time, I had managed to save my own life."

After the war, the taxes deducted without permission by the Dutch state from her father's bank account were finally repaid to Rosie and her brother after their long and continued insistence. It took until 1953 before the unjustified tax assessments related to 1943 were finally annulled. The money was returned without interest and had dropped considerably in value.

Throughout her life, Rosie kept in touch with her cousin Suzy Rottenberg-Glaser, one of her few family members who survived the war. After Rosie's death in 2000, Suzy remarked, "Rosie lived her life with optimism and flair, and rebuilt it in Sweden after the war. She didn't let the postwar fuss with the Dutch authorities preoccupy her for very long. She also never asked herself what it might have been like if she had joined Ernst in Switzerland. She lived life to the fullest, faithful to herself, even in prison. Her character remained unbroken. For Rosie, character was what it was all about."

August 1940

LEO CRIELAARS

At Rosie's behest, Leo was arrested after the war. He was imprisoned in Camp Vught, which was empty at the time and provided a useful prison facility. After an investigation, Leo was found guilty of treason.

Rosie had been forced to shut down her flourishing business after Leo had sent a letter to the *Kulturkammer*, the Chamber of Culture, informing them that she was Jewish. Her license was subsequently withdrawn. When Leo found out that Rosie had reopened her dance school in her parents' attic, he wrote another letter to the procurator general indicting his ex-wife a second time.

Den Bosch, October 11th, 1941

To Mr. Van Leeuwen, Procurator General of the Court of Justice, Den Bosch
Respected Sir,

The undersigned L. J. Crielaars, dance teacher and district administrator of the Dutch union of dance teachers, registered with the Dutch Kulturkammer, respectfully calls your attention to the following:

A few months ago, all bona fide dance teachers in the Netherlands were registered under the aforementioned organization; Jewish teachers were not permitted to register. As far as I am aware, all Jewish dance teachers have respected this ordinance with the exception of an exceptionally insolent Jewess by the name of Rosie Glaser. The said Jewess declared openly at the reorganization meeting in Utrecht, and in the presence of 147 dance teachers, that she had nothing to do with the new order and that she would continue with her activities, as you can see from the particularly Jewish style advertisements enclosed.

This surprised not only the dance teachers from my district, but dance teachers from across the country who immediately remarked that she had outwitted everyone yet again, and that you had to be Jewish to do so. First, she started to become Roman Catholic and told everyone she was not a Jew. Presently she has moved her teaching activities from the hotel ballroom she previously rented to the attic of her home, where she has set up a dance hall and continues as if nothing is wrong.

My district members are now complaining that this is unfair, because registered bona fide dance teachers are obliged to adhere to the new regulations, such as higher fees etc. This is in our own interests, of course, but I am sure you will see the injustice of the situation.

I reported the matter immediately to the executive board, which replied that I should settle things with the local authorities since they are presently unable to take action. The Kulturkammer is still in formation, and she is teaching in a private house. Yesterday I met with inspector Vos of the local police who informed me that the ordinance had indeed been published but without an indication of penalty. His hands are thus tied. He agreed to discuss the matter with the commissioner, but did not give me much hope. It is for this reason that I turn to you.

I politely request that you take measures to put an end to the illegal activities of that insolent Jewess.

Sincerely,
L. J. Crielaars

On May 25, 1942, he wrote yet another letter, this time addressed to the commissioner of police, stating that Rosie had been appearing in public without a Star of David and that he was personally certain that she had more than two Jewish grandparents. He concluded by asking how many Jewish grandparents one had to have before one was expected to wear a star. The letter was successful and led to Rosie's arrest and imprisonment for six weeks in solitary confinement in Wolvenhoek SS prison.

During his hearing after the war, Leo told the judge that he had not set out to harm Rosie and that he had acted only in the interest of the union of dance teachers, of which he was the district manager. If he had known that his actions were going to place Rosie in danger, he added, he would obviously have remained silent.

After serving nine months Leo was released and was free to continue with his dance school. He died in 1978. The dance school still exists.

MARINUS CRIELAARS

Marinus was arrested and imprisoned as a result, in part, of information provided by Rosie. The day after his brother Leo sent his letter to the commissioner of police complaining about Rosie's refusal to wear a Star of David, Marinus addressed the following letter to the NSB mayor of Den Bosch:

> To the Honorable Lord Mayor of Den Bosch
> May 26th, 1942
> Honorable Mayor,
>
> I hereby request that you intervene in the following matter.

A very impertinent Jewish woman by the name of Rosa Regina Glaser lives in your city and she prides herself on not wearing a Star of David. The said Jewess was also active as a dance teacher and was forced to put an end to her activities on account of her background. She is the daughter of Falk Jonas Glaser Philips, a Jew residing at Koninginnelaan 23 in Den Bosch.

The Jewess has made life very difficult for me on account of my membership in the movement by pitting the public at large against me. She herself hangs around with men from the Wehrmacht and even pretends to be a National Socialist.

It is high time that this impudent Jewess be subjected to severe interrogation. The police do not seem to mind that this Jewess does not wear a Star of David on her clothing. She appears to have wrapped a number of surveillance officers around her finger.

I politely ask you to root out the problem once and for all.

Waiting for measures to be taken.

Hou Zee [the Dutch equivalent of "Sieg heil"]
M. L. Crielaars, to the new order

At trial, Marinus declared to the judge that he was unaware that his brother had written a letter about Rosie the day before his. He also stated that he was unaware of any harmful consequences Rosie may have suffered on account of his letter. He had been a little confused when he wrote the letter, he said, and he certainly did not hate Jews.

In addition to his betrayal of Rosie, it appeared that Marinus had other crimes on his conscience. He had threatened Rosie's Jewish neighbor in Amsterdam, telling her he was a member of the Gestapo, and after she went into hiding he had her entire house emptied and took all her possessions. In court, he declared that he had saved the furniture from confiscation by the Germans and had risked his own life in doing so. But his excuse was flimsy; when the Jewish neighbor resurfaced after the war and demanded the return of her property, Marinus informed her that he didn't have it and didn't know where it was.

The judge sentenced Marinus to ten years in prison. A year later the sentence was reduced by half.

The postwar "purification" process in the Netherlands was launched under the slogan "swift, severe, and just," but due to the enormity of the project, the process of Dutch reconstruction, and the military actions in Indonesia, swiftness was quickly prioritized over severity and justice.

KEES VAN METEREN

Kees was also arrested, but not only as a result of Rosie's testimony. Kees's slate was far from clean. In addition to treason he was also suspected of fraud and collaboration. He had a large sum of money in his possession when he was taken prisoner by the Allies in Dessau. He insisted that the money was not his own and that his boss had asked him to purchase diamonds on his behalf in Amsterdam. He also stated that the Nazis had imprisoned him in a camp in 1943 as punishment for his anti–National Socialist attitude. He added that he had the good fortune to be able to escape when Germany collapsed.

The Allies handed Kees over to the Dutch authorities, and he, like Leo, was imprisoned in Camp Vught. Interrogation produced a substantial dossier. At one point reference was made to Kees telling the friend to whom Rosie had entrusted her gramophone and records that he had come to collect them at Rosie's

\- 1 -

Gemeente - Politie

Te s Hertogenbosch
Afd.: Politieke-Recherche
No. 954

PROCES-VERBAAL
Van Inbewaringstelling of internerring

Betreffende: C.M.W. van Meteren
Geboren te s Hertogenbosch den 22 Juli 1918
Wonende te s Hertogenbosch, Julianaplein 29
Bijlagen : zes stuks

Ter uitvoering der eerste/tweede algemeene Lastgeving//van een byzondere lastgeving van het Militair gezag inzake aanhouding, onderzoek en inbewaringstelling van bepaalde (groepen van) personen

heb ik, Johannes Evert Hulshof, Rechercheur der Politieke Recherche te s Hertogenbosch, tevens onbezoldigd Rijksveldwachter

Op den 18en Juni 1945 omstreeks 11 uur te s Hertogenbosch
aangehouden en verhoord

Naam: van Meteren
Voornamen, Cornelis Maria Wilhelmus
Geboorteplaats en datum: s Hertogenbosch, 22 Juli 1918
Nationaliteit: Nederlander
Burgerlijke Staat: ongehuwd
Beroep: Hotelhouder
Woonplaats en Adres: Hertogenbosch, Julianaplein 29

Als vallende onder het bepaalde, gesteld in voormelde Lastgeving onder,

Als verdacht van als tolk in dienst te zijn geweest bij de S.D.

Door mij gehoord, verklaarde hij:

Ik heb lager onderwijs genoten en vervolgens drie jaren gymnasium en Mulo. Ik ben niet in militairen dienst geweest. Ik had vrijstelling wegens kostwinnerschap. Ik ben nimmer met de Nederlandsche Justitie in aanraking geweest. Mijn vader had een Café en Restaurantbedrijf. (Hotel Lohengrin) te s Hertogenbosch. In 1938 is mijn vader gestorven. Ik heb toen, tesamen met mijn moeder, het bedrijf voortgezet. Voordien was ik als volontair in verschillende zaken in diverse plaatsen, ook in het buitenland. o.a. Duitschland en Hongarije in het hotelbedrijf werkzaam geweest. O.a. was ik in 1938 werkzaam in het Kasteel Oud Wassenaar te Wassenaar. Ik werd daar als bediende aangewezen voor de Sultan van Langkate, Sumatra. Voor deze diensten heb ik later op den dag van zijn vertrek een gouden medaille gekregen, die speciaal bij Begeer te Utrecht geslagen werd en uitsluitend voor bedieningspersoneel bedoeld was, met het recht tot het dragen van het hieraan verbonden eereteeken. Dit geschiedde tijdens het regeeringsjublieum van H.M. de Koningin. Kort voor het trouwen van Hare Koninklijke Hoogheid Prinses Juliana met Prins Bernhard werden er in Hotel Des Indes te s Gravenhage officieele feesten gegeven ter gelegenheid van de Koninklijke verloving. De Directeur, Henri Bey, stuurde mij als zoon van een collega altijd naar de beste plaatsen, zoo ook plaatste hij mij eens naast hem om Hare Koninklijke Hoogheid Prinses Juliana te ontvangen en gaf mij de opdracht uitsluitend voor haar bediening zorg te dragen en op haar wenschen acht te slaan.

Official police report on Kees van Meteren

request. The friend handed them over in good faith. Several witnesses characterized him as extremely unreliable. One report mentioned the German execution of a resistance fighter and a downed English pilot based on information provided by Kees.

In spite of the fact that Kees had pursued people and property dressed in an SS uniform, the judge found that there was insufficient evidence for a conviction. At the request of the defense, a psychiatrist had declared that Kees was not entirely sane. He was released.

Hotel Lohengrin, where he grew up and which had been so hospitable to the German occupiers, was destroyed by fire during the battle to liberate Den Bosch.

Rosie tried to track Kees down when she visited the Netherlands in 1947, but he had not returned to Den Bosch after his release from Camp Vught. Only many years later did she manage to trace his whereabouts and find his address with the help of the Amsterdam police. Rosie found out that he was married, had four children, and that he had left his family without a trace. What she did with the information is not known. Kees died in Cologne in 1996.

ERNST WETTSTEIN

After completing his assignment in Eindhoven, Ernst returned to Switzerland. Rosie tried to contact him after her arrest, but to no avail. It's possible that he wrote her back, but Rosie never heard from him again. He later spent time in Spain, where he worked as an engineer for a number of textile firms, introducing new techniques and mechanization with the help of modern Swiss textile machinery. He then returned to Switzerland. Rosie made no attempt to contact him after the war. Their engagement was never officially terminated.

HENK COLJEE

After the war, Henk was suspected of having collaborated with the Germans and having been responsible for the betrayal of

Rosie and her mother. As an NSB member married to a German wife, every finger seemed to point in his direction, and he was imprisoned. Magda employed high-priced lawyers to petition for his release, and to prioritize his case, but it did not help. At Magda's request, Rosie wrote a letter to the authorities informing them of her positive experiences with the Coljees. A church minister also submitted a statement confirming that after Rosie and her mother were arrested the Coljees had given refuge to two Jewish children, who thus managed to survive the war. The declaration made little difference. Henk was released after a year, but a number of his rights as a citizen were not returned. A disappointed man, he started the procedure to emigrate to South America, but it took a long time to obtain the required authorizations. He abandoned his plans and remained in the Netherlands. He worked as a milk vendor. Full citizens' rights were officially returned to him in 1952. He died in 1964.

MAGDA COLJEE

Magda remained in Naarden after the arrest of her husband. Returning to Germany—in ruins and under Allied occupation—was not an option. Her brother had died on the Eastern Front, and his children came to live with her. She had no children of her own. After her husband's release they enjoyed a number of good years together. When he died in 1964 she supplemented her income by taking in lodgers and running an ice-cream and candy kiosk. When she was too old to work and her brother's children had moved away, she found a place in a home for the elderly, where she remained until her death. She had little contact with the other residents, who found her sullen. Embittered, she suffered a minor stroke that affected her power of speech. This only increased her isolation. A couple from the local church came to visit her every Sunday inspired by a sense of social duty. Magda died at the age of eighty-three, isolated and alone.

JORG DE HAAN

Rosie and Jorg de Haan (fictional first name) never met again. According to a list of important functionaries in Westerbork, he was the representative of the so-called *Zentralstelle für jüdische Auswanderung* (Central Office for Jewish Emigration) in Amsterdam, the SS institution responsible for expelling Jews.

MARTHA

Martha (fictional name) met her husband after the war. They married and had three children. Rosie visited her several times in Knokke, where she lived. A stone was erected in Tielt in memory of Rachel (fictional name). Rosie and Martha remained lifelong friends.

KURT FISCHER

Rosie was unable to trace Kurt (fictional name) and never saw him or heard from him again. After the war, Kurt's hometown of Magdeburg was behind the Iron Curtain, further complicating investigations. Rumors abounded after the war that many SS officers were taken prisoner by the advancing Russians when they left Birkenau. Large numbers were sent to labor camps in Siberia.

THE THREE GERMAN SOLDIERS

After the war, Rosie tried to trace the three soldiers for whom she was exchanged at the Danish border. Lists probably existed with the names of those exchanged in such a manner, but she was never able to find them and was thus unable to identify the soldiers in question.

CARL CLAUBERG

Together with Josef Mengele, Carl Clauberg conducted countless medical experiments on camp inmates. He was captured by the Russians in 1945 and put on trial in the Soviet Union, where he received a twenty-five-year sentence. As part of an agreement between Russia and Germany, Clauberg was pardoned seven years later and returned to his native soil, where he lived as a free man, boasting of his "scientific achievements" at Auschwitz. Survivors pressed charges. He was arrested a second time in 1955 and died in 1957, shortly after the beginning of his trial.

ROSIE'S PARENTS

Rosie's parents, Falk Glaser and Josephine Philips, did not survive the war. On March 30, 1943, they left Westerbork on a packed

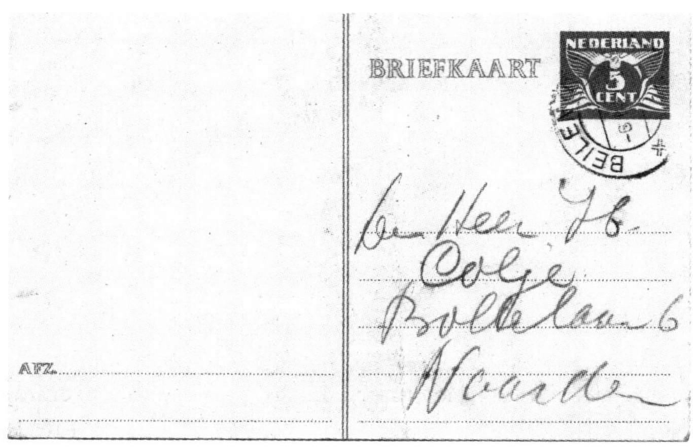
BRIEFKAART

NEDERLAND 5 CENT

BEILEN

AFZ.

train. The train made its way to Poland in the dark of night, its final destination Sobibor. Nothing was ever heard again of a single passenger. On the day of their departure, Rosie's father scribbled a note in pencil on a card and mailed it to Magda and Henk Coljee: "Just to let you know we're in transit. Best regards, and hope we see each other again soon."

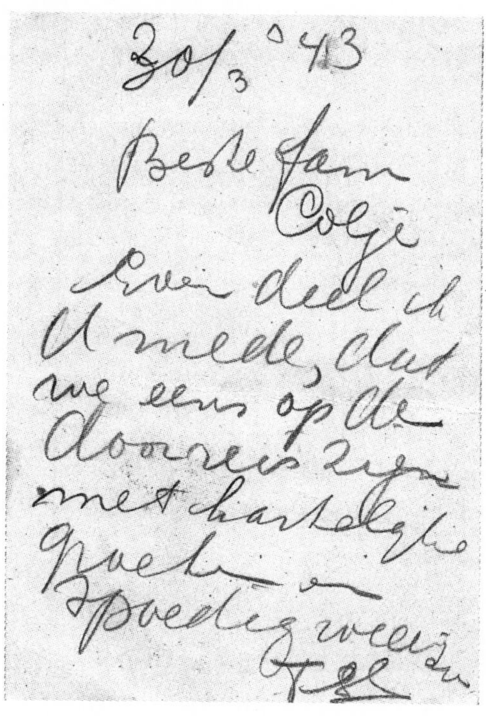

30/3 '43
Beste Fam
Coljé
Even deel ik
U mede, dat
we eens op de
doorreis zijn
met hartelijke
groeten en
spoedig weerzien

JOHN GLASER'S FAMILY

Rosie's brother, John, survived the war in hiding and proposed to his girlfriend, Elisabeth, in 1944 as soon as the Southern Netherlands were liberated. They married in 1945 and had five children: Paul, Marjon, René, Ernest, and Wouter. John and Elisabeth decided to keep their wartime past and John's Jewish background to themselves. John concentrated on playing the piano, working, and looking after his family.

Rosie visited John and his family several times after the war, but after a while they severed contact with one another. The war and its traumatic events were to blame for the rupture. John claimed that Rosie's carelessness had led to their mother's arrest. Rosie claimed that John evaded his responsibilities when he disappeared into hiding. An insignificant incident occasioned the break. In 1988, John wrote Rosie a letter proposing they resume contact. A brief correspondence followed, but accusations quickly prevailed, after which the siblings ceased communicating for good.

Elisabeth died in 2007.

ROSIE'S UNCLES AND AUNTS AND THEIR CHILDREN

Rosie had seven uncles and aunts. With the exception of one couple who spent the war in the Dutch East Indies, none survived the war. A few cousins also survived:

- First family, five children: Kitty, Jaap, Regina, and Jacob were murdered in Auschwitz; Joost survived in the Dutch East Indies.
- Second family, four children: Arthur and Maurice were murdered in Auschwitz and Herbert in Camp Dorohusk. Richard managed to reach Switzerland and survived.
- Third family, three children: Bernard, Irene, and Sonja were murdered in Sobibor.

- Fourth family, two children: Oscar was murdered in Auschwitz, Suzy survived in hiding.
- Fifth family, one child: Bram survived the camps; his wife was murdered in Auschwitz.
- Sixth family, two children: Regina and Hanchen were living in the Dutch East Indies and survived.
- Seventh family, two children: Regina and Rosetta were murdered in Auschwitz.

Many of Rosie's cousins were arrested while in hiding after being betrayed by the Dutch. Oscar was betrayed by his mother's doctor while he was visiting her in the hospital. He was arrested as soon as he left the building. His mother was ordered to leave the hospital, and because she was unable to walk she was brought to Westerbork on a stretcher. Oscar died in Auschwitz. After the war his sister Suzy, who survived in hiding, was completely alone. She tried to return to their parental home but without success. A former neighbor who had preserved the family's paintings, table silver, and other valuables refused to let her in and told her that her mother had said he could keep their property. Her mother had been murdered, and the neighbor closed the door. There was no possibility of appealing to the authorities and that was the end of it.

ROSIE'S SECOND COUSINS

Many of Rosie's first and second cousins can be seen in the photograph on the next page, which depicts a family get-together in 1939. Only two of her second cousins survived the war: Harry and Moritz. Harry returned from the camps (Auschwitz and Bergen-Belsen) by foot, and Moritz survived in hiding. Harry is still alive at the time of this writing. When he returned from the camps and rang the bell of his family's home, the former housekeeper opened the door and refused to let him in. It was already late in the evening, and he was sick and had nowhere to stay. When he said he was going to sleep on the front steps, where passersby might see, she finally allowed him to spend the night in his own house. The following day he was admitted to the hospital. It took two years before he recovered completely.

A family gathering in 1939. The only two survivors were Moritz Glaser (standing, second from left) and Harry Glaser (standing, fourth from right).

JEWS IN THE NETHERLANDS AFTER THE WAR

According to the official numbers provided by the Dutch authorities, 72 percent of the Jewish population of 140,000 perished during the occupation, an unusually high percentage compared with other occupied countries: in Denmark it was less than 1 percent; Germany 24 percent; Belgium 44 percent; and France 22 percent. (Sources: Israel Gutman, *Encyclopedia of the Holocaust* and Chris van der Heijden, *Grijs Verleden.*)

The actual Dutch percentage is probably higher than the official figure. During the occupation, several local authorities simply registered deported citizens as "gone abroad." On paper, therefore, these individuals were seen as emigrants and not casualties of war and were not included in the official death statistics. Experts thus dispute the official figures.

Many of Rosie's Jewish friends died in the war, and only a few survived. One friend, who also survived Auschwitz, left the Netherlands two years after the war because of anti-Semitism and the uncomfortable atmosphere and immigrated to Australia. She and Rosie kept in touch to the last. Thousands of other survivors immigrated to Israel and the United States for the same reasons. Others, like Rosie herself, never returned to the Netherlands.

AFTERWORD

WHEN I LEARNED about my family's secret, the first people I told were my friends. They were excited and curious and wanted to know how I felt about my rediscovered Jewish identity. But their questions seemed absurd. Had I been a different person prior to the discovery than I was now? Impossible, I thought. I am who I am. I couldn't suddenly become someone else. I became even more perplexed when a friend announced one evening that he had always thought I was Jewish. Why? Because of my name. It had never crossed my mind.

The question of my identity became even more prominent after I put pen to paper, cast the story in book form, and went public with it. The book has been the subject of a couple of television programs and was even adapted for the theater, where it had a sold-out run. Another theatrical program included performances of some of the songs Rosie wrote in the camps. Because of the book's success in the Netherlands, I'm regularly invited to give talks about Rosie. It became apparent in conversations following these events that many people in the audience simply presumed that I was Jewish. I had noticed the same thing during my search for additional information about my aunt's life. Jewish people tended to see me as one of their own.

Now that my book has been published, it seems that there has indeed been some change in my outward identity, although I was unable to sense it internally at first. So am I Catholic or Jewish? As an adult, I no longer attend Catholic services, and I am no longer an active Catholic as I was in my youth. But I still appreciate the culture associated with it. I sense its achievements: compassion, forgiveness, tradition, ceremony. In high school, we were taught religion by a young Jesuit. His classes were so fascinating, so full of historical awareness and worldly wisdom, that even non-Catholics came to listen. I went to the Jesuit monastery every week and discussed life's important questions in small groups. I learned a great deal from those encounters, which formed me to a certain extent, and I look back on them with affection. While Catholic culture doesn't define me, it is part of me. But under the Nazis, that would ultimately have made no difference. I would have been expected to wear a different identity on my sleeve in the form of a yellow star.

In the process of searching for information related to my aunt and her turbulent life, I made the acquaintance of more and more Jewish men and women, and some have become good friends. I felt at home with them from the outset. Why? It's hard to tell. I was curious about them, their fortunes, their life stories, the careers they had pursued, and the social positions they had obtained. But there was more. I felt familiar with the way they interacted, felt at ease in their company. Their seemingly disorganized and messy encounters with one another, the multiple conversations all vying for attention, the discussions and often extreme differences of opinion, the entrepreneurial spirit, the humor, the international orientation—this was all me. Whether or not what I experienced in these circles was specifically Jewish, I sensed a degree of kinship.

So am I a Catholic Jew or a Jewish Catholic? My personality

reflects both Catholic and Jewish cultural concepts. But I spent my formative years as a Catholic. A Jewish dimension has been added to my life, and I experience it as an enrichment. But though a new label can be applied, I'm essentially not a different person. I am who I am.

When my grandmother confirmed my suspicion that my family was Jewish, I changed the subject immediately and "forgot" to inquire further. The following day, I decided not to make it part of my life. It had no "new value," I told myself; what was I to do with it? On top of that, Jews were often directly associated with the State of Israel, with all its troubles and woes. That was all I needed! So I said nothing more about the subject and thought about it only sporadically. In spite of my inborn curiosity, I didn't feel the need to explore that part of my past any further. But deep inside, of course, I couldn't ignore the appalling truth that the majority of Dutch men, women, and children with Jewish ancestry were murdered during the war. Almost 73 percent of them. If I allowed that truth to get to me, I knew it would throw me off balance.

The same was true with Rosie's letters. I started to read them when I arrived home, but it was only later that I properly grasped their content, and it was then that the anger slowly emerged. Anger at the way my fellow countrymen and women—the good ones excluded—treated their fellow Jewish citizens during the war, and at how the Dutch government responded to the Jews who later returned from the camps. This was new to me. The history books and the memorial days focus on the powerlessness of the Dutch under German occupation and tell stories of heroic resistance and solidarity. But Rosie's story paints a different picture. At the beginning, I thought this was Rosie's own particular truth, unique to her, but further research revealed that the way she had been treated after the war was not exceptional. On the contrary, it turned out to be the standard. There wasn't much resistance during the war; people tended to be passive, to exploit the situation economically, certainly at the beginning of the occupation. Later, there were many examples of collaboration and outrageous betrayal.

An elderly man called me recently to say that he had found letters in an old linen closet from someone by the name of Glaser. They turned out to be from a cousin of Rosie's father who had gone into hiding with his wife and their children. He wrote the following from his hiding place:

> I'm sure this letter will come as something of a surprise. How are you? We are well, if you account for the circumstances. Times are hard right now, but we're confident they'll change for the better, and soon! We're staying "somewhere in the Netherlands." We'll tell you where when you come for a visit, but that will have to be after the war. It's not easy for us here as I'm sure you imagine. Time passes painfully slowly. When your husband and Eef last visited to bring that package we thought about leaving the country, but it wasn't to be. A lot has happened since then. We're no longer in Rotterdam. Please don't tell anyone [underlined] that you heard from us, because the betrayers never sleep, and destroy this letter as soon as you've read it. Warm regards from us all.

A letter in poorly written Dutch is dated shortly after the first letter. It's not from Rosie's cousin, but from the landlady who provided them with safe housing in exchange for money:

> This'll surely come as a surprise, a letter from Woerden. But not from the Glaser family. I wanted to let you know that the whole family was taken away. Such a pity. So you don't have to send the radio. It's terrible to be left with 6 children and no income.

She laments the loss of earnings from the Glasers as "terrible," but beyond that . . . nothing. Rosie's cousins were all deported and murdered.

After the war, people had little sympathy for the victims of the concentration camps. They were received coldly and told not to grumble. They were also discriminated against in terms of their legal rights: homes, property, and money were returned only in dribs and drabs, and in some instances not at all. The parliament even adopted a law that complicated the return of stolen property, a law that would have been more than at home under the Nazi occupation. The consequences were so horrendous that judges were forced to deviate from the law when they offered judgment in specific cases, in spite of the fact that it had been democratically enacted.

Anti-Semitism was worse in the Netherlands after the war than before it. Many survivors, Rosie's friends among them, emigrated after their return to rebuild their lives elsewhere. Rosie's decision to leave the Netherlands and live in Sweden was a good decision. Rosie observed, "Sweden is my new fatherland. Holland, no. In Holland I experienced too much sadness. When I visit the place I do so as a tourist, with the advantage that I speak the language. But that's all there is."

The Speaker of the Dutch parliament wrote me a very kind letter in which she told me that she had read my book and that Rosie's story had moved her deeply. She confirmed the shameless attitude adopted by the Dutch government shortly after the war.

I asked her if I could quote her for publicity purposes. She agreed, but not with regard to the reprehensible attitude of the Dutch authorities. The time was apparently not yet ripe. Government officials are thus seemingly still intent on sparing the authorities criticism. Confidence in government is the first priority. History students will one day write dissertations about what happened, and another fragment of the truth will drift to the surface. But some details will undoubtedly disappear under the dust and slowly be forgotten.

Going public with Rosie's story has also had an effect on my three daughters, their children, and the other members of my family—I have one sister and three brothers. I involved them at every step and kept them posted on new developments. But that wasn't enough. I noticed that they were struggling with it, more so my siblings than my daughters. My sister, who corresponded with Rosie on a regular basis, hasn't yet read the book, although she's attended a couple of my lectures. When I asked her why she hadn't read it, she admitted that she was afraid to read about the terrible things Rosie had gone through. She didn't want to sully her memories. One brother, who has his own business, told me he would never have gone public with the discovery. He's convinced that divulging such information can only be detrimental and is uncertain about the consequences the revelation of his Jewish roots might have for his client relationships. But when the children of Rosie's ex-husband—the man who betrayed her—contacted me on the occasion of the theatrical production, he became very upset. "How can you be in touch with the children of the man who destroyed our family?" he shouted angrily. Another brother, an artist, was annoyed that I had spoken about Rosie with one of his friends. He was afraid the revelation of our Jewish ancestry might negatively influence their friendship. Every now and then, my brothers, my sister, and I get together and discuss our concerns. The advice my father gave me still makes its presence felt: keep the family secret to yourself, otherwise it will be used against you.

My father would appear to be the least moved by Rosie's story. When I told him I was going to write about his sister he replied, "That's up to you" and shrugged his shoulders. I gave him a copy of the book when it was finished. As far as I know he hasn't read it, but I do know that he's had a look at some of the photos that accompany the story. He had no photos of his own from the period, neither of himself nor of his family. Rosie had taken them all to Sweden after she dug them up. When he saw a photo of his parents he smiled. I had the photo enlarged and framed. He still keeps it in his room.

Once in a while we're given a further unexpected glimpse into the past. Some older people have told me they remember Rosie from their younger years, and how they once danced with her. Some have a photo or a letter to share. It makes the past tangible and it moves me. I was perhaps most deeply touched by an encounter I had after I gave a talk in the city of Breda. When almost everyone had gone home, a young woman came up to me and told me she had come especially to give me something. She handed me a small piece of paper and said: "This belongs to your family." I opened it and saw a little Star of David. "It belonged to Sara Glaser," she said. "She's wearing it in the photo on page 123 of the book [page 103 of this edition]." I accepted her gift with gratitude, but couldn't stop myself from asking what made her so certain the pendant belonged to Sara. She then told me the following story:

I spent a great deal of time with my grandparents as a child; they were my second father and mother. I played a lot and every time I visited I asked if I could look inside my grandma's jewelry box. The only thing that really fascinated me was the little star. I would always take it out and ask Grandma why she never wore it. I was only a child, you understand. Then my grandma told me that it didn't belong to her, not officially. But the star continued to fascinate me and I constantly asked about it.

When I was a little older, my grandma told me the story behind the star. It had belonged to one of her neighbors, to her friend Sara. She had been forced to go into hiding during the war, and she had asked my grandma to look after it until she could come back and collect it. The sad feeling the star had always given me was immediately explained by my grandma's words. Sara never came back. She was murdered in the extermination camp near Sobibor. My grandmother didn't tell me this herself. I think she found it extremely painful. On her deathbed she bequeathed the star to me. It symbolized the bond between us, strong and unique. It remains so to the present day, even after her death.

The fact that this star didn't belong to my grandmother and was always hidden away in her jewelry box tells me it doesn't belong to me either, but to the Glaser family. They lost so much, and this little star is one small thing that has survived. When I heard about the book, about *Tante Roosje* by Paul Glaser, I didn't hesitate for an instant. The star is for you. This is what my grandma would have wanted.

When she finished her story, she handed me the little star that symbolized the close bond she had with her deceased grandmother. A tear trickled down her cheek. I was overwhelmed, didn't know what to say, and kissed her as a sign of my gratitude.

My father is still alive. Silence is the armor plating he uses to keep the horror of his past at bay. Part of that defense mechanism has been passed down to me, but it's no match for the profound emotion that overcomes me when I think of that last evening when Rosie, my father, and their parents were together in hiding—when my father, a man who had fought in the early days of the war as a Dutch soldier, sat down in silence in his mother's lap, and she caressed him. After that encounter they were never to see each other again.

Paul Glaser
Enschede, Netherlands, 2013

Author's Note and Acknowledgments

I began writing this book in 2008. My most important sources were Rosie's diary, the letters she wrote from the camps, the photos, and old films I discovered in Stockholm, and a variety of other documents, including poems, songs, and official reports from the Dutch State Police. I also used material drawn from conversations with my mother, Elisabeth, and of course from my meeting in Stockholm with Rosie herself.

Descriptions of Rosie's professional success brought me to the Dutch film archives, which provided me with a DVD containing a Polygon newsreel from the early years of the war. Dancing for newsreels, Rosie was elegant, had a good sense of rhythm, and looked particularly stylish in her rose-trimmed ball gown. The images brought her back to life, and I watch them again and again. She whirled and smiled until she danced out of view, not knowing what was about to happen.

I was able to supplement these materials with information from the Nazi archives about Rosie's time in the camps. Victor Laurentius deserves special mention for his excellent detective work. Ruud Weissmann's study of the Jewish history of the city of Den Bosch, where Rosie lived before she went into hiding, was of particular value. I made grateful use of Chris van der Heijden's important book *Grijs Verleden*, which detailed the measures implemented during and after the war with respect to Dutch Jews.

This book contains texts written by Rosie herself, taken from her diary and dealing with her youth in Kleef and Nijmegen. A number of quotations taken from Rosie's private archive have also been employed, and some of the letters she sent from Westerbork and Vught are included in their entirety. The poems were written by Rosie herself and came to light when I was going through her papers in Stockholm.

The people in this book are real people, some of whom are still alive. Since a number of individuals were unnamed in the documentation, I provided them with fictional names: Rachel, Kurt Fischer, Jorg de Haan (whose surname is actual), Pierre de Jaeghere, Lambiek, Betsy, and Martha. The nickname "Boy" refers to Hans Bickers. The remaining seventy-two names referred to in these pages are genuine.

Rosie herself was something of a magician when it came to names. The Lohengrin saga did not only haunt her life, it informed it. While she changed her name several times for security reasons, her motives were also sometimes aesthetic. She exchanged Glaser for Glacér, for example, which she continued to use in Sweden, because she thought it more stylish. At other points she went by Crielaars, Krielaars, Donkers, and Glacér-Philips. She also tried different first names, including Rosita, Rosa, and Lya. In her diary she refered to herself as Wanda, her brother as Charles, and her father as Frits. This may have been due to security concerns, as she started to write it in prison. For me she will always be Aunt Rosie.

Many people offered their assistance in the process of reconstructing Rosie's life and my family's past, and they deserve a word of gratitude.

My maternal grandmother, Jo de Bats, was the first to tell me what she knew about Rosie's family and, without realizing it, confirmed my suspicions about my family's secret.

Leny and Wolke Veenstra, who regularly visited Magda Coljee in the rest home in which she spent her final days, found the letters Rosie had written to her from the Dutch camps and went to the trouble of finding me.

My second cousin René Glaser told me about the family. His father, Joost, was Rosie's cousin, and he knew the family well. René took me to a synagogue for the first time in my life. Suzy Rottenberg, Rosie's niece, told me about her own life and what she remembered of Rosie. She invited me to meet the remaining family. Rosie's friend, Fran Beumkes, knew her from Den Bosch and told me shortly before she died about my grandparents and what it was like for them in the first years of the war. She was proud of the fact that her daughter, like Rosie, is an accomplished dancer. My father's second cousin, Harry van Geuns, told me about life in Nijmegen before and during the war, and about his imprisonment at Auschwitz and his return to the Netherlands.

Shortly before the end of her life, my mother, Elisabeth, added some details about what it had been like for Rosie and John's family during the occupation. Her sisters Riek and Joop confirmed her story and added further details.

I'm also grateful to my father, John, for his silence about the past, a silence that spoke volumes.

I set about writing this book armed with an arsenal of information. It would not have been possible without the encouragement of friends and family. Without their enthusiasm and support, Rosie's letters, diary, photos, poems, and papers might have been forgotten in a box in my attic.

My friend Franz Leberl, who lives in Boulder, Colorado, encouraged me to tell Rosie's story and my own to American friends. Their reactions were positive, and more and more friends of friends wanted to share this fascinating tale of exploration and discovery.

Joël Cahen, director of the Jewish Historical Museum in Amsterdam, encouraged me unremittingly to commit the story to paper, especially my own journey of discovery.

My wife, Ria, read the first chapters, and with her encouragement I put together a draft of the book. The complete manuscript was read by Hanneke Cowall, Judith Frankenhuis, Jeanne Willemse, Inge Sterenborg, Ruud Weissmann, Victor Laurentius, Bert Kuipers, and my daughter Lotte. Each went to the trouble of providing necessary feedback. Their observations and advice helped me to provide the story with greater depth. As a finishing touch I asked my wife, Ria, and my daughters, Myra, Barbara, and Lotte, to read the final manuscript. Their suggestions helped me to bring the book to completion.

I would like to thank Hella Rottenberg for her excellent editorial advice, and Gerton van Boom, who published the book in the Netherlands.

I would also like to thank Marianne Schönbach, who showed me the way to the United States, and Barbara Zitwer, who found a well-known publisher. Last but not least, I thank Ronit Feldman for her excellent support in the editorial process, and Nan Talese, who decided to publish the book.

Thanks to the contributions of many, my search has come to an end. The result is the book you have before you.

Additional Songs and Poems from the Camps

Animals
Westerbork, 1942

I wish I were an animal
It's hard here at the human end,
To be a person and be real,
And not just to pretend.

I'm very happy to intone,
I wish I were a bird,
I'd sing and sing for me alone,
I know it sounds absurd.

I wish I were a little pup,
So cuddly and so small,
They always lift your spirits up,
They're loved by one and all.

I'd have no need to be ashamed
To go where e'er I roam,

Out on the streets I can't be blamed,
For what's now done at home.

I wish I were a mighty horse,
So noble and so proud,
An animal of such great force,
His presence is quite loud.

I'd let the circus pamper me,
For one month or one year
And when I'd learned enough to flee,
I'd start a new career

I wish I were a donkey,
"Hee-haw" is all I'd say,
'Cause donkeys only know "haw-hee,"
That's all they say all day.

But if someone asked to marry me,
I'd say "no way," drop dead!
What a real ass I would be
To say "hee-haw" instead.

I'd be a chicken in its run
So plump and round and fine,
I'd cackle in the morning sun
And have a grand old time.

I'd bring my eggs to the market square
And sell them under the table.

Let the CCD* inspect my wares,
I'll just run as soon as I'm able.

I wish I was a tiny flea,
Then life would be the best.
To suck men's blood would be such glee,
I'd love to be a pest.

I'd pierce and prod and jab and prick
At men both big and small
I know exactly where to stick,
I'd drive them up the wall.

You do know what I mean, I'm sure,
Exactly what I desire.
But what can I do, I must endure,
I was born in human attire.

To live like a flea or a bird on the wing
Is as easy as one-two-three.
But to live the life of a human being
Is the hardest thing, mark me.

OTTOKAR

Vught, 1943

Some women long for a man in their lives.
A real man when the time arrives.

---

* Crisis Control Department set up by the Nazis to combat the illegal accumulation and sale of food.

Franca, she loves Ottokar.
Six months and a day so far.
But now and then if you get near
It's Paula whispering in his ear:
You're the dream of my sleepless nights.
Oh! Oh! Ottokar!
You know just how to make me swoon.
I love you in the morning, I love you at noon.
But I love you most by the light of the moon.
You're the dream of my sleepless nights.
Oh! Oh! Ottokar!

As it does, time has passed.
Six months have gone away at last.
Sweet Paula has been cast aside,
It's Ilse who's the blushing bride.
And now and then if you get near
It's Ilse's voice in Ottokar's ear.

A Little Longing

Birkenau, 1944, Text and Music by Rosita Glacér

I'm feeling a little longing, a little longing for you
I'm feeling a little longing, for my love for you is true.
Only those who know desire can understand my pain
Yet this is something for you and me, we two, and not in vain.
Leave me a little longing, a little longing so blue
Leave me a little longing, for your eyes, your mouth, for you.

We were forced to stay apart
long years, far too long for my heart,
But in my every dream I see
that you always return to me,
Yearning, waiting without rights,
many days and many nights.

Trouble is, I can't forget,
And people say I should regret.
But to you I will be true for life,
I promise to be a faithful wife.
Nothing will ever change my mind,
You know, admit it, you're not blind.

Before long, it will be forgotten,
A painful memory misbegotten.
For I know there's a time to build,
when all my dreams will be fulfilled.
We shall be strong and never bend
My love for you will never end.

Nothing can separate you and me,
We two together, linked and free.
I see our home in years to come,
A house for us, and me a mum,
I see a cradle full of love,
With there inside, our turtledove.

A Note About the Author

Paul Glaser was born in the Netherlands shortly after World War II. He has held management positions in a number of educational and health-care institutions, including periods as director of a psychiatric hospital and as CEO of a large organization working with the mentally handicapped. He has also been involved in the establishment of a historical printing museum, a regional theater, and a Montessori secondary school.

A Note About the Type

The text of this book was set in Requiem, a typeface designed by Jonathan Hoefler (born 1970) and released in the late 1990s by the Hoefler Type Foundry. It was derived from a set of inscriptional capitals appearing in Ludovico Vicentino degli Arrighi's 1523 writing manual, *Il Modo di Temperare le Penne.* A master scribe, Arrighi is remembered as an exemplar of the chancery italic, a style revived in Requiem Italic.